Conversations with Richard Wilbur

Literary Conversations Series

Peggy Whitman Prenshaw
General Editor

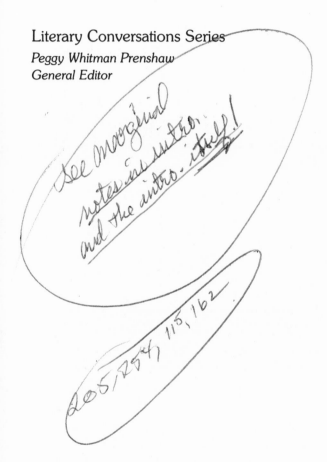

Conversations with Richard Wilbur

Edited by
William Butts

[handwritten annotation:] Abysmal! he's brilliant and SANE and sassy! (sometimes too kind, too hopeful(?)...

[handwritten annotation:] — However, see p. 189 for one of the biggest lies or self-delusions I've yet heard in the poetry biz — i.e., when Kunitz talks about the "poetry prison" and thinks, with Wilbur, that Berryman's suicide might be attributed to it. This kind of thinking is positively weird, coming from Kunitz and Wilbur whose publishing experiences have been vastly different!

University Press of Mississippi
Jackson and London

Library of Congress Cataloging-in-Publication Data

Wilbur, Richard, 1921-
    Conversations with Richard Wilbur / edited by William Butts.
        p.   cm. — (Literary conversations series)
        ISBN 0-87805-424-3 (alk. paper). — ISBN 0-87805-425-1 (pbk.)
        1. Wilbur, Richard, 1921- —Interviews.   2. Poets,
American—20th century—Interviews.   I. Butts, William.   II. Title.
III. Series.
    PS3545.I32165Z464   1990
    811'.52—dc20   89-28839
                                                       CIP

British Library Cataloging-in-Publication data available

Books by Richard Wilbur

The Beautiful Changes and Other Poems. New York: Reynal and Hitchcock, 1947.

Ceremony and Other Poems. New York: Harcourt Brace and Company, 1950.

The Misanthrope, by Molière (trans.). New York: Harcourt Brace and Company, 1955.

Things of This World. New York: Harcourt Brace and Company, 1956.

Candide, by Voltaire (trans. with others). New York: Random House, 1957.

Poems 1943-1956. London: Faber and Faber, 1957.

Advice to a Prophet and Other Poems. New York: Harcourt Brace and Company, 1961.

Loudmouse. New York: Crowell-Collier, 1963.

The Poems of Richard Wilbur. New York: Harcourt Brace and World, 1963.

Tartuffe, by Molière (trans.). New York: Harcourt Brace and World, 1963.

The Misanthrope and Tartuffe, by Molière (trans.). New York: Harcourt Brace and World, 1965.

Walking to Sleep: New Poems and Translations. New York: Harcourt Brace and World, 1969.

Digging for China; a poem. Garden City, NY: Doubleday and Company, 1970.

The School for Wives, by Molière (trans.). New York: Harcourt Brace and World, 1971.

Opposites. New York: Harcourt Brace Jovanovich, 1973.

Seed Leaves. Boston: David R. Godine, 1974.

The Mind-Reader: New Poems. New York: Harcourt Brace Jovanovich, 1976.

Responses: Prose Pieces, 1953-1976. New York: Harcourt Brace Jovanovich, 1976.

The Learned Ladies, by Molière (trans.). New York: Harcourt Brace Jovanovich, 1978.

Seven Poems. Omaha: Abattoir Editions, 1981.

Advice from the Muse. Deerfield, MA: The Deerfield Press, 1981.

Molière: Four Comedies (trans.). New York: Harcourt Brace Jovanovich, 1982.

Elizabeth Bishop: A Memorial Tribute. New York: Albondocani Press, 1982.

The Whale and Other Uncollected Translations. Brockport, NY: BOA Editions, 1982.

Phaedra, by Jean Racine (trans.). New York: Harcourt Brace Jovanovich, 1986.

New and Collected Poems. New York: Harcourt Brace Jovanovich, 1988.

Contents

Introduction ix

Chronology xv

An Interview with Richard Wilbur *David Curry* 3

Richard Wilbur: An Interview *Robert Frank and Stephen Mitchell* 17

An Interview with Richard Wilbur *Paul McKnight and Gary Houston* 36

Questionnaire to Mr. Wilbur *Paul F. Cummins* 42

Richard Wilbur *Joan Hutton* 46

The Window of Art: A Conversation with Richard Wilbur *Gregory Fitz Gerald and William Heyen* 56

An Interview with Richard Wilbur *Willard Pate and Panel* 66

Craft Interview with Richard Wilbur *The New York Quarterly* 86

Richard Wilbur *John Graham* 102

An Interview with Richard Wilbur *Philip Dacey* 115

An Interview with Richard Wilbur *Irv Broughton* 125

Interview: Richard Wilbur *Christopher Bogan and Carl Kaplan* 146

A Conversation with Richard Wilbur *Edwin Honig* 162

The Art of Poetry: Richard Wilbur *Peter Stitt, Ellessa Clay High, and Helen McCloy Ellison* 178

Here are two stand-up comics — alternating the role of the straight man. Rather duel, and probably not educational.

Introduction

The following conversations with Richard Wilbur, spanning some thirty years, offer generous testimony of a poet superbly versed in the traditions of his art and equally well able to place himself within those traditions. "Our most civilized, accomplished and heartening poet," the phrase by which Wilbur described W.H. Auden in 1972, now most aptly pinpoints Wilbur's own standing in his field. These interviews defend this claim. While outwardly they present the picture of Wilbur and his interviewers chatting cordially and leisurely, as if each were held in the poet's study, the subjects of these conversations are seldom so casual. In them Wilbur explains, with considerable wit and eloquence, the poems that have been his life's task and the subject of much discussion among critics. A caricature that Wilbur once drew of himself captures what he has had to justify in almost every interview: that the formal aspects of poetry are liberating, not limiting. In the drawing ("An idealized self-portrait," he labels it), Wilbur is carrying a pole bearing two flags, Meter and Rhyme, to the summit of Mount Parnassus. A road sign indicates his goal; other markers point the way to San Francisco and Black Mountain, the Meccas of free verse. The mood is typical of his poetry: the highest artistic aspirations tempered with humor and a certain topical pointedness.

The acclaim that greeted Wilbur's *New and Collected Poems* in 1988 and the awarding of a second Pulitzer Prize to him represent to an extent the triumph of Wilbur's stance in what he and his critics (and devil's advocate interviewers) have been debating since *The Beautiful Changes* was published in 1947. Hyam Plutzik, reviewing Wilbur's *Things of This World,* summed it up in his now famous charge: "How can he be so damnably good-natured in an abominable world?" The traditional form of Wilbur's verse continues to incite some critics with its "abominable" subject matter and excite

others with its mixture of "thinginess" and metaphysics. Wilbur's
unusually finished work endures.

When Wilbur first came on the poetry scene at age 26, critics such
as Louise Bogan marveled at his "remarkable variety of interest and
mood," his "seemingly effortless advance to a resolute conclusion,"
his "gift of fitting the poetic pattern to the material." Exploring and
affirming a "mystical" experience of everyday life and everyday
objects using these talents has always been a concern to which
Wilbur returns. As he notes in an essay on Emily Dickinson, "the
subjects to which a poet returns are those which vex him." What
"vexes" Wilbur, in the sense that he feels compelled to strive for it
again and again, seems to be the relation between the things of this
world and the things of another, spiritual world, capturing the
"difficult balance" that is the topic of his "chestnut" poem, "Love
Calls Us to the Things of This World." As he tells one interviewer, "I
can believe in angels by way of and in the laundry. . . . I don't really
want to have much truck with angels who aren't in the laundry, who
aren't in the everyday world." Fellow poet Thom Gunn, reviewing
Wilbur's *Advice to a Prophet,* remarks on the danger of this course:
"The public prefers a wild and changeable poet to one who has
pursued a single end consistently and quietly," especially an end that
continues to vex. The extent to which Wilbur has succeeded in
consciously striving for this "single end" through the decades may be
measured by the extent to which his interviewers keep returning to
those same concerns—and by the fresh insights that inform his
responses to such questions as: What can rhymed verse offer that
free verse cannot? Why the almost obsessive search for the spiritual
in the physical in your poetry? How does the form of your poetry
relate to its function? What effect does translating drama have on
your poetry? None of these questions appear verbatim in these
interviews, but so far as Wilbur's work reflects continuing variations
on these themes, a great many of them are addressed repeatedly.

Perhaps this continual and formalized quest for vexing aspects of
existence helps to explain Wilbur's relatively small output. The fear of
appearing to harp on the same issues demands a great deal of
forethought. Only in this painstaking manner can Wilbur ensure the
freshness of what he writes. "It looks as though I were getting terribly
choosy," he observes to more than one interviewer, "and terribly

anxious not to repeat myself." He is fond of telling the story of the time poet Richard Eberhart told him he could not use a certain word in a poem—he had used that word before.

The first interview in this collection—indeed, the earliest located—dates from 1962. By this time the 41-year-old poet had a number of books, translations and prestigious awards to his credit as well as a secure reputation. An interview from a dozen years previous, when Wilbur had but one slim poetry collection to his name, would be most interesting. Would that young man be as articulate and self-assured as Wilbur in his early forties? (It's interesting to note, too, that were some 26-year-old to bring out a collection of the quality of *The Beautiful Changes* today, an interview or two might well follow in *Interview* or *Rolling Stone*.

The questions asked Wilbur over the course of three decades shift subtly, just as Wilbur's responses to recurring questions change with time. Naturally a number of topical questions crop up. Those from the late 1960s and early 1970s return often to the Vietnam War and political activism, Ferlinghetti, Ginsburg and the Beat poets, the rock lyrics of Bob Dylan. Along with the more informal tone of these interviews, typical of the times, comes the most pointed, almost hostile questioning of Wilbur's structured verse, so antithetical to the trends of the day. Interviews of the last ten years tend to accept Wilbur's work with less suspicion as the country's pendulum swung back towards a more conservative posture and certain excesses of the 1960s grew out of favor—even, perhaps, as Wilbur's continued productivity proved the validity of meter and rhyme in modern times. Also noticeable is Wilbur's changing attitude toward his teaching methods. While not forcing his classes to actually compose samples of various poetry forms, he appears to grow more stringent before our eyes about their knowledge of the forms and of poetry's history and traditions, as if attempting to make up for the laxness and demand for "relevancy" of curriculum in recent years. Most noticeable of all is the snowballing effect that Wilbur views his translations as having on his poetry, a shift from the witty towards the dramatic.

Throughout, Wilbur remains disarmingly open, more liberal in his views than his establishment image and the false aura of his "traditional" (read "old-fashioned") verse leads some questioners to

[handwritten marginalia: No! the pendulum of a hardfelt of the best poets before, during and after the upheaval in the 60's (mostly 60's). The in—]

[handwritten note at bottom: Credibly swift ascendancy of Williams as the leader of the free-verse tsunami — and Williams did not exercise that leadership! — was simply because one needed no technique to write (what became known as) free verse !!]

expect. Wilbur defends his work with the graciousness of his thought
and the persuasiveness of his reasoning. He comments on other's
work with the same humane, ever-reasonable standards. When the
rare sting of his venom is felt, it is with force. The malice which
certain interview subjects such as Truman Capote thrive on (and, it
would seem, even cultivate for the press's sake) is totally foreign to his
generally benevolent nature. In one instance Wilbur discusses
Lyndon Johnson's rejection of a painting of him (the subject of his
poem, "A Miltonic Sonnet for Mr. Johnson on His Refusal of Peter
Hurd's Official Portrait"): "I think he rejected it because he said (in
the painter's presence) that it was the ugliest thing he had ever seen.
Whereas he could have found that in a mirror." Immediately he feels
compelled to add, "Enough: I'm being nasty" by way of apology. A
bit later in the same interview Wilbur remarks that viewing *The
Godfather* and *The French Connection* almost back to back left him
with "enough of that kind of nastiness for a lifetime." Wilbur is not
blind to this kind of harsh realism, but clearly he prefers a realism that
places man in a loftier light.

   Thus Wilbur's defense of formal poetry begins not by excoriating
free verse but by admiring free verse's successes and demonstrating
the deceptive difficulty in writing it. Again and again he shows the
versatility and virtuosity that has distinguished his poetry as he argues
that rhyme, meter and grace have as much a place in today's poetry
as ever, that poetry cannot be reduced to the equation that free verse
equals daring and formal poetry equals timidity. One wonderfully
effective response to a question about Randall Jarrell's well-known
criticism of his work ("Mr. Wilbur never goes too far, but he never
goes far enough") characterizes Wilbur's courteous method of
countering such charges. Besides offering the expected explanation of
how "far" he goes in any poem, he adds the revealing information
that at the time of Jarrell's review Jarrell had been injecting a new
tone into his work, placing him in a frame of mind that could hardly
lead him to come to any *other* conclusion about Wilbur's work.
   The interview as a form has always encountered criticism, the more
so as its popularity increases. One young critic, Bruce Bawer, recently
went so far as to dismiss most literary interviews as "unpremeditated
yammering" and "extemporaneous chatter" in reaction, it appears, to
having been interviewed himself on a college radio station as a 24-

year-old teaching assistant and having faked a relaxed appearance and recited a prepared text.[1] This critic goes on to astutely analyze interviews, though he relies largely on interviews with noted gossips and assorted hams to make his case, and closes with a grudging acknowledgment that a few interviews actually manage to be both entertaining and edifying. But for all the possible weaknesses of interviews—the over-edited, cut-and-paste interview, the under-edited interview that preserves every *um* and *ah,* and so on—the form known as the literary interview has come into its own, with no less potential for strengths and weaknesses than any other form.

No one is more concerned about the inevitable amount of repetition in interviews than Wilbur himself. He admits, "I am neurotic about repeating myself: I even feel a bit funny when I say the same thing to two different correspondents." Just as the subject who enlarges and expands on his views in interesting ways in successive interviews supplements our understanding and apprecia-tion of that person's work, the subject who proves unreliable about factual matters, garnishing or altering through whim or memory lapse, distracts, as does the subject who changes his opinions from interview to interview. It worries Wilbur that he is often asked about his artist father or how his work was "discovered" by André du Bouchet or other topics where he has little choice but to repeat himself. Such matters are relatively few, though, and Wilbur never differs from account to account. Every interview is intended as a self-standing piece, so some repetition inevitably occurs, but this is organic to the form.

Like a story that tells the same plot several times, each time from the point of view of a different character, the delight in Richard Wilbur's interviews lies in observing the poet's shifting responses over the years, how they vary and complement each other. The challenge to the reader, and the enjoyment, is to construct a composite portrait of Wilbur out of his various views. Of course the circumstances of the interviews should be correct: the right interviewer asking the right questions to the right subject. To that end the interviews in this collection achieve varying degrees of excellence.

I do not claim the literary interview as an art. Nor is it what Bruce Bawer says: "an entertaining hodgepodge of personality, public relations, and primary source material."[2] Who would deny that a creative, articulate mind can partake in a series of thoughtful, provocative conversations? Or that the simple, spontaneous insights of two people discussing what concerns them most offer something not preserved in the artist's studied creations? Properly handled, the literary interview (as these interviews with Richard Wilbur amply attest), even in its repetition, remains an invaluable aid in the study of a person and that person's art. It is what George Garrett calls "the scholarship of experience." What even our interview critic wouldn't give to read some newly-discovered interviews with Pope or Coleridge!

As with the other books in the Literary Conversations series, the interviews in this book are faithful to the original text. Often the biographical and bibliographical sketches appended before some interviews, little more than a rundown of dates and titles, have been omitted, or only relevant portions retained. Such information may be found in the chronology of this book. Typographical errors and mistakes in transcribing have been silently corrected. A modest number of footnotes have been provided where explanation seemed warranted; these are followed by *Editor* to distinguish them from footnotes that appeared in the original publications.

I am grateful to all the interviewers and publishers who freely granted permission to reprint these interviews. Special thanks are due the following for their advice and assistance with this project. To the man who may know more about Richard Wilbur than Wilbur himself, Jack W.C. Hagstrom, M.D., who with John Lancaster went above and beyond the call of scholarship in lending expertise and material from their bibliography-in-progress. To Professor Alan Hager, whose critiques from the start of this project lent shape and focus. To Professor Thomas Daniel Young, whose fine *Conversations with Malcolm Cowley* provided inspiration. And most of all to Richard Wilbur, who answered the questions.

WB
July 1989

1. Bruce Bawer, "Talk Show: The Rise of the Literary Interview," *American Scholar* (Summer 1988), pp. 421-429.
2. Ibid.

Chronology

1921   Richard Purdy Wilbur born in New York City on 1 March to Lawrence Lazear and Helen Ruth (Purdy) Wilbur

1923   Wilbur family moves to stone house on farm estate of J.D. Armitage in North Caldwell, New Jersey.

1926-38   Attends Essex Falls Public School, Grover Cleveland Junior High School and Montclair High School

1929   "Puppies" appears in *John Martin's Book,* a children's magazine—his first published poem.

1938-42   Attends Amherst College and receives B.A. degree. Contributes to *Touchstone* and serves as chairman and columnist for *The Amherst Student.*

1942   Marries Mary Charlotte Hayes Ward in South Berwick, Maine, on 20 June

1942-45   Serves as cryptographer with U.S. Army, 36th Infantry Division, 36th Signal Company, in Africa, southern France, along the Siegfried Line, and at Cassino and Anzio in Italy

1946-47   Attends Harvard University Graduate School on the G.I. bill and receives M.A. degree

1947   First book of poetry, *The Beautiful Changes and Other Poems,* published. Begins three years as Junior Fellow of the Society of Fellows at Harvard University.

1948   Lives in Paris and Grasse, France in spring as Junior Fellow. Awarded the Harriet Monroe Memorial Prize by *Poetry* magazine.

1950   Second book of poetry, *Ceremony and Other Poems,* published. Awarded the Oscar Blumenthal Prize by *Poetry Magazine.*

1950-55   Briggs-Copeland Assistant Professor of English composition at Harvard University

1951   Awarded the Golden Rose Trophy from the New England Poetry Club

1952   Receives honorary M.A. degree from Amherst College

1952-53   Attempts to write verse play while in New Mexico as a Guggenheim Fellow

1954   Wins O. Henry Award (third prize) for "A Game of Catch"

1954-55   Awarded the Prix de Rome Fellowship of the American Academy of Arts and Letters. Resides in Rome.

1955   Verse translation of Molière's *The Misanthrope* published. Compiles *A Bestiary,* "An anthology of prose and poetry on various beasts, with drawings for each animal" by Alexander Calder. *Modern American and Modern British Poetry* published, edited by Louis Untermeyer in consultation with Wilbur and Karl Shapiro.

1955-57   Associate Professor of English at Wellesley College *und so weiter*

1956   Third book of poetry, *Things of This World,* published

1957   Elected to the National Institute of Arts and Letters.
           Voltaire's *Candide* published, with lyrics by Wilbur and
           others, book by Lillian Hellman and score by Leonard
           Bernstein. *Things of This World* awarded the National
           Book Award, the Pulitzer Prize and the Edna St. Vincent
           Millay Memorial Prize. *Poems 1943-1956* published in
           London by Faber and Faber.

1957-63   Professor of English at Wesleyan University

1959   Named general editor of the Laurel Poetry Series by Dell
           Books. Steinman Poetry Lecturer at Tufts University. Edits
           and writes introduction to *The Complete Poems of Poe,*
           and lectures on "The House of Poe" at the Library of
           Congress. Wins Borestone Mountain Poetry Award (first
           prize) for "Advice to a Prophet" and Boston Arts Festival
           Award for poetry.

1959-77   Member of the Poetry Board of Wesleyan University Press

1960   Receives honorary L.H.D. degree from Lawrence College

1960-61   Receives Ford Foundation Fellowship; works at The Alley
           Theatre in Houston, Texas.

1961   Elected chancellor of the Academy of American Poets.
           Travels to U.S.S.R. with Peter Viereck as State Depart-
           ment cultural representative. Fourth book of poetry,
           Advice to a Prophet and Other Poems, published.

1962   Wins the Melville Cane Award from The Poetry Society of
           America for *Advice to a Prophet.* Active in the National
           Poetry Festival at the Library of Congress.

1963   Receives second Guggenheim Fellowship. First book for
           children, *Loudmouse,* published. *The Poems of Richard
           Wilbur* published; includes contents of first four collec-
           tions. Verse translation of Molière's *Tartuffe* published, is
           co-recipient of the Bollingen Prize for best translation of
           poetry.

1963-77   Olin Professor of English at Wesleyan University

1964   Takes part in Smith College Vanderbilt series on modern
           poetry. Receives honorary L.H.D. degree from Wash-
           ington University. Travels to Finland as State Department
           cultural representative.

1965   Wins Borestone Mountain Poetry Award (second prize)
           for "On the Marginal Way." Earlier Molière translations
           published together in paperback edition as *The Mis-
           anthrope and Tartuffe.*

1966   With Alfred Harbage, edits and writes introduction to
           Poems of William Shakespeare. Addresses International
           Poetry Forum in Pittsburgh, Pennsylvania.

1967   Receives honorary D.Litt. degree from Amherst College

1968   Wins the Sarah Josepha Hale Award

1969   *Walking to Sleep: New Poems and Translations* published.
           Receives honorary D.Litt. degree from Clark University.

1970   *Digging for China; a poem* published

1971   Awarded the Bollingen Prize for Poetry, the Brandeis
           University Creative Arts Award and the Prix Henri
           Desfeuilles. Verse translation of Molière's *The School for
           Wives* published.

why is this mentioned ?/.

1972   Elected to the American Academy of Arts and Letters

1973   Second book "for children and others," *Opposites,*
          published. Wins the Shelley Memorial Award from The
          Poetry Society of America.

1974   Receives honorary D.Litt. degree from American Interna-
          tional College. Limited edition of *Seed Leaves* published.
          Edits Poe's *The Narrative of Arthur Gordon Pym.*

1974-76   Elected president of the American Academy of Arts and
          Letters

1975   Receives honorary D.Litt. degree from Williams College

1976   Receives honorary D.Litt. degree from University of
          Rochester. *The Mind-Reader: New Poems* and *Re-
          sponses: Prose Pieces, 1953-1976* published.

1976-78   Elected chancellor of the American Academy of Arts and
          Letters

1977   Receives honorary D.Litt. degrees from Marquette Uni-
          versity and Wesleyan University

1977-86   Writer-in-Residence at Smith College

1978   Verse translation of Molière's *The Learned Ladies* pub-
          lished. Edits *Selected Poems of Witter Bynner.* Wins the
          Harriet Monroe Poetry Award.

1980   Receives honorary D.H.L. degree from Carnegie-Mellon
          University

1980-81   Elected to second term as chancellor of the American
          Academy and Institute of Arts and Letters

1981   Writes introduction to Poe's *Eleanora*. *Seven Poems* and
        Advice from the Muse published.

1982   Receives honorary D.Litt. degree from Lake Forest
        College. Verse translation of Jean Racine's *Andromache*
        published. Collected Molière translations published as
        Molière: Four Comedies. *Elizabeth Bishop: A Memorial
        Tribute* and *The Whale and Other Uncollected Transla-
        tions* published.

[handwritten in margin: publisher of too many Irish versifiers]

1983   Appears at the Library of Congress in program celebrat-
        ing the fiftieth anniversary of the Academy of American
        Poets. Wins the Drama Desk Award for *The Misanthrope*,
        the PEN Translation Prize for *Molière: Four Comedies*,
        the Chevalier Ordre des Palmes Academiques and the St.
        Botolph Club Foundation Award.

1986   Elected honorary fellow of the Modern Language Asso-
        ciation. Verse translation of Racine's *Phaedra* published.
        Receives honorary D.H.L. degree from State University
        College at Potsdam.

1987   Appointed second Poet Laureate of the United States,
        succeeding Robert Penn Warren

1988   *New and Collected Poems* published. Wins the Aiken
        Taylor Award for Modern American Poetry from the
        University of the South, the Pulitzer Prize for Poetry, the
        Bunn Prize from the Seattle Public Library Foundation
        and the Los Angeles Times Book Prize.

1989   Wins the Grand Master Award from Birmingham-South-
        ern College. Robert Frost Professor of English at Amherst
        College, fall term.

[handwritten: — Well, what didn't he receive? and why?]

Conversations with Richard Wilbur

An Interview with Richard Wilbur
David Curry/1962

From *The Trinity Review,* Vol. XV, No. 1 (December 1962), 21-32. Reprinted by permission of David Curry.

The interview was held at the poet's home in Portland, Connecticut, on a Sunday afternoon late in October.

Approaching the Wilbur home, we drove through an area of conventionally modern homes, then turned onto a private drive, deep with leaves that anyone else would have swept aside, went through a veritable forest of trees, and met the Wilbur home itself, an old, rambling, unpretentious and unconventional place—a bit of the country within the city.

The Pulitzer Prize winning poet met us at the door in a splash of yellow, a jacket that called the colors of the driveway leaves back to mind. He led us to a screened porch where he had been reading and had intended to have the interview. There was no outlet for our tape recorder on the porch, so we were led to the living room. ("I've never used one of those things before," was all he had to say about the recorder.)

While we assembled the recorder, Mr. Wilbur went upstairs to hunt a manuscript for us. While he was gone, we noticed an odd assortment of items in the room. On a table were two magazines, a copy of the *New Yorker* and one of *Life Magazine.* On the mantel was a small, gold-framed triptych, which the poet later explained had cost less than a dollar in some foreign market. A gilded wicker chair dominated one corner of the large room. Mrs. Wilbur, we learned, is engaged in a hobby of gilding old wicker items ("to impress the New York crowd.")

When Mr. Wilbur returned with the manuscript, he pointed out his own favorite items in the room, three stones found on the ground in Russia ("so perfect that they seem to have been done by hand.") The stones were a bluish-grey, with deep, white circles that did indeed seem designed and engraved. There were a large stone and two small ones ("to unbalance the large one.")

For the interview, Mr. Wilbur sat on a sofa before a large,

3

floor-to-ceiling bookcase. (There are almost as many bookcases in the Wilbur home as there are portraits of ancestors.) He spoke in a deep resonating voice that must compliment his poetry readings very well. His speech was broken frequently by long, thoughtful pauses. His humor was accented now and then by a slight grin.

Let's begin with a question that is probably pretty familiar to you. You rarely depart even partially from a traditional form in your verse. You never depart totally. Is this simply a question of what you find most comfortable, or do you have definite feelings against free verse?

Wilbur: Well, I would have to answer that in about three parts. With what I do (and it's true that I use a lot of meter and rhyme) I feel most comfortable. And that's the reason for it. I could, of course, give arguments for the greater technical effectiveness of poetry that's written within and against meter and rhyme. But that would be critical, and I never pretend that what I do I do on principle. I do it because it feels right that way, just as Adrian Quist thought it was right to use both hands on his back-hand.

Now, as to whether what I do is traditional, I would take exception to that a little. It is undoubtedly traditional to have recourse to tetrameter and pentameter and to use rhymes. But I don't very much follow established forms such as the sonnet. I've *written* them, but I don't tirelessly turn out sonnets, villanelles, ballades. Often the forms I choose (the stanza forms, say) are arrived at rather intuitively or by luck. The line lengths will be chosen much as a free verse writer chooses his line lengths, according to the way the words want to fall. And the rhymes will occur if they *do* occur. If they do occur, then in the remainder of the poem I'll keep to rhyme as well as to the metrical pattern which is naturally developed. So my work, in general, is likely to start out in something of a free verse spirit. And because my poems are usually not very long (I think the longest one is about ninety odd lines) it's usually so, I think, that the stanza form, first chosen in the light of what the rhythm of the utterance wants to be, will interpret the spirit of the poem successfully throughout. I could argue, in other words, that, however artificial many of my forms seem, they are *organic* in origin and, when successful, organic throughout—in the same sense in which a free verse poem may be said to be organic.

And the third thing I wanted to say is that I haven't anything against free verse at all. I think it's extremely hard to write. I've been satisfied only three or four times with anything I've done in free verse. But I hope that I'll continue to try to do it. I'd say in general that the body of free verse poetry in English contains very few successes. One's criterion has to be very subjective. You have to say about a free verse poem not that it fulfills some set of arbitrary rules and interestingly conflicts with those rules, but that it just somehow seems right. You can use the toney word *inevitable* to make this sound more authoritative, but it's still perfectly subjective judgment. But I'm not afraid of being subjective in this matter, since everyone has to be, and I would argue, for instance, that most of Ezra Pound's free verse does not seem to be inevitable, does not seem to me perfectly to work—though he has some triumphs in that kind. It's trying to do a rarer, harder thing, to write free verse. And you could argue that there are certain effects which the varying of rhyme and meter can get, which free verse cannot possibly get with the same sureness and emphasis, however lucky it may be. The example I usually give is the fall of Satan as described in *Paradise Lost*. Milton makes Satan fall for about nine lines, and the reason he makes Satan fall so hard is that he disappoints the reader's expectation of pauses at the ends of lines. Now there aren't any such expectations to disappoint in free verse, or, at any rate, they're not so strong. And so the effects of free verse can not be so powerful. This is one reason, I think, why free verse writers, even the best of them, fall back on exclamation points.

Your objection to the term traditional is interesting, since I read recently a review of your latest volume—in Poetry Magazine—*in which the reviewer complained of your unqualified use of traditional devices as mere decoration. I couldn't accept her complaint, particularly since I had just returned to your poem, "Next Door," and noticed your extremely careful use of rhymes there. All rhymed words in the poem are important words that should be accented; in a number of instances, paired rhymes within quatrains serve to contrast the old with the new, the old-age home with the lawn next door. Do*

*you often find yourself dissatisfied with critics who, not seeing the
purpose of your devices, complain of them as unnecessary?*

Wilbur: Well, I think so. When people who are averse on principle
to formal verse of any kind light into me, I feel that often they are
prevented by their prejudice from distinguishing mere doily-making,
mere fulfillment of arbitrary form, from the expressive use of the
form.

If I understand you rightly, you are saying that in this poem, "Next
Door," I rhyme only important words generally or get contrasts of
meaning out of words that are paired by the rhyme. And I hope that I
do that. I have a strong objection to rhyming on words that are of no
importance. I hope that I have written some poems that are
successful in respect to completely consuming the form and turning it
wholly to expressive purposes. I don't have any patience—any more
than, say, Robert Duncan would have any patience—with the tinkling
villanelles of the eighteen nineties. I can't think, however smoothly
such poems move, that they are any achievement. And I can
sympathize with the free verse rebellion of the teens of the century
when I go back to the poetry of the nineties and the tens, of the
nineties and the first ten years of the century, and see what inanely
formal work was being done by many poets who were in favor then.

*Along this same line, how much do you feel that your work as a
poet has been influenced by your living and working in Academia?
Do you think this might have something to do with your traditional
bent?*

Wilbur: Oh, I suppose it might have at any rate confirmed ways of
doing things I already had. I suppose the first things I ever tried to do,
when I started writing at the age of eight or nine, were in verse, tried
to be in stanzas.

I just can't say how much proximity to the academies would make
for adherence to meter and rhyme. Some of the most radical
innovators in respect to form are or have been attached to the
academies. I don't think it necessarily goes along with Bohemia.
There's surely been no more academic poet in the twentieth century
than Ezra Pound. The fact that he's not spent a number of years in
the academies is an accident. They *threw him out.* He's surely the
most pedagogical personality and the most pedantic personality in

modern poetry. And you associate Pound with formal freedom from the beginning to the end of his career.

Were you asking mainly about whether nearness to the academies is conducive to formalism? Well, I've more or less dodged the question, I suppose. But I don't think I can answer it. You think of Cummings who stayed away from the academies and sat down there in Greenwich Village for most of his career, resisting us all and writing in *sonnets,* sometimes disguising the fact that he was using traditional forms by typographical means, but surely as literary and as formalistic as most of his brothers in the academies.

Do you teach a course in writing at Wesleyan?

Wilbur: I've taught courses in the short story, which I suppose I'm not remarkably well qualified to teach, since I've published only one short story in my life. I also teach a course in versification.

What do you feel are the merits and the weaknesses of such a course? Did you yourself, when younger, take a course of this sort that you feel you profited from?

Wilbur: Never.

Never took one, or never profited from one?

Wilbur: Never took one.

But it has to be said in the first place that if a student is not talented, you can't do very much for him—and that if he *is* talented, you *still* can't do very much for him. You can encourage him. You can, if you're lucky, manage to identify yourself with his objectives, which he may not as yet fully realize. You may be able to help him discover what his emerging capacities are and push him a little toward an earlier discovery, an earlier development of them. You can sometimes communicate some small technical trick or suggest some fresh, imaginative approach to material.

I use a number of exercises in my versification course, ask people to do perhaps eight or nine exercises in the course of a semester. Most of these are time-tested by now. And they will very often encourage a student to look freshly at things in a way which he can later make solid use of. The exercise itself may not be much, but it perhaps will have the effect of *shaking the student up.* An example would be this: I often say to a class of poets, "You probably were brought up to feel that poetry should be ennobling, that therefore

So much for "workshops" then! Hear, hear.
(One teacher one *defined*, *if possible*, *finds* to speak to *receptive reader(s)*)

streetlights should be compared to stars, rather than stars to streetlights. Try comparing stars to streetlights or making similar comparisons between supposedly high things and things supposedly low." That's a very simple suggestion, and very specific, and people very often in taking it find themselves profitably shaken up and freed from confining habits of imagination.

The fundamental excuse for writing courses, I think, is that they authorize the busy undergraduate to give some time to writing and to feel that it might be as important as learning lists of the kings of Britain.

A last thing that happens in these writing courses, if you teach them as I do with considerable class participation, is that the developing writer is given an audience—and usually a fairly friendly audience, since everybody feels a bit vulnerable.

Those are the few things that one can do in teaching writing, the few advantages I think one can claim for it.

This may be getting a bit personal. How do you feel about the New Yorker, *where most of your poetry first appears? Do they interfere with you?*

Wilbur: Not at all.

Your word is quite final with them?

Wilbur: Yes. I gather that they interfere considerably with their prose writers, even their best prose writers, their most celebrated writers. They will quarrel with their prose writers on points of grammar, on points of fact, on points of internal logic. But the poets are allowed to do pretty much what they like. This isn't to say that the editors of the New Yorker don't look over your poem with Fowler's *Usage* in one hand and tell you that your system of punctuation is very idiosyncratic. Every poem comes back, in proof, covered with queries. But they are only queries, and if you like, you can simply write *stet, stet, stet, stet* down both sides of the page.

Only once, I think, in all the time I've been publishing poems in the *New Yorker,* have they ever given me an ultimatum and said, "You must change this word, or we will not print the poem." And this, amusingly enough, had to do with what they regarded as an antique spelling which would give the impression of being a misprint. They're very sensitive about misprints. I had used the word *clocked* instead of the more common word *clucked* to describe what hens do.

I wanted to say *clocked* for various reasons and was stubborn about it. But they were even stubborner, and finally, because I was *broke,* I let them print it as *clucked* and then restored it to *clocked* when I put the poem into a book. That is the only time they've been anything but handsomely concessive.

Where do you feel that the best poetry in America is being published today? Or do you even have such a feeling?

Wilbur: I wouldn't know how to localize it right now. Things are getting very spread out. Magazines like the *Saturday Evening Post,* which for decades printed nothing but junk in the way of poetry, are now printing a quantity of good verse and paying handsomely for it. The *Ladies' Home Journal,* I believe, has been printing people like Auden, for example—and Nemerov. I suppose—I don't read these magazines very much—I suppose that most of the poetry in the *Post* and the *Journal* would still be of an undistinguished kind. But, at any rate, the sort of poetry that Auden and Nemerov and others I could mention write is getting spread out considerably into middle-brow and slick magazines. It's impossible nowadays for the little magazines to feel as embattled as they used to feel, and to feel that they are fulfilling a function which no one else will fulfill.

I don't know how I'd choose among the little magazines right now. I always admire *Poetry Magazine* for its readiness to open the doors to new talents. The taste of *Poetry Magazine* has never, under any editor, been infallible, but I think this is because of their admirable catholicity, because they are willing to represent poets of all kinds and to take a chance on poets they've never heard of and no one else has heard of.

It strikes me it's not at all hard to get poetry published nowadays. It would be hard for us to sit down to look at a poem and guess, agent-fashion, where it ought to go. I might go to the *Saturday Evening Post.* The same poem might go to the *Kenyon Review.*

One of your poems, "To an American Poet Just Dead," leads me to believe that you might have something to say on a certain matter. Randall Jarrell has had a great deal to say in the way of lamenting the absence of a very large or very discriminating audience for poetry in America. What are your own views on this matter? Do you see any ways in which the situation might be bettered?

Wilbur: I like a lot of Jarrell's criticism very much. I think he overdoes it sometimes in berating the American public, complaining of their neglect of poets. Even Whittier, Longfellow, and those beloved poets of the last century were not known to a very large public, and it was not their best work which was prized by the public which they did have. I suppose it could be said that there have been times when poetry was better received by the public and was more attuned to the public taste and comprehension. But I shouldn't say that the present situation is a bad one at all. Public buying habits favor the anthology rather than the individual book of poems, but anthologies sell pretty well. It may be that the poetry public is far too much a school-made, college-made public right now, that the public itself is far too academic. But it's still a rather good and bright public, and one has to be grateful for it.

I suppose the thing that encourages me most right now is the popularity of the poetry reading as a form of—what would you call it?—entertainment, I suppose. I called the poetry reading a form of entertainment when I was visiting in Moscow and talking to some poets, among them Yevtushenko, and Yevtushenko said, "Why do you call it entertainment?" He was very offended by that, because he wanted it to be a higher word. Well, of course poetry *is* a higher thing than entertainment, but I couldn't think of a better word for it. And I explained to Yevtushenko that I prefer to use modest words for what poetry is and does, and he accepted that. In any case, I think that the popularity of the poetry reading since the late forties is a very good sign, a very hopeful thing. I'm astonished at how many people will turn out, sometimes at the cost of a *dollar,* to hear the work of someone whose poetry they don't know very well. And then I think that the constant opportunities one has to read poetry, not only at colleges and universities but in museums and other places less strictly academic, are bound to have an effect on one's writing, to affect it probably for the better and turn it toward the *dramatic,* in the broad sense, and once again toward the simplicity of the song.

I don't suppose I've covered the whole range of the topic you brought up, but it's a big subject.

Do you think a case could be made that the work of certain poets—Eliot and Pound, for instance—has reached the point where it exists only for poets—by poets and for poets? Could it be that poetry, being so highly refined a medium, reaches a point in these men

where the general public, unable to interpret its devices, cannot get
through the framework of the poem to its substance?

Wilbur: Some poetry, especially the poetry of Eliot's and Pound's
generation, clearly could be grasped, initially at least, by a small
audience only, and that audience was likely to consist in fair part of
poets. I think that's less and less the case nowadays. You know these
symposia on the subject of the Poet and his Public which are held all
across the continent every year. I've noticed that indignant questions
from the audience about obscurity are rarer and rarer each year. And
I think that there's a reason for this, that actually there is less and less
obscurity to complain of, that the poets of my generation are far
easier to understand than Eliot and Pound. And also I suppose that
we have a more trained public at present, which is better able to cope
with whatever difficulties there are in the poets of my generation and
younger.

Are you writing for a particular audience or for everyone?

Wilbur: Well, here I would have to talk as a critic and not as a
poet, because I think that when you write, as when you talk, you're
not really choosing your words according to your audience—unless
you're talking, say, to children. You talk the way it seems natural for
you to talk. But, speaking as a critic and trying to figure out what it is
that I do when I choose my words, I suppose that I am using a
lexicon and a field of reference that belongs not to the public as a
whole but to that part of the public which has had about as much
education as I've had . . . Oh, maybe—since I'm a college
professor—I'd better not say that. But let's say people who have had
a certain amount—a full high school education, and people who
have done a bit of reading. I refuse to be done out of the privilege of
referring to Hephaestus if I like. If that's what I want to say, I will refer
to Hephaestus, regardless of whether a large part of the population of
southern California doesn't know who Hephaestus is—for economy's
sake, for the sake of saying with point and resonance what you want
to say. You can't be forever attuning yourself to what that admirable
fiction, the average man, may be supposed to know. Of course you
try to be as simple as you can. You do this for the sake of making
yourself clear to yourself. And so some kind of availability to the
general public ought to be a by-product, a natural by-product, of the
natural inclination of poetry to arrive at a maximum clarity, a

simplicity and condensation of thought. I don't see how you can worry about the public. I don't see how you can worry about your own implicit suppositions about your public. Of course there are implicit suppositions in your choice of words and in your range of references. But I can't think that it is very useful to be very aware of what these implicit suppositions are—because they can't be changed profitably.

When did you begin to write poetry?

Wilbur: Age eight.

When did you begin to think of yourself as a poet?

Wilbur: As a poet in the full sense? Well, I suppose I began to think that way when my first manuscript was accepted—in 1946. I had been piling up a lot of poems prior to that time, sending them from this war zone or that to my wife and a few friends, but I didn't think of myself as a *professional* poet. I was proposing to be quite strictly a scholar and a teacher. It just happened that a friend of mine saw some of my poems, asked to see others, sent them to a publisher, and got them accepted—whereupon I decided to put my head down and concentrate a little more on writing poetry. And I suppose that made me a poet.

Periodically I have doubts as to whether I'm a poet, and I suppose it has something to do with whether I'm writing or not. Right now, I haven't written any poetry for six months, so I don't feel much like a poet. You have to be writing, and I think also that you have to be showing it to people and having it published in magazines in order to feel that the word properly applies to you.

Why did you decide to translate Molière? What do you feel that you gained from translating him?

Wilbur: Well, I can give a simple biographical answer to that. I told the Guggenheim Foundation, back in 1952, that I wanted a fellowship under which I would write a poetic drama. At that time the Poets' Theatre was getting started in Cambridge, and I wanted to write a play for them. I got down, with the Guggenheim Fellowship in my pocket, to the desert of New Mexico and started trying to write poetic plays. And they didn't come off. They were very bad, extremely wooden. I had no luck at all bringing characters on stage and making them talk in anything but the most stereotyped manner. I turned to Molière because I thought I might learn something about

what poetic drama might be by translating him. I also turned to
Molière because I'd been in love with the *Misanthrope* for some
years. I wanted to translate it for its own sake, as well as for the sake
of instructing myself.

Well, I'm fairly satisfied with that translation from Molière, and I'm
fairly satisfied with the translation of *Tartuffe* I've just done. And I'm
glad I did them insofar as I did them for their own sake. As for what
instrumental value the translations have had, I really can't now tell—
because I'm still no good whatever at writing original poetic plays. I
see no signs of *improvements* on that side. Perhaps, however,
translating Molière, communing with him as I've necessarily done in
translating some four thousand lines of his poetry, I've come to be
more open and dramatic in my own poetry. That's a possibility. I
know that it *has* happened that I've become more open and
dramatic. Whether I can trace it to Molière or not, I don't know.

*Judson Jerome has admired your adherence to what he calls the
"American Tradition" in poetry, a natural imagery, natural expression—nature—running through Whitman and Dickinson to Frost and
then to you. Jerome feels, as a matter of fact, that you are our finest
living poet. Is there some conviction behind your strict adherence to
natural imagery? Do you lament the absence of natural imagery in
many major poets of the day?*

Wilbur: I suppose we have a lot of urban poets at present in
whom there's little nature to be found. And, as Geoffrey Grigson
pointed out a while ago in one of his BBC broadcasts, there are a
great many modern poets who use natural imagery with a blithe
inaccuracy—no botony or zoology in it, you know. Dylan Thomas
was mentioned by Grigson in particular, though I suspect that
Thomas, coming as he did from a country part of England, actually
had a better, solider knowledge of nature behind him than many
current poets.

I use natural imagery because I was raised on a farm. I don't think I
have any feeling that nature belongs to poetry more than urban
materials. In fact, I had rather not (I've come around to feeling this) I
had rather not make the distinction between nature and the city. I'd
like to see cities as objects quite as natural as bee-hives. Cities are
natural things for men to construct. I have no *cause,* in other words,
for using as much natural imagery as I do. I don't rebuke Delmore

Schwartz, for instance, for being an urban poet or for writing about city scapes. And I attribute my use of natural imagery to simple affection and long acquaintance.

How seriously have you considered writing in other mediums? You've mentioned the short story and the drama this afternoon. Is poetry your favorite medium? Marianne Moore has said that she prefers the drama. I still find that impossible to believe.

Wilbur: I was just reading a quotation in today's *New York Times Magazine,* from Nathaniel Hawthorne. Hawthorne was saying that the sort of book he enjoys reading is exactly the sort of thing he does not write, and that he feels he would find it very difficult to read the works of anyone who wrote like Nathaniel Hawthorne. I wonder if Miss Moore's attitude might not be similar, because I don't think of her as a dramatic writer—in *any* way. I think that this is probably the last of her virtues, the least—I don't know exactly how to say that. It's the virtue she has the least of.

My favorite field *is* poetry, though of course I have a belly full of it every now and then. Everybody does, I think. There are times when I don't want to read it, don't want to hear about it, and had far rather read botany—or mystery novels.

I've tried, in addition to writing poetry and an occasional short story, to do some literary criticism—especially in nineteenth century American poetry. I've written about Poe and about Emily Dickinson. And then I've had a go at writing Broadway show tunes. I did or revised about eighty per cent of the lyrics for *Candide,* the Bernstein-Hellman show of a few years back. I might like to try it again if anything similarly high-toned came along. There's a lot of excitement in comic opera or musical comedy, a lot of possibilities which still haven't been realized, and I do think that the appearance of institutions like the Lincoln Center may make it more and more possible for composers and lyricists and book-writers to be boldly high-toned and not knuckle under to Broadway standards. That's what spoils most of it, and I must say I have *no* interest at all in writing straight Broadway musical comedy.

Who do you feel are our finest poets writing in America today? And who outside America interests you? In particular, what younger poets seem to you to be particularly promising?

Wilbur: That's a dreadful question.

Actually, my tastes are fairly catholic. I would have to name, if I wanted to name all the poets whose work has in some measure pleased or instructed me—I'd have to name most of those in any standard anthology. There are few poets whose names are generally known that I would altogether reject. There are a few less well-known than they should be whom I esteem very highly. One of these would be J. V. Cunningham. Another would be Howard Nemerov. Another would be William Meredith. All of these people are *recognized* poets, but they deserve even more recognition than they have. I would say that there is nobody writing better poetry in this country than Howard Nemerov.

There's no use my naming all the names you would expect me to name, because they are the eminent names in any standard anthology. I *would* name them, and cheerfully and honestly name them.

The foreign poets who have most interested me are chiefly French. And I suppose my most curious taste, because the poet is not too well-known in America, is for the French poet whose name is Francis Ponge, whose first book was called *Le Parti Pris Des Choses,* and who writes constantly from the point of view of things. He's even more of a "thing poet" than Dr. Williams or Marianne Moore, and he's more *prosaic,* I should say, than either of them is.

I'm being evasive again, but I just have so long a list that I don't want to name it off.

Before one final, broadly generalized question, I want to pose a topical question—for those who like things topical. How have you received the news of Steinbeck's being awarded the Nobel Prize? There's much comment on this, and I thought it would be interesting to have your own comment.

Wilbur: Well, I'll say flatly that I wanted Robert Frost to get it, and think that Frost deserves it, and understand somewhat why he didn't get it. Frost is hard to translate. In Russia he has a good translator, a fellow named Sergeyev, and I think the Russians see him properly, see his *magnitude.* It strikes me that he's not been so fortunate in other countries. And then he's not the kind of poet you associate with social protest, with generous social feelings of a kind which people in other countries can easily respond to. His politics are rather subtle, and of course in his earlier poetry his politics are so conservative, so *laissez-faire* conservative, as not to have any likely appeal to Europeans. His colloquialisms ask for some magnificence of talent in the translator, and I'm sure that he hasn't transpired in the translations he has been given in most countries.

Thinking back on Steinbeck, whom I *hadn't* expected to get the Prize, I remember how much I liked *Tortilla Flat* and *Of Mice and Men* and *Grapes of Wrath*—and I can't think that any important injustice has been done. The latter books of Steinbeck I simply haven't read, so I can't weigh his work as a whole. I suppose what one asks of the Nobel Prize is simply that it be given to somebody who's good. And Steinbeck is good.

Now for that last, broadly generalized question. Your comments this afternoon make it clear that you think carefully. Your poetry shows that you write it carefully. You've said that it's been six months since you wrote your last poetry. Obviously, then, there's something that you want to do and that you do with care. You're a young poet—in your early forties, published for about fifteen years. For a generalized question, nothing suggests itself better than to ask just what you intend to do with your career as a poet. What do you see before you—or hope before you?

Wilbur: Well, you can probably anticipate what I'm going to say, because I've more than once during our conversation denied conscious purposes, denied that I write in order to adhere to projects or principles. I don't *know* what I'm going to do. Of course, what I want to do is to write more poems. What they'll be like, I don't know. I hope that they'll be like what I've already written, insofar as what I've done is good. But I'm quite ready to surprise myself by doing something odd or—by writing *free verse*, if you like.

All I can say is that I want to write some *more*, and hope that it doesn't come too hard, and that the decline will not be too terrible.

Richard Wilbur: An Interview

Robert Frank and Stephen Mitchell/1964

From *The Amherst Literary Magazine*, Vol. 10, No. 2 (Summer 1964), 54-72. Reprinted by permission of Richard Wilbur and *The Amherst Student Review.*

Mr. Wilbur lives in Portland, Connecticut, with his wife (an alumna of Smith College) and his four children, in a large, old frame house hidden by evergreens and tall maples from the new development that has grown up around it. When we arrived for the interview he came out to meet us wearing a white shirt (open at the top), slacks, and tennis shoes. Although he is forty-three years old, he strikes one, by his appearance, manner, and speech, as a man in his mid-thirties. He has the same kind of charm, eloquence, and aristocratic grace that one finds in his poems. The interview, which took place in the Wilbur's living room, lasted the better part of an afternoon, during the course of which we were occasionally interrupted by Aaron, his youngest child, who could not stop marveling at the rotating reels of the tape recorder. ("Our two younger children are Aaron and Nathan—we probably have the only pure Anglo-Saxon Jewish family in Connecticut," Mr. Wilbur laughed after the second such interruption.) We began by talking about his recent experience with theatre ("I haven't done any acting since I was Scrooge in the eighth-grade play")—the production of his verse translations of *The Misanthrope* and *Tartuffe,* the reaction to his libretto for *Candide,* and a translation he has been working on recently. The discussion then shifted to an educational program on poetry that he is preparing for the Voice of America. This led to a question on his classes at Wesleyan, just across the Connecticut River from his home.

What kinds of things do you teach in your writing course? In fact, what can you teach about writing?

You clearly can't do anything with people who are untalented. With people who are talented you can sometimes be a little bit of

help in seeing, somewhat before they do, what it is that they do best,
and encouraging them to do that. I think it's also possible to shake
people up in their imaginative habits, by means of exercises. I assume
that no one can be creative every week of the year, and so, on the
odd weeks, I ask my students to do exercices calculated to make
them see in a slightly different way. The usual thing, for example, is
to suppose that nature is more poetical than man-made things;
therefore that it is an enhancement to compare streetlamps to stars
but a degradation to compare stars to streetlamps. So I ask my
students to do something like comparing stars to streetlamps—to
compare something supposedly exalted and spiritual to something
supposedly man-made and low. This often shakes people up a bit.
It's very odd that it should be so ruffling, so surprising nowadays to
find oneself obliged to compare in that direction. It's well over a
hundred and fifty years since the Bowles controversy, in which Byron
was involved—the controversy over the poetic status of man-made
things. I think it's pretty clear that criticism nowadays believes one
thing to be as poetical as another. We all readily accept this as theory;
but still, the imaginative habit is to enhance by comparing man-made
things to nature.

Does teaching interfere with your writing?

Oh yes, I think so. Teaching is probably the best thing one can do
if one has to do something else, something in addition to writing. But
teaching does in a great many ways interfere with writing. It uses a lot
of the same kind of mental energies. It makes you go stale on words.
It makes you considerably less chaste in your use of words. You
develop the habit that all teachers have of settling for the merely
adequate word. That attitude simply won't go with the writing of live
poetry. And it takes an enormous amount of time. I have a feeling
that teachers put in a longer work day than most people in America.
Most of my nights during the week are spent in preparing classes, and
I think this is true of a lot of teachers; whereas my friends who are in
business can't understand why I can't run out and play tennis as
soon as I get home from work.

*Aside from the financial aspect, is there anything in teaching that
helps you in writing?*

Yes, I'm sure there is. I'm really grateful towards teaching. It's a
thing I like to do, and it was initially the thing I most wanted to do. I

don't believe that there is any such thing as a good poet who is also
an ignorant poet, and I don't think that I can name a good poet
nowadays who doesn't have a grasp, not a scholarly one necessarily,
but a good dilettantish grasp of the whole range of English poetry.
Most of the good poets I know are acquainted, either directly or
through translation, with quite a lot of the literature of other cultures
too. And if you're a teacher, this kind of knowledge comes to you as
a matter of course. There may be some harm done in one's having to
treat the material so analytically, in one's having to discuss it when
one doesn't feel like discussing it. It would be nice to be more
dilettantish, but it's nice to be pushed into activity too. And the
teaching profession gives you all sorts of deadlines before which or
by which you will know something about Edmund Spenser. That's a
help.

Getting to your writing itself . . . When did you start to write verse?

Well, I started to write earnestly and frequently during World War
II. One has an awful lot of leisure during any war, mostly waiting
around; and I think, as I've said in a couple of places, that a time of
disorder is likely to provoke anyone with any verbal abilities into
writing. You use your writing as a way to put things provisionally back
together—as Robert Frost said, as a "momentary stay against
confusion." When I started writing poems during the War, I used to
send them every now and then to friends, and always to my wife.
Sometimes I would send poems to Armour Craig; and I sent them
once or twice to other people at Amherst, but particularly to Armour.
The poems just piled up. I almost never thought of sending a poem to
a magazine. Then when I went to Harvard Graduate School in 1946,
just after the War, I ran into André du Bouchet, an Amherst man,
who was poetry editor of the magazine *Foreground,* which ran for
two issues in Cambridge, Mass. It was being financed by the
publishing house of Reynal and Hitchcock, who were doing it partly
out of high-mindedness, and also because they thought that
ownership of a little magazine might help them to scout for new
talent. All of the editors, André among them, were committed to find
new talent for them. André, therefore, wanted to see my poems
when my wife gave out the dirty secret that I had a drawerful of
them. He took them home with him and reappeared at our
apartment about two hours later, rushed in, and, with a marvelous

display of Gallic fervor, wrapped his arms around me, kissed me on both cheeks, and declared me a poet. He then sent my poems to Reynal and Hitchcock. Much to my surprise they wrote back that they would like to publish a book. I guess I had the most painless introduction to publication any writer's ever had.

It's obvious that you have a distinctive style even in the earliest poems in The Beautiful Changes. *But most poets have extremely derivative styles at first—Eliot's and Stevens' undergraduate verse, for example—and aren't original until later. How does it happen that a poet seems suddenly to find himself—to find the style that is himself?*

I can't guess how that happens. I can guess how it is that some people take a long time getting to an original style. It can be very bad for people to be snowed under by the influence of any one writer for a long time. I keep telling my students at Wesleyan to get excited above five or six poets at once, if possible, and also to read contemporary poetry and the old fellows at the same time. It's not that there is really a serious risk of one's writing *Paradise Lost* over again, but I think it's good to have a confused set of enthusiasms, to prevent one from getting frozen in the vocabulary and in the pet attitudes of any one poet. For a while, I remember, every young poet, among those just starting to publish, was making a noise like Yeats; and to some it was paralyzing for several years. During the recent high celebrity of Yeats, I think a number of people were really slowed down in their development by devoting themselves to writing poems in which they impersonated old men defying death, and the like—in which they used the Yeats vocabulary from . . . well, the only word I can think of now is "rage."

Whom were you excited about at college? What poets were you reading?

Actually, I read almost no contemporary poetry. I suppose that I started reading T. S. Eliot in high school, and I had read James Joyce's poetry in high school. But I don't think I was particularly excited about contemporary poetry or about the possibilty of becoming a poet when I was at Amherst. I read with pleasure, in courses, a good deal of the poetry of the past. I think I was more excited about criticism and about journalism when I was at Amherst than I was about poetry. Indeed, I was more interested in cartooning than I was in poetry. I didn't start to read very hard in the way in

which a poet reads poetry until I was in the army and carrying
around in my musette bag a strange mixture of books. I remember
that I had Gerard Manley Hopkins' poems and a little pamphlet of
Dylan Thomas' poems and Tennyson's poems. I also had a barracks
bag following me—at a distance—it sometimes caught up with me—
and in the barracks bag was *Finnegan's Wake,* for heaven's sake!
(Laughter.)

So you did have limited contact with modern poetry?

Quite limited, really. I wasn't at all as up on who the interesting
younger poets were as most of my students are now. John Berryman
has just published his 77 *Dream Songs* and my students at Wesleyan
know about that. I didn't know the corresponding things that were
happening in poetry when I was at Amherst.

*Almost everyone says that you have been influenced by Marianne
Moore. When did you start to read her?*

I think that I read her first just a little after the war, and I remember
being stimulated to read her by Ben Brower's enthusiasm. At least
that was contributory. And I was for several years very charmed with
her poetry and I think undoubtedly influenced by it. I don't think I
have been influenced by her for quite some time. But it's possible to
find a few poems in my first book.

Do you read criticism of yourself?

I guess I do, really. That is, when there is some fairly sustained
piece of commentary, someone will tell me about it, and I find it
pretty hard not to go and look. I know that you're supposed to say
that you don't read criticism about yourself, but I find it necessary at
least to read anything that is said about me by anyone that I find
interesting. And I don't see any reason for pretending that I'm not
interested in what they say. I remember going to see E. E. Cummings
one time in the Village. We had an awfully nice conversation, mostly
about Cézanne's correspondence with a young man who was
extorting statements about nature from him. Then we got off onto
poetry briefly, and he said that he remembered some article,
somewhere, by a fellow who he thought was named Blackmur, and
he thought the article might be found in *Hound and Horn.* Well, this
is one of the most celebrated essays on Cummings, of course, and
Cummings could not have failed to know it better than he indicated.
By the time we were finished with the conversation, I let my eyes roll

over his bookshelves and there was a complete stack of *Hound and Horn*. He was bound to have read that article with displeasure more than once.

Several critics—Randall Jarrell was the first—have criticized you for not taking chances in your poetry. Jarrell says that most of your poetry "consents too easily to its own limitations," that you "never go too far, but never go far enough." What is your reaction to this sort of criticism?

I always feel that I take enough chances. And so instead of taking Jarrell's criticism seriously, what I've done has been to try to explain it away in terms of his attitudes of the time. At the time he wrote that criticism, he was commencing to write long, unrhymed narrative poems, often quite loose in their rhythm and relatively prosaic in their language. He was moving away from the sort of cleanly executed formal poem that he'd written during the War. I think that he saw himself as making a daring departure and was glad of it. He noticed that Lowell was being influenced by the direction that he was taking. Lowell said as much, and I think it's probably true that when Lowell got into writing long narrative poems in comparatively relaxed rhythms, it was Jarrell who started him off. And I think Jarrell felt that there I was, still back writing iambic pentameters, and frequently rhyming them, and not running on at his length. I think that's what he meant by not running for "touchdowns," settling for "short gains."

If you will excuse what Auden calls a silly question, whom do you write for?

Well, of course that is a question for which every poet has figured out a pat answer. I would say that I write for the, by now, largely anonymous . . . no, no . . . let me start over. I write for a lot of people who have influenced me and whom I have admired and who are in my head. When I start to write, I don't say, "Now I'm going to see if I can write a poem that Theodore Baird would approve of." But he is one of the witnesses in my head. He is blended with fifty or a hundred other people I'd like to be understood by and would like to please. Not all of these people in my head are teachers or poets. A lot of them are just people, you know—lively people, people whose sensibility one admires, perhaps more than one admires their intellect.

Perhaps your children?

My children would qualify, although they're pretty bright. (Laughter.) But I think that that is an accurate answer and that it really does explode the question of whether one writes for oneself or for others. One does both, because, whatever the Self is, any proper definition of it is going to have to include the idea that the Self is constituted of other people—of the influences of other people.

About your children—what do you have them read?

I try to get my children to read almost anything. I suppose that I haven't been a great bully in this way, just because I've felt that it's bad enough for their father to be a writer, and that if he were a writer who bullied them to read, it might put them off some of the great pleasures of life. So I haven't pressed them very hard to read, or to read this or that. But when they've said, "What shall I read?" I've often pulled down from the shelves quite adult books. And I have encouraged them all to disregard their teachers when their teachers tell them such-and-such a book is too old for them. All of my children have enjoyed reading poetry in some measure, and I've tried with moderate success to get some of them to memorize poems. It seems to me that while one has a good memory, it's an awfully good thing to get a few poems of certified merit into the head. I did get my son Christopher once to memorize Frost's poem "Nothing Gold Can Stay," that being a short one; and he grudgingly memorized it and said it to me a couple of times. Then when this time of year came around he came running in from our maple tree and said, "Nature's first green is gold! It's true, Daddy!" (Laughter.)

Do they know any of your poems by heart?

I think that may be the case, but I'm not sure. I certainly haven't made them recite such things for me.

How does a poem start for you?

Well, I should say almost never as an idea, and almost never as a mere descriptive possibility, and almost never, I think, because of some interesting word that I've encountered and want to use. It's got to be a sudden and surprising conjunction of all those things before I can get going. Generally what starts me off is a perception of something in the external world in which I feel the potentiality of an idea, not perhaps fully realized, but felt to be there. And then I suppose I can't go ahead unless something in the way of an interesting series of words comes to me. There are some people who do write poetry without words, some of the time, but I can't. I have to be interested by the words, and feel that the words are new. I remember one poem I contemplated for a long time when I was at Harvard about the winter aspect of the yard in front of Apthorp House. I had a study in Adams house that looked out across the yard at Apthorp House. There were a lot of trees in that little yard, and in January the trees would often be covered with ice; they'd thaw a little at midday, and then they'd freeze again as the light failed. This always interested me as a sort of résumé, in a couple of wintry hours, of the progress of the seasons. As the trees thawed, they often had globes of water on the twig ends which fell as fruit falls. I felt a poem in that, but I couldn't simply start writing until I found a word that made me want to do it. And leafing one day, I confess it, through the *Oxford English Dictionary,* I came across the word "gemmation," a wonderful word which suggests jewelry but means budding. It was clear to me at once that I could now write that poem.

Do you work your poems over a lot?

A very long time. I suppose there are one or two which I have written in an afternoon. But in many cases I've taken five years to finish a poem—five years of picking it up and putting it down again. The last one I finished I began in 1960 in Houston, got stalled on it, picked up again and finished it this year.

Is that the one dedicated to Robert Frost?

No, it's one that's coming out in the *New Yorker,* called "Complaint," a poem about a neurotic courtier. The one I've dedicated to Frost I started to write not long after his death. I was trying concurrently to write a memorial poem to Frost and that didn't work. But the poem about seed leaves turned out to be a Frost-like poem, I felt. It seemed to me to have enough of Frost in it so that I could honestly dedicate it to him and call it a memorial poem.

Both you and Robert Lowell have said that all poetry of the highest quality is religious. In what sense do you mean that?

I think there are various ways you could argue for that position. You could say that all poetry, however much it may be irrational, moves towards clarity and order, that it affirms all that is clear and orderly in the world, affirms the roots of clarity in the world. Then, you might say that poetry is given not only to saying that this is like that, as in the simile; it's given also to saying that this *is* that, to

affirming rather nervily that prosaically unlike things are to poetry's
eye identical, con-atural. I think there is a natural disposition of the
poetic mind to assert that all things are one, are part of the same
thing, that anything may be compared to anything else. And if
anything may be compared to anything else, the ground of the
comparison is likely to be divine.

Then poets believe in metaphors?

I think so. Did you say a poem of the highest quality? I think that in
poetry of the highest quality, in poetry of great genuineness and
seriousness, the metaphors are believed. I remember that my friend
Joseph Beach, who is chiefly remembered as a critic, but was also a
poet, used to talk a great game of atheism; and in his last book, called
Involuntary Witness, I was surprised to find a poem of his which
ended with a thumping religious affirmation. I took it around to him
and I said, "Look, Joseph, I thought you were an atheist. What about
this?" and he said, "If it says I believe in God, it must be true,
because you never tell lies in poetry." I think that's right. It seems to
me that poetry is one's way of talking at one's most serious, and that
you outdo your prosaic mind. You do better than your prosaic
apprehension of things in poetry.

*When one reads "Love Calls Us to the Things of This World," one
finds that one does believe in angels.*

(Laughter.) Well, I can believe in angels by way of and in the
laundry. I find laundry a great help to the conception of angels, and I
suppose one thing I'm saying in that poem is that I don't really want
to have much truck with angels who aren't in the laundry, who aren't
involved in the everyday world. It's a poem against dissociated and
abstracted spirituality.

*One reviewer has said of you, "The best of Mr. Wilbur's poems
always resolve themselves in favor of the concrete reality—which
would lead me to label him 'classic' as opposed to 'romantic.'" I
realize that these terms have been much abused, but do they have
any meaning for you in this context?*

In connection with what you're saying they do have some meaning
for me. In connection with what you're saying, the word romantic
makes me think of Novalis, for example, of Jena School German
romantic imagination, and its preference for vagueness, and its love
of the blue flower that's in the blue distance. I prefer not to situate the

beautiful and the spiritual at a vague distance. I prefer William Blake's classical eye. I think of William Blake as a classicist in this sense. He can see all the spiritual truth he needs to see in the sand grain near at hand, and in the other immediate properties of his world.

You said in your lecture on Emily Dickinson, "The subjects to which a poet returns are those which vex him." Do you find that true in your poetry?

Yes. This is probably something which I can't testify about, but undoubtedly it's the things you find yourself affirming over and over again which are the things you feel yourself in danger of not affirming. You remember probably more accurately than I a thing Wallace Stevens said about Dr. Williams. He said that Williams' poetry represented an inclination towards the sentimental, corrected by a passion for the anti-poetic; something like that. Well, I don't know what inclination of mine is corrected by a passion for the concrete, but there is an inclination I keep correcting. I'm sure of that.

Are there subjects which used to interest you and no longer do, or subjects which interest you now and wouldn't have before?

I've never figured this out and so I don't know whether I can testify. I wouldn't be surprised to find out that I've always been writing about the same thing, but that I now see the subject wholly differently or project it before the mind's eye with quite different properties from those that I used to use. By properties I mean, well, things like Robert Frost's walls. He was always worrying about the subject of walls, and whether they were good or bad, and what things they were protecting us from or keeping us out of; and he really thought in walls for a long time. I think that at all times he was concerned with the subject of human limitations. But he shifted the properties in which he talked about the subject. I undoubtedly have shifted the properties in which I talk about the things that vex me, but I should guess that I haven't completely abandoned any subject that ever interested me.

I was wondering about the abundance of Latin-root words in your poetry . . .

Maybe I really do have a lot of Latin roots, but I'm in love with Anglo-Saxon words too.

Well, I was wondering particularly about what John Ciardi calls

your Latin-root sense—in lines like "the maples with a stiff/ :
Compliance entertain the air," where you're consciously taking
advantage of the words' history.

Yes, I know that I do that. And I know it's something I've enjoyed
in John Crowe Ransom and Wallace Stevens. They're the two people
I think of when I think of that kind of play with the root meaning of
Latin words. But I should be interested to see just how far away I am
from whatever is normal in English verse, with regard to the balance
between Latin and Anglo-Saxon. I know that people have figured out
what was normal in 1600 or so, for Marlowe and Shakespeare;
perhaps Josephine Miles has already done the same for the present
day.

Have you ever been tempted to write free verse?

Well, I've published one or two free verse poems. I have in—I
forget which book—a poem called "Apology." It's a little love poem
in free verse. I think I have one or two others, somewhere. Mostly, I
haven't been able to please myself in my efforts to write free verse. I
agree with Ezra Pound when he says that free verse is harder to write
than formal verse. It's very clear that however much one masters the
formal elements in a formal poem, however much one makes them
do just what one wants, they are a little bit of a crutch and a comfort.
They may not end by looking so. I hope to heaven they don't look so
in my poems. But at any rate, they feel so during the process of
composition. You say to yourself, "Well, there's another pentameter;
I'm right at home." But with free verse, you have to have a kind of
intuitive assurance that what you've done is right. In spite of Yvor
Winters' efforts at codification, I don't really think that there are any
rules for writing free verse, or that one can say why a free verse
poem is successful. I have a feeling that the best free verse is likely to
be written by people who have mastered formal verse. I think that
there I am agreeing with Pound and Eliot. Nevertheless, I think that
the writing of formal verse is likely to delay one's progress towards
the writing of free verse; because, however difficult it may be, formal
verse is in some ways emotionally comfortable. It requires fewer
arbitrary decisions, fewer intuitive conclusions that one is somehow
mysteriously right.

Among the poets of your generation there was a rather evident return to formal verse—a tendency which was predicted by Eliot, I think in the Thirties. Do you see any significance in this return to form?

I don't, no. In spite of what I've been saying, I don't associate free verse with daring and formal poetry with timidity. It doesn't seem to me that a prevalence of formal verse indicates that poets are unnerved. I realize that the word "stanza" means "room," and that one can imagine the formal poet as huddling within a room, hiding out from the turbulent world. I don't really think that's true.

Then could you say what the positive elements are in formal verse?

Are you thinking of the end product or the process?

Either, or both.

Well, I think that the process of writing formal verse is very likely to be a slow one. If one is hard on oneself, if one is demanding of one's poetry, it's very likely to be a slow business. Finding the right rhyme can slow you down. Finding the right way, the right live way, to counterpoint a basic meter can slow you down considerably. And since you are slowed down by these technical difficulties, you are also likey to be slowed down in your choosing of words. Now, the ideal free-verse writer—I don't think he exists, but I think he's a possibility—the ideal free verse writer would be perhaps even more slowed down by the demands of his organic kind of form, by his need to feel that he has achieved perfection in that sort of form, than the formal poet is by his kind of formal restraint. But, in general, I think free verse doesn't work that way. The free-verse poet inclines to write faster, inclines not to choose his words so carefully.

How about the end product?

In a rhyming poem, one has, of course, an infinitely better chance of governing the reader's voice than a free-verse poet does. There are the line beginnings and the line endings to require emphases of the reader. You have the rhyming pattern to dictate further emphases, you have the possibility of rhyming hard and soft on the same sound, in such a way as to require very precisely a giving-out of the voice, of the tone. A diminuendo. There are lots of means of control of the reader in a formal poem—a rhymed, metrical poem—that the free-verse writer can't have. This is one reason why free verse is full of repetitions. Repetition is one way of heightening that is still available to you if you have thrown away all emphatic rhythm. You can continue to begin your lines with the same three words. One sees this in American free verse from Whitman right through to the present. Another thing you can do—something that even so good a practitioner as Dr. Williams did—is to use question marks or exclamation points all the time.

Getting to the process of writing . . . First, I wonder if you ever compose on a typewriter?

Never on a typewriter! Something happens to what you've written when you put it on the typewriter. It gains a sudden objectivity and authority; and if you compose on the typewriter, you forego the pleasure of transforming your work, of externalizing your work, by putting it on the typewriter. Once I've typed something out, I find myself at once more impressed with it and more capable of judging it. If it fails to impress me on the typewriter, I know it won't do. But there's just too much speed and noise to a typewriter. I really don't believe the story about T. S. Eliot composing on the typewriter—a man who has written as few poems as he has cannot have rushed them off on a machine.

There's such a density of sound in your poetry, do you read your poems aloud when you write them?

Oh, I think I probably read everything aloud, and over and over and over. And I write everything over and over and over. I was amused the other day to find out that in this respect, Dylan Thomas and I have the same habits. He, when having another go at a poem on which he was stalled, would write it all out from the beginning, even if it was the "Ballad of the Long-Legged Bait" and it was going to take a number of pages. He would sit down and write the whole poem out up to the point where he got stuck, in hopes that the impetus would carry him on for another few words. I do that—write the poem over and over again and say it over and over again. I never, I think, apply any sort of speech-class analysis to what I'm doing, but I just see if it sounds right to me. I didn't use to do this, and when I look back at my earliest poems I notice how, quite often in them, there are clots of consonants that make some lines unpronounceable. It's clear that when I began I was a lot less concerned with the ear than I am now, and it's not hard to see why. If you have some experience as a Broadway lyricist and then do a lot of running around the country reading your poems aloud to people, it's going to modify your sense of words and of poetry.

It's been said that in post-War American poetry there have been two schools—the Lowell School and the Wilbur School. Donald Hall made the distinction in an excellent introduction to his anthology of comtemporary verse . . .

The Penguin one?

Yes, in which he distinguished two schools, the Lowell School and the Wilbur School.

Hmmm.

I suppose that one of the main distinctions would be the intentional line-cluttering of the Lowell School, as opposed to the more musical quality of the . . .

Maybe that's true. I certainly think that Lowell gets very exiciting, violent sound effects. I don't know that he errs on the side of being hard to pronounce. It seems to me that a line can be quite violent, cacophonous, and still be very sayable. And I think he's quite a wonderful technician. I don't know whether I'm more melodious than he is. But I think that he and I are probably about the same in respect to pronounceability. He has become a very good reader aloud of poems, and I think he's become more and more aware of sound, of the ear—has more of an actor's sense of the ear than he used to have.

Hall said that the typical ghastly poem of the Fifties was a Wilbur poem not written by Wilbur. Would you recognize a Wilbur School at present?

I'm not at all conscious of being a member of or a founder of a school. It seems to be the custom at the moment among people who are making a general survey of the poetic situation to put Lowell on one side and me on the other. I'm all grace and charm and short gains, and he's all violence and . . .

Touchdowns?

Well, he's Apollo and Dionysus locked in a death grip. (Laughter.) I've heard Donald Hall and Leslie Fiedler and Randall Jarrell saying this, saying that I have had a lot of imitators. I can only say that my powers of recognition aren't very good if I do have a lot of imitators. We don't see ourselves very readily in our children. It's other people who do that for us. Maybe Jarrell and Hall and Fiedler are right and I

just can't or don't see these things because they are so like me. But I
have no sense myself of being part of or being leader of a school. I
don't think I want to be. When I teach poetry I never encourage
anybody to write as I do. I find that when I'm reading poetry just for
the hell of it, sitting around opening magazines and books, I don't
turn by preference to any one kind of poetry. I just want it to be
good. And I have a distinct taste for variety.

*If you don't think of yourself as founder of a school, do you
consider yourself a disciple of any poet in particular or a continuator
of any particular tradition?*

I don't think so. I can manage to enjoy something about many
different kinds of poetry, and it has always been that way with me. I
do fall out of love with people from time to time, but then I go back
to them again. At various times, I've been fond of the poetry of
almost anybody of quality you might name. And I don't regard
myself as the continuator of any particular one of them.

Would you say you have any favorite poets?

I'm going to be evasive again, because it would be quite a big list.
And it would include a lot of individual poems which I've picked up
along the way and have an odd feeling for. Everybody is stubborn
about a certain number of unfashionable poets or poems, and it's
always fascinating to discover what the special tastes of writers are.
They're never what the critics would predict. The critic always wants
to size up the period in terms of three or four influential figures to
whom there have been certain recognizable tributaries and from
whom passes a set of clear lines of influences. But if you go and ask
Elizabeth Bishop, for example, what poetry she reads often, it will be
George Herbert, and not Marianne Moore—whom the critics call a
major influence on her. They would like her to be influenced by
someone immediately her senior, and it confuses the chart if you go
back to Herbert more than to Marianne Moore. I remember the first
time Theodore Roethke came to see us. After we had read his new
poems, we got around to reading other people, and he began
spouting, very handsomely, the poetry of Charlotte Mew, about
whom I knew nothing at the time. She, I think, was of more
consequence to Roethke than a lot of people Roethke's critics will be
talking about. As for myself, I read a lot of Herbert, a lot of Marvell, I
read the prose of Traherne; and I do this for simple pleasure, not at all

in a scholarly spirit. Those are three people I never tire of. With other people I tend to have my on and my off moments. Though I suppose Dr. Williams has never wearied me. I don't know just what it is about him that doesn't weary me, but he doesn't.

You mentioned during a reading at Smith College that while you were living in Rome you put in an eight-hour day. Were you serious when you said that?

Yes, I did make myself write about eight hours a day. It's possible to do that if you have a job of translation under way. That's one good thing about translation. It's something you can do if you're not feeling original and inspired. Of course, it's very hard to adjust the claims of poetry and translation once you get to translating. In fact, you're likely to find yourself doing translation because it's the easiest thing to do. Mr. Molière has already figured out what the subject matter will be.

It seems that the poet-translator has two extremes to synthesize: on the one hand, to efface himself before the original; or on the other hand, to use his own voice and not be overly concerned with preserving the voice of the original. While your translations are recognizably in your style, they are quite faithful, as opposed to the translations of Pound, or to Lowell's Imitations.

Well, I think it's probably true that all translators who really are poets—who are poets first and translators second—are drawn to the jobs they do because they want to take over something that is in the original and incorporate it into the body of their own work. Perhaps they claim, by way of what they are translating, some kind of utterance, some kind of emotion which doesn't come easily to them in their own poetry. But I think some go farther than others with this. The Pound tradition, in which Lowell is writing, is a tradition of adaptation—of adapting the original to the taste of the present moment, to the style of the present and to the style of the translator, making the original available to all those who are in communication with the translator as a poet. It's this approach to translation that Eliot was talking about when he said that Pound had invented Chinese poetry for our age. I know that I share some of the imperialistic approach of Pound and Lowell in translation, but I think I have a little less of it and am very much more reluctant to put my own material into what I'm translating. I enjoy the illusion that I'm bringing it back alive, that I'm getting it over with nothing left out. Now, I know this is always an illusion, but that's what compensates me for being less imperialistic than Lowell.

How did you come to write your ballade for the Charles d'Orléans contest? Is that an example of bringing something back alive?

Well, I don't know. I don't think I felt that I was writing a ballade for a contest in the fifteenth century. I've never liked to write exercises or feel that I was writing anything but a poem of my own, in contemporary language. Some of my poems have been mistaken for exercises, to my sorrow; but I have never meant to do that sort of thing. I don't like to write something simply in order to have used a meter, or a certain form. And my poem "Junk," which you referred to a while ago, is not at all meant to be a virtuoso performance in Anglo-Saxon meter. It's meant to be a poem which I felt, rightly or wrongly, called for Anglo-Saxon alliterative meter.

Has that been called an exercise?

Dudley Fitts, with whom I agree in almost everything, reviewing the book in which that first appeared, called it an exercise in Anglo-Saxon meter, as did some other reviewer. I am aware that the meter and the alliteration are a little odd, that a bit of adjusting is called for, and that it is likely to look at first like an exercise. But it seems to me a fairly fervent poem, and I would be sorry if anyone who had read it twice still felt that it had been written as a technical workout.

Don't you consider that taking a chance?

Yes, I suppose I could have mentioned that sort of thing when you asked me about Jarrell's "short gains" and "touchdowns" remark, because I do think that a thing like that amounts to taking a chance, and clearly I've suffered for it! (Laughter.)

Do you usually discuss your poems with other poets before you publish them?

I generally show anything I've written, first to my wife, and then to some friend or other. I've shown a great many poems to Bill Meredith, and have shown some things to Lowell and to John Brinnin, who's an old friend of the family. I don't know whether I've ever gone so far as not to print a poem because someone didn't like it. That's another matter. I think in general when poets show poems to each other, they're looking not for criticism but for praise. I remember one friend of mine—a man who ordinarily is a good writer—had written a perfectly dreadful long poem, which he showed to John Holmes, to Lowell and to me. And we all said, "Never let this see the light. Never publish it. If you do, make the following changes." We all gave him enormous lists of changes to be made. He accepted all the criticisms cheerfully, and all of the specific recommendations with gratitude, and then went and published the damn thing without a single alteration. I think that actually is normal procedure for poets. I recall Frost's saying about this matter, "I understand that you and Ciardi and others have been meeting in Cambridge and reading poems to each other. What is it that you're after—praise?" I said "Yes," and he said, "Well, that's all right. I was afraid you were going to say criticism."

Have you ever received unusual requests, in the vein of Marianne Moore's correspondence with the Ford Company?

Oh, yes. There was a request a number of years ago that was so strange that I've forgotten the details of it, really, but it amounted to this: There was an admiral in the navy who had fallen in love with either the Arctic or the Antarctic—I think it must have been the latter—and he thought it beautiful. He wanted to take a poet to the Pole with him—he wanted it to be a professional poet, a person of proven verbal grasp—and to pay this poet to encompass the Pole with words. I was very tempted by the idea of a Polar voyage, but I just couldn't bring myself to promise that I'd measure up with poems. It's very strange. The man simply wanted it done, and felt that the Pole had never yet been done in poetry. I suppose it hasn't. . . . It is rather flattering to be compared to a photographer, you know—someone who might really get it down.

Then people do respect you, even though you're a poet!

Yes. In fact I think there's been a rather cliché notion going around for a long time in America that writers and authors are not respected. I truly think that there is considerable respect for the practitioners of arts in this country, and that it isn't necessary for a poet to be self-conscious about what it is that he does. I find I can come right out and tell people what it is that I do, and I don't then have to tell war stories to prove that I'm a man.

Archibald MacLeish has been speaking recently about the problems raised by the awarding of the Bollingen prize to Pound in 1948. The major one, of course, is the problem of belief in poetry, how much the reader must assent to the ideas in a poem . . .

What you want in poetry is not rightness or wrongness of belief, but adequacy of attitude, a sufficient comprehensiveness and richness of attitude. The trouble with Pound is that he has, for all of his virtues, a kind of cranky emotional dryness, and doesn't seem to me to be interested in enough things. I suppose that may sound a little absurd, considering how active a man he is and how broad he's been within the arts. But really, it's within the arts that he's been broad. I do find him emotionally and intellectually narrow. . . . It seems to me that what you want of poetry in respect to ideas is not convincing argumentation, or the attractive presentation of ideas in which you already believe, but a demonstration of how the world would look, how you would feel, if you dwelt in the presence of a certain idea. Dante is a good example to think of here. It's by no means necessary to accept a Catholic theology, or Catholic conceptions of the relative gravity or nobility of the vices or of the virtues, in order to be possessed by Dante. He can show you what it would be like to see the world in a certain way, what it would be like to think and feel as a medieval Catholic. And that for me is quite sufficient. The issue of reading the poem is not conversion, but enrichment of experience, a stretching of one's sense of the possibilities of the world.

May I ask you a typical closing question? It's on the order of, Do you have any advice for the young poets of today?

Oh, I don't think I can give any advice beyond reiterating some things I've already said about reading a lot and all over the place at once, so as not to get under the thumb of any one admired writer. I suppose one might give any young poet the least difficult advice: that he not set himself any schedule for writing, because that's making poetry grim, as it oughtn't to be; but that he make sure that he allows himself at reasonably frequent intervals to sit down and do nothing and see whether he has anything to write. You could sit down and do nothing once a day, so long as you were sure to do nothing if nothing wanted to happen. I think generally poets are mistaken when they say, "No nonsense now, let's get down to business. Every morning at six o'clock I'm going to go to my desk." It does make for increased production, but I think it makes for forced work and the spoiling of a lot of good ideas.

An Interview with Richard Wilbur

Paul McKnight and Gary Houston/1966

From *Thistle*, Vol. IX, No. 1 (December 1966), 22-27.

The following interview took place from 9:15 to 9:45 A.M. on April 30, 1966, in a parlor at the Wooster Inn, shortly before Mr. Wilbur was to participate in a panel discussion with Lewis Mumford and Howard Hanson. The weather was wet, Mr. Wilbur's humor was dry, and so excellent spirits prevailed throughout.

Thistle: Mr. Wilbur, could you account for any past or present literary figures who have influenced your work?

Wilbur: That's really hard to say, hard for *me* to say, because I've read a quantity of poetry in the past, and responded to a whole lot of it at one time or another, and rejected very little of it. And I feel pretty much the same way about most of the main names you'd encounter in any anthology of contemporary poetry—that I found something in most of them to respond to, and doubtless have been influenced by them. It's no shame to confess that one's been influenced, because no poet has ever thought up the idea of poetry for himself. He got the notion of writing poetry from seeing a wonderful poem sometime. He wanted to do something like it.

Thistle: Is it true that you reject Eliot and Pound in favor of the tradition of Yeats and the more musical poetry?

Wilbur: I tend to sound a little sassy about T. S. Eliot—sometimes using words like "promiscuous" about his echoing of previous literature—but actually I have the greatest respect for him, and I can remember that when I was in the twelfth grade of high school I hauled around Eliot's poems under my arm everywhere. And it was "Ash Wednesday" that particularly took my imagination then, and still does. I think it's the best of his poems.

No, I don't feel against anything, really. The extremely melodic, the extremely contrived poetry of some poets I can enjoy and profit from.

The very prosaic poetry of William Carlos Williams, for example, I can also enjoy. In fact, Williams—although I recognize his technical limitations—is one poet of whom I never tire at all.

Thistle: Can you remember any outstanding personal experiences, such as your wartime experience, which have influenced your work?

Wilbur: I don't think I can remember any *moments* which influenced me, turned me into a poet, or gave me material for poetry, but I think there were certain sustained experiences or exposures which did affect me one way or another. Being brought up in the country had a lot to do with the way I feel about the materials of poetry—it comes natural to me to use, in particular, botanical materials. And then, being brought up in the house of a painter gave me a busy eye, I think, and made me responsive to painting. If you've looked through the paperback of my poems, you'll notice that there really are quite a number of references to painters and to painting. And then World War II, of course, had doubtless a greater effect on me than I could possibly account for. I said once, in writing a little biography of myself, that I thought I had come to take poetry seriously for the first time as a soldier in World War II. War, as Evelyn Waugh said, is mostly *waiting around*. You do a lot of waiting, and it's a waiting both anxious and boring. And during these periods of anxious and boring waiting you contemplate a personal and an objective world in disorder. And one way of putting the world to rights a little bit, or at least articulating your sense of the disorder, is to write poetry. So I commenced to do it for earnest therapeutic reasons during World War II—not with any eye to publication, of course. In general, I sent the poems to my wife and friends, and a couple of my teachers at Amherst whose good opinion I desired.

Thistle: Would you consider yourself a moralist or primarily an agent through which we expand our awareness of the things around us?

Wilbur: Of course you're talking about the way in which the poetry should be used by the reader. The relationship between the poet and the reader is a very *oblique* one, and I think one has to insist on that. You simply do not write for an audience directly, with a direct consciousness of the audience and a desire to influence the state of things. And yet, of course, if there were not the possibility of an audience, you'd probably write a good deal less. You have the audience and your likely effect on it, and your commerce with the audience is your sense of the language and of its range of experience. In the back of your mind, as you write, what you're really thinking about is how you can get down on paper what it is that's eating you at the moment, in a form satisfactory to you. Now, I guess I've evaded your question, but from the point of view of the reader, I should like poetry to have the effect of putting everything into one language, as it were, of introducing the aspects of life which are likely to be separate in everyday, scattered experience—of introducing these aspects of life to each other, yoking them together with grammar, making some kind of unity of sensibility possible at least for a moment. Is that clear?

Thistle: Yes. But what place, then, should poetry take in the life of the reader?

Wilbur: Well, I think that I. A. Richards is right in saying that poetry is the most comprehensive use of language. That is, poetry, at its best, can contain more of experience at one time than any other style of using the language. And therefore, for people capable of using poetry, for trained readers who know how to use it, I should think that it would be very central. I can't think that it would be something to do on Sunday afternoon. It would be something to do whenever one felt the need of putting the world in order, and something to remember having done, something to be permeated by.

Thistle: Have you ever put before yourself the dichotomy suggested by Plato between poetry and philosophy, and, having questioned yourself with this dichotomy, chosen the latter, just the way Plato did?

Wilbur: You know, to talk about poetry with a capital "P" can be very delusive. One should talk about *poems,* I suppose, and try to think of individual poems. As soon as one does that, the claims become more capable of examination. But to go back to the question, it seems to me that ideally poetry can contain the kind of thought which goes by the name of "philosophy" and not falsify it by a loose, passionate sensationalism, as Plato feared that poetry would do. He excluded it from his *Republic,* I think, on those grounds—that it excited the lower part of man and destroyed his contemplative serenity. Philosophic language, in general—I'm not speaking of existentialist philosophy, but of classic philosophy—is an abstract kind of language in which things are put in order at the expense of excluding the concrete, the particular, the everyday. Now it seems to me that philosophical poetry, at its best, manages to be abstractly orderly and at the same time to test its abstract ideas in something that *looks like* the felt world of experience. I'm thinking, in particular, of Dante. In Dante, you're at all times aware of a philosophical, theological structure derived from Aristotle and Thomas Aquinas. Philosophically, Dante is always perfectly clear, but all of his general ideas are instantly embodied, and their validity is tested by the probability, and convincingness with which these ideas can be physically represented.

Thistle: The question was asked because, when you spoke of your desire to bring order out of disorder, as from your World War II experience, the context gave the impression that you may have beheld two paths before you. One would be poetry, and the other would be the more prosaic form, philosophy.

Wilbur: Well, I've never felt drawn to the idea of being professionally a philosopher. I have been drawn in other directions, I confess. I thought for a while of being a painter until I convinced myself that I lacked the delicacy of hand for it and that I was probably a little blue-green colorblind. And I thought of being a cartoonist, a newspaper cartoonist, a policial cartoonist, and I thought strongly of being a general journalist, because there's a long tradition of that in my family. And then I got the hankering to be a teacher, and the fact that I was a poet and was to take myself seriously as a poet didn't burst upon me until I was already in graduate school, getting to be a teacher. And thus, becoming a poet complicated my life, because, you see, I can't take the teaching lightly. It's something I started out to do in earnest, and if I could slight my teaching, I'd find it easier to pay attention to my poetry as I'd like to do.

Thistle: How do you teach poetry in the classroom?

Wilbur: Poetry appreciation, that is?

Thistle: Yes.

Wilbur: Well, I'm not much interested in critical theory, myself. I think what you do is to look at the work and see what seems to need explaining in it, what it seems to be up to. You interpret it as far as you can in its own terms. And, really, that's all I can say about it. I have no feeling that analysis is damaging to poetry. I know that there's a lot of objection to so-called "close reading" as a teaching technique. It seems to me that that's about all you *can* do in class, unless you resort to a lot of generally irrelevant historical and biographical background, or unless you restrict yourself to OH's and AH's—unless you place yourself, as one of my Amherst teachers said, in the "wet pants" school of literary criticism. It seems to me what you *can* do, in teaching a poem, is to analyze it in the light of what it seems to be trying to do, with a maximum of sympathy, and then, having done all that, read the poem over and hope to read back into it all that you've taken out of it in the way of analytic conclusions and paraphrase. Bury the paraphrase in the original. Then, if it's a good poem, it will survive the process. You can't kill a good poem. Heavens, I've read endless, boring essays on the imagery of "Lycidas," but when I go on to "Lycidas" itself, it's still perfectly fresh.

Thistle: Do you feel that poetry should be a spoken tradition rather than solely a written one?

Wilbur: I don't know about the "should"—of course you knew I would object to your use of the word "should" there. I think that poetry suffers a little when the sound aspect of it is neglected. About the time that I was starting to write poems, the influence of the "new criticism" was very strong, and there was a great, general relish in the academies and among critics and students for poetry of maximum density, maximum irony, maximum ambiguity. Now, that kind of poetry is not necessarily capable of good dramatic performance. Dramatic performance is likely to oversimplify that sort of poem, the William Empson sort of poem. I started out writing under the influence of that kind of stress in criticism and classroom teaching. And I think, therefore, that some of my early poems are written with a tin ear or with no ear at all. I was interested in the words, in the interaction of the words, but not in the dramatic tone of the poem and with no interest in the matter of articulation. I've got some terrible clots of consonants in my early poems that are very hard to talk. But as I've come to travel around the country and read poems to people, and as I've written Broadway lyrics, I've become more aware of sound, and I think my poetry is the better for it. I do think poetry in general—everybody's poetry—is the better for some awareness of sound. On the other hand, poetry written for declamation is likely to be rather thin on the page. I think, for example, Lawrence Ferlinghetti is *damn* thin on the page. And most poetry written to be howled against a jazz background is pretty poor reading. So that one can go too far in that direction.

Thistle: Along with this general notion of "direction," do you foresee any future crystallization of a distinctly American literary culture?

Wilbur: You know, I don't think very well on this level of punditry. I'm not likely to say anything worth hearing in the way of cultural prophecy. As for whether we will come to cohere in the deepest sense of the word "cultural," I don't know. Poets and pundits and priests cannot put us all together in a *live* culture. In a live culture, people understand each other by looks, by gestures, by postures. There are all sorts of subverbal things which express their solidarity and their intuitive understanding of each other. And the United States is the sort of country in which, when men go into the men's room, nothing is said; no one ever speaks to anyone else in a men's room in America. There's a terrible mistrust, and we don't know what we're about; we don't trust each other. Isn't that true, in your experience? That in men's rooms and bus stations and comparable places, Americans tend not to talk to each other? They look at each other with a certain anxious curiosity, but not with the kind of instant understanding Italians feel when looking at one another. Italians know each other's signs.

Questionnaire to Mr. Wilbur

Paul F. Cummins/1967

An excerpt from *"Difficult Balance": The Poetry of Richard Wilbur*, a University of Southern California doctoral dissertation (1967), 229-33. Reprinted by permission of Paul F. Cummins.

Cummins: As I read your poetry I notice a general absence of explicit references to Christian theology and yet your poetry seems to present a rather orthodox view of man and reality—that is, that man is neither brute nor angel, but partakes of both; that the Divine is neither wholly transcendent nor wholly immanent but present in both dimensions; that man is imperfect yet worthy of celebration. If this is so, then why do you—who seem so deeply aware of and respectful of Western traditions—avoid explicit references to Christian symbolism, doctrine, themes?

Wilbur: My view of things, though not steady, is some sort of Catholic Christian, but I don't as you note make much use of Christian symbol or doctrine. This is because I cannot bear to borrow the voltage of highly-charged words, as Edith Sitwell did in her post-conversion poems full of lions and suns and crosses. It is seen through at last, as one sees through the panoply of a stupid ceremony. Poetry full of ready-made emotional value will also not represent the movement of the mind and heart toward understanding and clarification, and poetry has to be discovery rather than the celebration of received ideas.

Cummins: You have stated that some of your early poems "may at moments have taken refuge from events in language itself—in word-play, in the coinage of new words, in a certain preciosity." Are you disturbed by any other stylistic or thematic characteristic in your published poems? Are you currently striving to overcome any specific weakness?

Wilbur: Am I currently striving to overcome any weakness? I suppose I feel, just now, a little more than the usual dissatisfaction, but I shall not know what dissatisfies me, for certain, until I find by accident what will improve upon it. I don't deliberately operate on my style. To be a *little* more specific, *one* thing which now vexes me is an inclination to think too readily in rhymes—the result, I suspect, of translating 3,000-odd lines of Molière into couplets.

Cummins: Are you dissatisfied with any particular poem for any particular reason?

Wilbur: I am satisfied, up to a point, with all the poems I haven't destroyed.

Cummins: Several critics have accused you and other so-called "academic" poets of evading the responsibility of dealing with the socio-political problems of our times. I have my own rebuttal for these critics, but I would like to know how you react to this.

Wilbur: I don't think my poetry does avoid philosophical matters, but I haven't written too many explicitly political or "social" poems. "Speech for the Repeal of the McCarran Act," "After the Last Bulletins," an earlier poem called "To an American Poet Just Dead"—and more recently "Advice to a Prophet" and "On the Marginal Way." I don't think I shall ever again strike the note of the third poem mentioned, although some readers are very fond of railing and indicting in poetry; I have Robert Frost's preference for writing about immedicable woes rather than merely complaining. Most political poetry is complaining and speechifying, and doesn't come out of the whole and intricate self. But I agree with my friend André du Bouchet that any full poetry is bound to have an implicit political dimension.

Cummins: What philosophers and theologians have made the greatest impact on you? Do you think any particular works have influenced you?

Wilbur: Augustine. Thomas Traherne in his "Centuries." Pascal. The first and third one feels in such a poem as "Beasts."

Cummins: What poets, novelists, critics, men-of-letters do you find yourself reading most?

Wilbur: I read poetry in a general and open way, and enjoy something in any able poet you might mention. I like novelists who write prose and write it well: Waugh, for example.

Cummins: As I read your complete poems I see many parallels with Wallace Stevens: for example, spirituality without God; a sense of the dynamic nature of reality; an impulse to reconcile opposites; a quest for order; the perception of correspondence between man and nature; the primacy of the imagination. Do you think these qualities

are too broad to establish such a parallelism? Do you think you have
been directly influenced by Stevens? By any other twentieth-century
poets?

Wilbur: I'm sure that my enthusiasm for Stevens, circa 1948-52,
has affected my own work, although I can't say just where. Of late I
have found his work too undramatic, connoisseural, and in-
conclusively ruminative, but still pick it up with pleasure and may
have another spell of enchantment, in time. For all his stress on the
ding an sich, I find him too hothouse subjective right now.

Cummins: Do you think it far-fetched to say that the use of
traditional forms (in your poetry as well as others') has a ritualistic
quality: that is, that the use of form itself is a ritualistic means of
celebrating the continuity of human experience? I ask this because I
feel that there is a universality in your poetry which is absent in many
modern poets who reject traditional forms—perhaps there is some
sort of cause and effect relationship here. I ask this also because I
sense that your almost total self-restriction to traditional stanzaic
forms goes beyond your published explanations—namely that form
provides aesthetic distance, that it provides a yardstick with which to
measure deviation, and so on.

Wilbur: I don't think I generally have a ritual intention in using
rhyme and meter, unless there is a kind of ritual which begets what it
celebrates, having started in ignorance. I don't make much use of
"traditional forms" in the sense of writing sonnets, Spenserian stanza,
villanelles, and all that. I do use meters and rhymes most of the time,
but generally let the words of a developing poem choose their own
form.

Cummins: One critic (Donald Hall) has said that suffering in your
poetry is always "understood and discussed but not presented in the
act." Other critics take you to task for not expressing a tragic sense of
life, for not projecting anguish, torment, etc. And James Dickey
includes you in what he calls the "School-of-Charm" poets who lack
personality. What are your thoughts about such criticism? Have you
ever or do you anticipate writing poetry that is more personal,
confessional, autobiographical?

Wilbur: I suspect that I have, rather often, expressed "a tragic
sense of life," but I don't advertise my actual private life or "project
torment." The *Berkeley Review* published some remarks of mine on

this subject a few years ago, and the remarks were included in a book edited by Tony Ostroff and called, roughly, *The Poet as Reader and Critic.** I vote for obliquity and distancing in the use of one's own life, both because I am a bit reserved and because I think these produce a more honest and usable poetry.

Cummins: Are you publishing another volume of poetry soon? When?

Wilbur: I have perhaps one-third of a new volume, and can't guess when I'll be ready to publish again. It looks as though I were getting terribly choosy, and terribly anxious not to repeat myself. I've never written quickly, and so don't fear that I'm drying up; but I'd be grateful for a spate.

The Contemporary Poet as Artist and Critic: Eight Symposia. Boston: Little, Brown and Company, 1964. *Editor.*

Richard Wilbur
Joan Hutton/1968

From *Transatlantic Review,* 29 (Summer 1968), 58-67.

JH: Childhood would seem the right chronological place to begin talking about a poet's feeling for words and the world they represent. I suppose that every poet's love affair with words and forms begins early and has a great deal to do with physical surroundings?

RW: From the beginning it was a love affair not merely with words but some of the other arts, too. My father was a painter, and naturally I played around with the idea of following in his footsteps. I also played around with his paints and brushes, and drew a great many cartoons, in the manners of the *New Yorker* and the *New Masses.* I was forced to do a little music, and though I had no talent for it, I was interested enough in it to feel that that was one of the dimensions of my childhood. To tell the truth, I was still drawing, and thinking I might be a newspaper cartoonist, in college. The poetry was rather marginal. But taken hard. I don't think I became especially a writer of poems until sometime after World War II, because it wasn't until then that anybody took me very seriously. On the whole, the excitement at Amherst during my undergraduate years was about criticism. I imagine that here or there in the world, the New-Critical excitement had already broken or was yet to come, but for the Amherst I knew, it was at high tide. What you wanted to be was a critic, and I put most of my energies into that, so as to please my teachers.

JH: Surely you grew up in gardens?

RW: Yes. In a sense, too many. My mother had too many roses, and too many flowers generally, and I was made to work amongst them and weed them, and do the back-breaking things that you have to do for a lady gardener who is always changing her mind about where she wants the beds to be. It convinced me that I didn't like flowers. Right now, my tame-flower vocabulary is very limited, and I make mistakes about candytuft and something that's like it. But there was nature of other and wilder sorts around, and that's what I really reacted to. We had (I guess it couldn't have been virgin forest, but the owner of the farm on which I grew up used to pretend it was) lots of woods; and then the farm was an unprofitable but beautiful under-taking, and on it you could find something of everything: cherry trees, plum trees, peach trees—

JH: And water and birds and animals, to judge from your poems?

RW: In the way of water, we had a few streams in the woods which culminated in ponds calculated to look unpremeditated; and lots of animals; one bull, cows, pigs, chickens and—I'm making this sound like a toy farm; it was in a way; it was the plaything of an industrialist; but all the things that happen on real farms happened there. I got to ride on the haywagon and play hide-and-seek in the corn field and to see the chickens beheaded and the pigs have their throats cut, and all that.

JH: Hoping to get at some of the ways in which you work, I'd like to ask about the composition of your poem, "Mind." Did the rhyme scheme lead to the thought or the thought to the rhyme scheme? In tightly and formally wrought poetry of this kind, it is the double strand of poetic reason and rhyme working together which delights and mystifies the reader.

RW: I'm sure that before I started writing that poem I was thinking about the resemblance between bat activity in a cave and thought activity in the mind, which has so often and conventionally been compared to a cave, and that I felt something was going to happen at the end to explode the metaphor. What I've just said is almost as conjectural as something a critic might say, because I'm so far from the poem in time; but I'm quite sure that the rhyme would not have led me to the final thought of that poem. Good poets do not, I'm certain, ever allow themselves to be led into important statements by the rhyme. No poet whose work I admire ever seems to be forced into telling a lie by the structures he's using.

JH: Rhyme, then, could be considered as a test of your honesty?

RW: Indeed. You sit in judgment on all the mad little suggestions that the rhyme gives you, and you are very strict with them and with yourself. Sometimes there's a fortunate accident, sometimes some-thing is proposed by the rhyme that will really tell you what it is you are after. Or give you a local felicity you don't want to pass up because it really does belong in the poem.

JH: That recalls Mr. Frost when he talks about "letting the poem unfold." You are off on a discovery. Need you necessarily see where you're going when you start out?

RW: I like the word "unfold" in this connection, because if you unfold something, it's all there from the beginning. It's just a matter of getting to the end of it. If you unfold something, you can't find something in the middle that wasn't implied. (I believe that I've just used the word "implied" in a splendid way.) You don't, of course, know everything the poem is going to be when you start out . . .

JH: But you have the form in mind?

RW: You have the trajectory of it in mind. I almost always know about how long the poem is going to be, what it's tone, or tones, are going to be, and if it's going to "turn," I know that too; but I may not know what the individual line is going to say; of course I don't.

JH: Are there any "constants," any clichés you could propose about the way you work?

RW: No, because I can immediately think of exceptions to anything I might propose. I very seldom write anything fast. I've only got about two poems in the nearly two hundred I've written (my Johnson sonnet was one) that were composed in a single day. Many hung in the air three years, five years, before I could find out where they wanted to go. Sometimes, because I'm a slow thinker, the big problem is not to find some handsome image that will finish it off, but to concatenate, to take the next logical step. I know that I resemble another terribly slow writer, Dylan Thomas, in that I'll sit and poke away at a poem until the page begins to look stale to me, and then I'll have to take another sheet of paper and write the whole poem out from the start. I expect I do this out of a childish feeling that I'm building up speed and will make a broad jump at the end of the copying out.

JH: In reading your poetry, I am always struck by the presence of a poet who rarely speaks directly of himself. Would you characterize this as an effect of reticence or as a conscious theory of art? One recalls Eliot's essay, "Tradition and the Individual Talent," in which he speaks of the progress of the artist as "a continual extinction of personality." Might this have something to do with your notions?

RW: Well, it certainly did at one time. I was starting to write in earnest at a time when Eliot was every other word from the people who were interested in poetry. His doctrine of impersonality was, on the whole, unchallenged. On the other hand, my own reticence made it very easy for me to admire this doctrine of Eliot's. Then, I'm both a balked scholar and a poet; I've done a lot of reading and I am likely to be conscious of where I derive from and border on other poetry of this and earlier times. So although I don't feel like an imitative person, and don't feel I've borrowed culpably, I am aware that not all my conceptions are absolutely peculiar. I had a letter recently from the Argentinian poet, Borges. I'd been translating some of his poems and he said, referring to the work not yet translated, that if I could improve on anything, he'd be grateful. I think Borges exemplifies better than anyone I can think of now, that attitude towards literature which considers it a product of the whole society and also of the whole republic of letters. Of course there is a great originality of voice in his poetry as well as in his prose, but everything he writes is full of a conversancy with other people and he is not in the least disturbed by the fact. I think that writers who are obsessed by the idea of originality deceive themselves as to their dependence on other people.

JH: Yes. One thinks, to take the obverse side of the poetic coin, of the solitary voice which often dramatizes itself by speaking directly from the madhouse. Do you see this as a consequence of our messed-up world, or lack of other, meaningful backdrops or, to let Miss Dickinson phrase it, that "much madness is divinest sense"?

RW: Some poets do try to exemplify that idea, the idea that much madness is divinely sane. And I recall that Allen Ginsberg recently asked an audience whether they would consent to the proposition that the United States government, in its foreign policy, is psychotic. Something like a third of the audience voted for that idea. They and Mr. Ginsberg are setting themselves up as super-sane.

JH: And prophets?

RW: Yes. Prophesying against a sick society less divinely sick than they. Actually, I think that many people who take that position are prophesying not merely against the faults of our institutions, but against institutions themselves. Insofar as they do that, I can't sympathize with them. Though I can share all their objections to our Viet Nam policy, I'm all for institutions, for working in and through institutions, and if that means being in the establishment, why there I am.

JH: I suppose that you can't talk about the "mad voice" generally, that you have to take the particular poet into consideration because each one says it differently; that there is probably more variety than similarity in what has become known as confessional poetry. But we would agree, surely, that your poetry stands at an opposite pole?

RW: Yes, though I just wrote a poem which is about to come out in the *New Yorker.* It's called "Running," and it's literally about me, though I very seldom do that kind of thing. I think that you passed from the subject of mental disturbance to confessional poetry by an obvious route, because many of the people who write that class of poetry have had their spells in the asylum. In general, I feel that such poets are, when writing at their best, not merely setting up their own hurt against society but are taking themselves as representative of, as peculiarly sensitive to, the general janglement of our culture nowadays. That's the best excuse for it, I should say; that's when such poetry is strongest: when the poet is a kind of representative victim. Of course, sometimes, that stance can seem pretentious or fashionable, or a matter of emotional habit. It may seem in the particular case that what, for the poet, was merely a bad Tuesday, is being too forcibly presented as evidence against the age.

JH: Many of your poems seem to me concerned with a quest for what might be called "a difficult balance," to borrow a phrase from "Love Calls Us to the Things of This World." You seem to come to a point in your consideration of the relationships between things and ideas, reality and imagination, between the act and the vision, between what we see and what we make of it, in which an exciting and unifying awareness takes place. It is as if you are tensely situated in the middle of a paradox, looking both ways on it.

RW: Yes, that sounds right. I know that I keep riding those subjects, and that I have often ended poems not so much with affirmations as with declarations of what is there. And what is there seems, very often, a clarified contradiction, or balance. A lot of my poems, like the one having to do with laundry as angels, are arguments against a thingless, an earthless kind of imagination, or spirituality. My critics tell me so, and I believe them. Having written out of that position for years, I find myself totally unprepared to admire psychedelic visions, for example.

JH: You want to earn your vision?

RW: I like resistance. I like it in art, as Gautier did: "vers, marbre, onyx, émail."* And I like the world to resist my ordering of it, so that I can feel it is real and that I'm honoring its reality.

JH: I wonder if it would interest you to be conversational about the moral and ethical dimensions of nature? Most poets are uneasy about these terms, but I think they are there in your poems. In "Junk," for example, you write, "Yet the things themselves/in thoughtless honor/Have kept composure,/like captives who would not/Talk under torture." Nature does seem to have "prodigious honesties," to quote from "Clearness," to teach.

RW: Yes. Well, certainly in the case of "Junk," I can see that I'm ascribing something to nature that is the basis of a human virtue; an inclination to make things and to make them properly. I suppose that I'm not talking about nature in any limited sense, but rather about nature as a creation. What I'm saying there is finally religious. Not a statement about "nature," but a religious statement.

JH: But by inhabiting nature and inviting nature to inhabit us, we somehow learn integrity? Or is that misstating your intention?

RW: I guess that if you've invested a lot of attentive imagination in nature, you're likely to be able to express your honesties in terms of nature, and with no sense of imposition. But I don't think that I conceive a nature so instructive as William Cullen Bryant's.

JH: I'm not suggesting that for a moment. Emerson's notion of the outer expressing the inner, "the universe is the externalization of the soul," he wrote, is a kindlier way of putting that, and I think that every fine poet comes to feel this to some extent; this intervolvement.

RW: If Emerson's Nature means that kind of a circuit, in which the mind is attuned to nature, rather than simply learning from it; if the mind properly finds its figures out there, is co-natural with the world out there, yes, I can go right along with that kind of Emersonianism. I don't for a minute think of the human creature as isolated from nature and so, although it's possible to use a tree or an animal or a sea in a cavalier way, a way not *immediately* true to the facts of nature, almost any poetic use of natural things is going, finally, to have to have some truth in it, because the imagination does belong in the world.

JH: Wallace Stevens, I believe, bluntly states that the ethical has no more place in poetry than it has in painting.

*Verse, marble, onyx, enamel. *Editor.*

RW: When Poe said something of that sort, he was complaining of the rhymed moralizing into which Longfellow sometimes fell, and there was some justice in the complaint. As I remember, Poe goes on in the same piece to formulate his attitude more broadly, saying that the good should be recommended by poetry not for its ethical value but for its comeliness. If that means that poetic quality shouldn't be sacrificed to the preaching impulse, fine. But if you turn from Poe's abstracter criticism and judge him by his tastes and his own poetry, it's plain that he had a damned narrow view of poetry. Are we to rule out satire as a kind of poetry? Alexander Pope? Satire that really is satire is always written out of a firm sense of how people ought to behave. Now as for Stevens' statement, I don't pretend to have grasped his thought as a whole, but I don't see how there can be a supreme fiction which lacks ethical content. I am put in mind of a couple of lines of his, in this connection; I believe I can quote them:

> How gladly with proper words the soldier dies
> If he must, or lives on the bread of faithful speech.

Don't I hear the ring of collective values in that? Surely those proper words are not only handsome but dutiful.

JH: Let me ask you a question that is usually put somewhat defensively, often by people who do not read much poetry and who mistrust analogy because it's only logic of a sort. Do you think poetry makes things happen?

RW: That's a rough one. I do think it does. It does in proportion as it's really in touch with the present feelings of people. I do think there is poetry that doesn't make anything happen because it's too personal, perhaps, or for reason of some incapacity.

JH: It's not "veracity." This is getting back to Emerson again. He said, I think, that the value of genius to us is in the veracity of its report. Poets must keep telling us what's "true."

RW: Yes, and if you think (and it's very unpopular to think so at present) of the poet as an agent of society and as a servant of the language, why, then, what the poet does all the time is to see what ideas and what words are alive and, insofar as he can, to go right to the center of the words that represent the things that are vexing us. Now, if you do that, you're bound to make things happen, because you'll help people to clarify their feelings. They'll have to know, a little better, what it is that they're feeling. The path from that kind of clarification to action is not necessarily an immediate one. You don't necessarily read a poem and pick up the telephone. But something you might call "tonalizing" does occur, a preparation to feel in a certain way, and consequently to act in a certain way. That does occur, I think, when you read a poem which goes to the words that are bothering you. I suppose you can't expect, by means of a poem, to produce a perfect volte-face in anybody; that would be very presumptuous; even a propagandist doesn't expect to do that; but you can help a man to see what he may be about to see.

JH: Do you think, perhaps, you've done this in your poem, "Advice to a Prophet"? Might some people have read this and looked at fear in a different way?

RW: Possibly.

JH: Because it's about the words, in part, that stand for the facts which we really don't know how to face, isn't it?

RW: Yes. I believe that what I was trying to do in that poem was to provide—myself, of course—with a way of feeling the enormity of nuclear war, should it come. The approach of that poem, which comes at such a war through its likely effect on the creatures who surround us, is a very "thingy" one. It made it possible for me to feel something beside a kind of abstract horror, a puzzlement, at the thought of nuclear war; and it may so serve other people. I hope so.

JH: To go back a bit to Mr. Stevens, wasn't it finally the mind's mode of perceiving itself in operation that fascinated him; the cognition, or at least a sense, of how the poet comes upon his comparisons?

RW: Yes, I think Stevens once said that he regarded the essential thing in poetry as comparison. Metaphor would be the highest-voltage kind of comparison. I suspect that that is what most poets are up to although you can think of exceptions. Most poets are up to the enforcing of such resemblances as they see as having some truth in them. This is one reason why I've always felt, and annoyingly said, that poetry is essentially religious in its direction. I know a lot of people, poets, who are not consciously religious, but find themselves forever compromised by their habit of asserting the relevance of all things to each other. And poetry being a kind of truth-telling, (it's pretty hard to lie in poetry), I think that these people must be making, whether they like it or not, what are ultimately religious assertions.

JH: Religious assertions?

RW: I'm using "assertion" in a loose sense; perhaps in a Marshall McLuhan sense. If the medium is the message—then I think that all poets are sending religious messages because poetry is, in such great part, the comparison of one thing to another; or the saying, as in metaphor, that one thing is another. And to insist, as all poets do, that all things are related to each other, comparable to each other, is to go toward making an assertion of the unity of all things.

JH: You aren't talking about the redemptive quality of form in rendering chaos intelligible?

RW: That wasn't my drift, although I think, there too, that however destructive or negative the spirit of any poem is, the fact that it insists upon shape and harmony and incidental graces makes it optative in character. It's on the side of order. The medium is on the side of order.

JH: Would you say that chaos exists or only inexact vision?

RW: Chaos certainly exists for everybody, subjectively, at certain times of his life. One of the most interesting, general statements I've encountered about poetry was made by Stephen Spender when he talked about the rhythm which one finds in the work of almost any poet. For a time, he'll feel as if he had his hands on all the ropes, he'll have a confident vocabulary and, perhaps, an inclination to affirm; and then, it'll all get away from him, and though he may not lose his grasp of the world entirely, something of his confidence in it will vanish. Perhaps there'll be new things in his awareness which disorder his sense of the world, and require him to re-integrate things once again. I do think all artists oscillate between a chaotic sense of things and an orderly sense of things.

JH: So that by "religious," you mean simply the unity which most poets find through analogy; or would you define it in a more orthodox way?

RW: I mean that poetry makes order and asserts relations (sometimes of a surprising kind) out of a confidence in ultimate order and relatedness. Nothing more orthodox than that.

JH: So, in one's desire to relate your poetry and your worldview to others that are relevant and comparable, one might not be wrong in saying Plato and Emerson, to give you some very distinguished company?

RW: You frighten me. Like most poets I'm not a philosopher, and am frightened of coming to a position too fixed and too articulate. May I let that question go?

JH: Of course. Perhaps the fairest summary of your aesthetic lies in your own observation:

"The beautiful changes
In such kind ways,
Wishing ever to sunder
Things and things' selves for a second finding, to lose
For a moment all that it touches back to wonder."

RW: A kind and gracious summary. Those lines are so old that they seem someone else's; and so I can assent to them without embarrassment.

The Window of Art:
A Conversation with Richard Wilbur

Gregory Fitz Gerald and William Heyen/1970

From *Modern Poetry Studies,* Vol. I, No. 2 (1970), 57-67.

The present conversation is edited from Mr. Wilbur's appearance in the *Writers Forum* series on the SUNY campus at Brockport, March 12, 1969. With Mr. Wilbur appear Gregory Fitz Gerald, director of the Forum, and William Heyen, recipient of the Borestone Mountain Award for 1966. The conversation begins after Mr. Wilbur's reading of his poem "The Lilacs."

Heyen: Mr. Wilbur, "The Lilacs" is, for a contemporary poem, rendered in an unusual form: the heavy alliterative Anglo-Saxon meter. In this way it resembles your poem, "Junk." What is it that has attracted you to this form?

Wilbur: Well, I took both Anglo-Saxon and Beowulf at Harvard Graduate School, and I was the odd one who liked those courses. I love the Anglo-Saxon language and find the rhythms of the alliterative line very catchy. There are other virtues in alliterative poetry which I recognize but can't define. The form compels, or at least enables, you to write a certain kind of poem. I can't possibly tell you why two of my poems have fallen into that form. I don't write exercises. I let the poem, as it comes out, find what form it's after. All I can say is that in the back of my head was the alliterative line, and for some reason a poem about junk and a poem about lilacs wanted to come out that way. I don't think that this makes my two poems "antique" in any way. It's always seemed to me that elements of technique, like meter and rhyme, are in themselves meaningless and timeless, though particular forms may have particular capabilities.

Fitz Gerald: "The Lilacs" is from your new book, *Walking to Sleep,* isn't it?

Wilbur: Yes.

Fitz Gerald: Could you tell us a little bit about the book and what one will find inside it?

Wilbur: I should preface any remarks by saying that I never make a book, in the sense that a poet such as William Butler Yeats made a book. For him a book was a set of related poems. You have a strong feeling, looking through a Yeats book, that he's written a few of the poems purely to complete a pattern. With me, a book is simply the clutter of poems which have accumulated over a certain number of years. *Walking to Sleep,* because I was interrupted by various projects, represents about eight years' worth of poems. I trust I don't repeat anything I've done before. At the same time, I can't be sure of reporting great departures here, either. I've got my longest poem—the longest ever for me—in this book—the title poem. I've run on for a couple of hundred lines, which for me is interminable, considering my slow rate of composition. And also the book includes about eleven translations from various languages.

Fitz Gerald: What specific translations do you include, Mr. Wilbur?

Wilbur: There are three sonnets from Jorge Luis Borges, three poems of Villon, a little rondeau from Charles d'Orléans, a poem from Akhmatova, and three poems from Voznesensky.

Fitz Gerald: It seems to me that a great deal of very good translating is being done by our best poets today. Would you agree that translating is undergoing a great resurgence?

Wilbur: Yes, it is. And, of course, it's much more highly organized now and encouraged more—publicly—than it was in the days of Longfellow. Longfellow's the person who did it for the 19th century. He did a great service in translating so much from so many European literatures. Today we have Rockefellers and Bollingens behind us. We have programs which not only pay us a bit for translating but actually urge us to translate specified works. A publisher will decide, for instance, that a book of translations from certain Russian poets should be done. He sets it all up, arranges for the linguistic mediation, contracts with the appropriate poet. The results are often very good. Furthermore there are programs like Paul Engle's translation shop in Iowa City to encourage this kind of work.

Heyen: Mr. Wilbur, you said that much of your own work may be understood as kind of a public quarrel with the aesthetics of Edgar Allan Poe. I know you've been attracted to his work. You've written much about him, yet you've said that his theory of the nature of art seems to be *insane.* Would you comment on this?

Wilbur: We're often drawn to things about which we're of two minds. It seems to me that's what the recurrent subjects of a poet are likely to be—the things that trouble him, that make him feel double. I feel double about Poe. I think he's a much better writer than he's generally allowed to be. It's his fiction I'm thinking of rather than his poetry. But I am greatly put off and put out by his aesthetic. It looks at first glance like a variation of transcendental aesthetics, but really is not, because of its world-annihilating character. In a transcendentalist poet, like Walt Whitman, the world of concrete particulars is always present; indeed it's delighted in; it's recreated by vivid language. But the whole direction of Poe's poetry tends toward brushing aside and annihilating everything in the natural world, everything that stands between Poe and the realm of pure spirit. That seems to me to be aesthetically bad. Isn't it also morally and religiously bad to brush aside the realm of nature and drive impatiently toward what one supposes to be the realm of pure spirit, as if one were an angel? I'm thinking, of course, of Allen Tate's essay on Poe, "The Angelic Imagination."

Heyen: You once made a metaphorical distinction between considering art as a window as opposed to art as a door. You indicated, and I agree, that the latter is not the proper way to consider art.

Wilbur: I vote against art as a door, because I value the resistance of the world, its independence of the mind, its interaction with the mind. I don't want vision to usurp reality.

Heyen: In your own work, I think such poems as "Love Calls Us to the Things of This World" and " 'A World without Objects Is a Sensible Emptiness' " bring this issue into focus.

Wilbur: I'm sure they do. I'm not terribly conscious of myself as constructing a body of doctrine, of course. I think we all try to avoid that kind of sense of ourselves, so as not to grow confiningly consistent.

Heyen: You yourself have summed up one of your general themes as the "proper relation between the tangible world and the spirit." I think that's the way you put it.

Wilbur: Yes.

Fitz Gerald: I'd like to shift a little bit, if I may, to another subject. Mr. Wilbur, do you still feel as you said in an anthology essay five or six years back that there is an increased responsiveness toward poetry in America?

Wilbur: I don't know whether I've noticed any increase in the last five years since that essay was written, but if I compare the present situation, let's say, with that of the late 40's, I think it's obviously true that for the hearing of poetry we have a much larger audience in America now. Of course, the audience is chiefly supplied by the universities, which provide more and more courses in the literature of the last three minutes.

Fitz Gerald: True. I teach one of them. But do you think that this rise in oral presentation of poetry has affected the poem itself in any important way—in structure or in aesthetics?

Wilbur: I think it has, yes. I think it's had a considerable effect. I know that my own early poems are strictly on-the-page poems. They're written with a tin ear. Some of them are very hard to speak aloud. There will be particular lines which are extremely hard to deliver, a tenor couldn't handle them. But more and more, I've been reading aloud to audiences, as almost every poet does nowadays. For a while I was involved also in the writing of Broadway lyrics. As a direct result, I've developed an automatic sense of what is pronounceable, as well as an increased feeling for variation of sound in vowel sequences. I don't go about it analytically or programmatically, but I know that my results are a good deal more speakable and more sonorous than they used to be. There are other effects, too. It's not only a matter of appealing to the ear, though more and more now the poem is conceived of as something to be heard. Performance also gets into it now. I am willing to bet that most poets who do a good bit of performance reading find themselves insensibly becoming more dramatic. The effort is all toward getting a real speaking voice into their poems, much more than they used to do.

Fitz Gerald: Do you think that oral presentation will ultimately reduce the complexity level of poetry? In other words, won't a poetry oriented to the ear have to be written so as to be more easily grasped by the audience?

Wilbur: I should guess so. At least in its emotional spine, a poem which is written, perhaps not with an audience in mind, but written by a poet who has been reading aloud, is going to be simple. There are going to be simple tonal progressions, or simple progressions of attitude, of emotion—the whole thing will tend to be simpler. I know that my own poems have become more dramatic, more like the speaking voice. Perhaps this development has come in response to my experience in reading my poetry aloud. Some people have responded very conspicuously to the increased audience. Back in 1956, I went out to San Francisco just after Allen Ginsberg had read his poem "Howl" for the first time. It was played to me on a tape. I felt that the first performance of "Howl" was very much like the work of a high-toned standup comedian. Ginsberg really works with an audience the same way a comedian does, though in a higher sense perhaps. A lot of poetry of that character is being written today—the sort of poetry that would amuse an audience, and often it is delivered in the manner of a comedian, perhaps with a jazz backing.

Fitz Gerald: As Ferlinghetti does frequently.

Heyen: I can't resist asking you a question, since you mention it, what do you think of "Howl"? I ask because to a good many of us, in certain senses Richard Wilbur and Allen Ginsberg represent the antithetical poles in contemporary American poetry.

Wilbur: Yes. Ginsberg is supposed to say "no" to me, and I'm supposed to say "no" to him. Actually, I consider him a person of great talent. I do think that he throws it around loosely sometimes. From my own position, given my habits, I have to feel that if I possessed his material, I'd handle it a little differently. I wouldn't be quite so exhibitionistic, or so loosely Whitmanian. Still, I am glad Ginsberg is on the scene.

Heyen: Mr. Wilbur, one critic says that "public issues have not been particularly fruitful sources of subject matter for Mr. Wilbur." Would you agree with this statement?

Wilbur: I can think of exceptions to it. That is, I wrote a poem called "Speech for the Repeal of the McCarran Act," and also I have a poem called "Advice to a Prophet," which is concerned with offering the reader a means of being afraid of nuclear warfare. And what else? Oh, I have a poem against Lyndon Johnson. That may exhaust, however, my public or political poems.

Heyen: Many poets today are writing war poems, George Starbuck, Robert Bly, and W. S. Merwin. I do sense the background of the times in your new book, but the poems are not directly topical.

Wilbur: Yes, that's right. I think that in a poem like "On the

Marginal Way," in this new collection, the Viet Nam War and World War II and much else is in the background; but the poem isn't strictly or specifically topical. It isn't in a narrow sense politically *engagé;* it uses politics as circumstance, as part of one's inevitable awareness at a time like this. It seems to me that most of the protest poetry being written now is pretty awful. It has a posterish simplicity which keeps it from honoring the subject. My idea of a really good political poem is Yeats' "Easter 1916," which does transform, in a very moving way, MacDonagh and MacBride, Connolly and Pearse, before it's through. But it's full of qualifications. It says the English "may keep faith/After all is said and done." If it had less force and sweep at the end, it could seem like a quibbling poem, especially to someone passionately and simply committed to the Irish Rebellion. But for me, Yeats' "Easter 1916" does what poetry ought to do with public matters. It should not surrender any of its complexity.

Heyen: Yeats was interested in the "lonely impulse of delight," as he puts it in one poem, and there is also his poem "On Being Asked for a War Poem," in which he says the poet who pleases "a young girl in the indolence of her youth,/Or an old man upon a winter's night" does enough. Would you read a poem for us that is not a war poem? The particular one I have in mind is "The Death of a Toad."

Wilbur: All right.

Heyen: This is one of your classic pieces.

Wilbur: It goes back a way, yes. I think it must have been written some time around 1949.

> A toad the power mower caught,
> Chewed and clipped of a leg, with a hobbling hop has got
>   To the garden verge, and sanctuaried him
>   Under the cineraria leaves, in the shade
>   Of the ashen heartshaped leaves, in a dim,
>   Low, and a final glade.
>
> The rare original heartsblood goes,
> Spends on the earthen hide, in the folds and wizenings, flows
>   In the gutters of the banked and starting eyes. He lies
>   As still as if he would return to stone,
>   And soundlessly attending, dies
>   Toward some deep monotone,
>
>   Toward misted and ebullient seas

And cooling shores, toward lost Amphibia's emperies.
Day dwindles, drowning, and at length is gone
In the wide and antique eyes, which still appear
    To watch, across the castrate lawn,
    The haggard daylight steer.

Heyen: I was reading the other day Randall Jarrell's essay on your work. As you know, it's filled with praise and filled with blame. At one point, in regard to this poem, he says that it seems to get *too poetic,* words to that effect. But more generally, how do you react to reading reviews and critical essays on your work? Are they helpful at all? Are they amusing? Do they anger you?

Wilbur: In the first place, I must confess that I do read them. I remember visiting E. E. Cummings once in the Village, and he referred in a kind of offhand, vague way to "some article" on his work written by "a fellow named Blackmur maybe." I remembered precisely what article it was, and also that it had come out in *Hound and Horn.* I couldn't help noticing that Cummings had a sizeable stack of *Hound and Horn* in the corner on his bookshelves. He was, like so many poets, defensively pretending not to be up on what had been written about him. Yes, I confess I read anything about me that I happen to turn up. I am not sure I am instructed by it. Even when it's very intelligent and sympathetic criticism for which you're grateful, you can't be helped much. You're compelled to go on and persist in your own quirks. After all, nobody approaches his own work in the language of criticism, that's the language in which poetry comes out, not the language in which it's put in. It seems to me that the writing of poetry is at once a more stupid and a deeper process than the critical operation.

Fitz Gerald: This does sound as if contemporary poetry may be in the hands of a small group of scholars and critics. Is this a kind of an elitist group?

Wilbur: It may as well be admitted, relative to the other arts, that poetry has always been an elite form. No matter how much we teach it, no matter how much we spout it from platforms, it's going to be the necessary art for a comparatively small number of people. If we start looking around for great audiences as Whitman did, I think what we're likely to do is to depress our expectations of poetry itself. I'm not in the least encouraged by the great sales of Rod McKuen's books, because his writing is absolutely insipid and doesn't, for me, qualify as poetry. It may be rather nice with a guitar, I don't know, but it's no good as poetry. I'm not led to feel that poetry is enjoying an increased popular appeal because of McKuen's sales or because of popular interest in the lyrics of Bob Dylan. You have to draw a line somewhere, as Garfunkel did recently—you know the lyricist of the Simon and Garfunkel team? He said, "what Wallace Stevens writes is poetry, what I write is lyrics." Having written both lyrics and poetry myself, I think I can chop them apart—in fact, if not with a handy definition.

Fitz Gerald: Is it bad, then, that Voznesensky sells 225,000 copies of a book?

Wilbur: No, that's fine. I think one can find reasons for these extraordinary sales in the Soviet Union, reasons for us to feel a little better, for us to feel not wholly daunted about it. For one thing, in the Soviet Union there's considerably less trashy distraction and trashy entertainment than we have here. There's a good deal less to take your eye off poetry, off reading that has some value and demands some effort. I do think that that cultural difference is extremely important. For another thing, and here I'm borrowing something that Newton Arvin said in his book on Longfellow, the Russians are now at the stage we had reached in the middle of the last century. There is a new general literacy in Russia, and they're very excited and highminded about it. People in America have been literate for several generations now, and so people with excellent educations can sit around reading "whodunits" with no sense of shirking. But so many people in Russia today represent families which are reading for the first time; they can be appealed to on the highest level.

Firz Gerald: So often we hear the charge that contemporary American poetry is pretty much a prisoner in the hands of an elitist group of scholars. We even have a term "academic poetry." You, of course, are yourself associated with Wesleyan University and have been a teacher almost all of your professional life. What sort of substance do you think there is to these charges that the academy is somehow destructive of the poetic impulse?

Wilbur: I don't know where poetry can better situate itself at present. Yes, there are disadvantages to poetry's being written by teachers as much as it is, and also consumed by them and students.

I, myself, would like to stir in the whole community, if I could. But there seems to me no disadvantage to poetry's being intellectually sharp, and to its having some knowledge behind it. Good poetry always has had that; there have never been any good ignorant poets. So there are virtues to the attachment of poetry at present to the academic world and to scholarship. If I looked around the country trying to find a wild man who had nothing to do with the universities, and who was at the same time a good poet, I am very much afraid I couldn't find one. All of the wild men we might think of have been teachers or are teachers now. Charles Olson was even a college president, for heaven's sake.

Fitz Gerald: Of course, Ginsberg has an academic degree and Ferlinghetti a doctorate.

Wilbur: Yes, and I believe Gary Snyder may have an advanced degree in Oriental studies.

Heyen: You don't think that your long connection with academia has hurt you in any way?

Wilbur: It probably has; it probably has. But as I say, I can't imagine any *perfect* situation.

Fitz Gerald: Do you have any special eccentricities in your working habits? Hemingway, as you know, would write standing up and Joyce wrote on colored paper and so on. Do you have any of these idiosyncracies?

Wilbur: I wish I had something really colorful to report. The one thing I know is that as a writer I'm very, very slow. I'll take any excuse whatever to get away from writing, because I've made it so painful a process. Between picking it up and laying it down, it sometimes takes me five years to finish off a poem. And whenever I go back to work on an unfinished poem, I do what Dylan Thomas used to do; I have to write it all out from the very beginning, and come up to where the next line is going to be, providing I can think of it. I never do leave any gaps to be filled in later. Of course, I have no grounds for being proud of that. Shelley and Keats left lots of gaps, and they came out all right.

Fitz Gerald: That sounds quite the opposite from the "automatic writing" we're hearing about these days. It does sound as if you've spent a good bit of time on revision.

Wilbur: I don't revise, no. I write so horribly slowly that by the time I do advance, by the time I do go on ahead in a poem, I'm satisfied with what I've finished so far. I feel I may risk progressing. But I write very slowly, and it's very far from being automatic, which isn't to say that there isn't a lot of the irrational in my writing, just as there must be in everybody's. I think that one reason why I'm so slow is because I sit there half dreaming, letting rhymes suggest idiotic ideas to me, trying to stay loose and irrational. But, at the same time, because of the nature of poetry, it is essential to sit judicially on top of the process.

An Interview with Richard Wilbur
Willard Pate and Panel/1970

From *The South Carolina Review,* Vol. 3, No. 1 (November, 1970), 5-23. Reprinted by permission of Furman University and Willard Pate.

Richard Wilbur visited the Furman University campus on February 9-10, 1970. During his visit, he appeared with a panel of students who questioned him about American poetry. These pages are a record of that session.

Panel: Mr. Wilbur, I think we want to start with a general question pertaining to the tradition of American poetry: What do you feel is peculiarly American about American poetry? What makes it American?

Wilbur: I don't know whether I can distinguish between poetry and prose fiction in this respect. But I do think that America is different from England. That's the main distinction to be made. America is different from England in not having a long and coherent, relatively unmixed tradition. And I'm not speaking of literary tradition merely. I'm speaking of the culture as a whole. So that I think the American poet—the American artist generally—is likely to feel out on his own and very close to the wilds, if you compare him to his English or European counterpart. Wright Morris wrote a book about the American novel called *The Territory Ahead*—that's Huck Finn setting out for the territory ahead. There's always some impulse in the American writer to set out for the frontier in some sense or the other—to head for the savage, the original, the uncivilized, to stand loose from whatever cultural coherences people may try to thrust upon him. William Carlos Williams' sensibility is, it seems to me, impossible to imagine in England. I'm thinking, of course, of that poem of his that begins—that savage poem of his that begins, "The pure products of America / go crazy" and ends "No one / to witness / and adjust, no one to drive the car" ("To Elsie"). That's a big part of the way America feels: "No one / to witness / and adjust, no one to drive the car."

You can pretend it's not true; you can pretend that what Brooks Adams called "the incoherence of American democracy" is not a fact. You can write for a few cultured friends down the block in Cambridge—there have been American poets who did this—but mostly I think the American writer, both with regret and with attraction, acknowledges the fact of a great diversity of culture, of considerable anarchy in this country, and the presence—if not in the sense of woods, in other senses—of the wilderness still amongst us.

Panel: Well, then, you lay a great deal of emphasis on the qualities of audience, the type of audience the poet has to play for. In other words, the diversity in American culture makes a difference in the reception a poet gets.

Wilbur: I suppose I don't think of a poet as deliberately addressing an audience, in the sense of giving a performance. It's rather more oblique than that. And yet you do represent other people to yourself in the process of writing. You are indirectly talking to your fellow citizens, and maybe a few other people if you are lucky. Mostly I think what you do is talk to yourself in the presence of the language. And the American language is, if you are using it in a lively way, a pretty good reflection of the state of American life. If you use the existing live American language faithfully, you are going to have to cope with the facts of our culture.

Panel: Where do you think modern poetry in America is today, especially in terms of the tradition of American poetry?

Wilbur: I just taught a course in American poetry that started with Anne Bradstreet and collapsed in the middle of T. S. Eliot. I didn't get down to the present moment. So circumstances have not forced me to be lucid about the immediate situation. It does seem to me an extremely chaotic one. As always, the best talents are quite individual, and yet not freakishly so. And they are sitting off by themselves in some town or other, writing their poems and hoping to be read by each other.

You could distinguish a school of writers and call them confessional, and there would be some truth in that. People like W. D. Snodgrass, Robert Lowell, Anne Sexton, the late Sylvia Plath, and others could legitimately be grouped as poets who have made a great deal out of frank autobiography. Mostly, I think these people are most justifiable, most useful to us as poets, when they are treating themselves as representative sufferers in the modern age. I don't care much for confessional poetry when it is just the sort of whining that you get at a bar from drunks. You can distinguish that tendency, and I don't know whether it is playing itself out or not. I expect that it may.

John Berryman is way off by himself carrying the rhetorical tradition in American poetry to a wonderful extreme, writing in about three dialects at once in such a way as, freakishly and wonderfully and humorously, to make an impression of a whole personality, or let's say a jarring personality which is fully articulate in all its persons.

You know, Marianne Moore is still with us, though I think probably she's done the major part of her work. And a wonderful poet, Elizabeth Bishop, who started somewhat as her disciple, is still with us also. They are great descriptive and more or less overtly moralistic poets.

There is a group of people who lately lost one of their leaders, Charles Olson, who have been classified as the Black Mountain School; and I think that they are probably the best poets in America who *consider* themselves as constituting a school. Most American poets are ashamed to think of themselves as belonging to a gang. But these poets do—that is, they refer to each other with maximum seriousness and respect. They feel that the way they go about it is the way it should be done. I've never completely understood their aesthetics, but I think some of the results, especially in the best work of Denise Levertov, can be handsome.

There is a school—and I suppose it *is* a school—of writers called the New York School. A couple of them are very amusing, but I don't think that they are of sufficient consequence to deserve such a magnificent title as the New York School. They are a group of people who hang around the art galleries and write for art magazines. In general they feel that the live modern tradition comes down from Tristan Tzara and Lautréamont. You know, it's surrealism and dada, and if you're not with that, you are not with the modern at all. The late Frank O'Hara was a member of this school, and he wrote one of the funniest lines that has ever been written. It won't sound funny out of context, but I'm going to say it anyway—the line goes: "Ah, Jane, is there no more frontier?" And then there is John Ashbery who isn't really very funny, but who writes in the manner of this school, attempting, I think, to accomplish something of the nature of abstract painting in poetry. And then there is Kenneth Koch, who is funny as the devil. The limitation of this school is the limitation which the dada tradition has—the inclination to silliness. And in the poetry of this school generally you find a hidden sentimentalism—they all think childhood was the best of times; there's no sadder sound in nature than the sound of a running-down nursery music box.

I haven't covered everything. I left out all those people with the guitars in their hands. But, you know, one thing about America—to refer again to Brooks Adams—Brooks Adams pointed out, in a lecture called "The Incoherence of American Democracy," back in 1916 that if George Washington had had his way, there would have been a canal from the Potomac to the Ohio, and the produce of the west would have come into Washington, D.C., and Washington would have been a great commercial as well as governmental center, and we might have had a city like Paris. As it is, we don't have any one city that is the central city of America to which you go if you are a young man with talent in one of the arts. And that really does affect our art—that we're not in great physical proximity, we poets of America. The fact that you don't see over a period of ten years someone who lives on the west coast is going to have something to do with his power to influence you.

Panel: What do you think of the effect on poetry—anyone's poetry—of activism, political or otherwise?

Wilbur: Well, I should think that anybody's free to write about whatever is his natural subject; and it is possible to drop out of the public scene and write about nature, God, and love, and that's enough—isn't it?—for some people. But I think I should be disappointed in any very productive poet of the modern period who didn't react in some measure to some of the things that are happening about us and to us, some of the things that are being done by us. When you pick up books of poems about the Vietnam war or about the assassination of President Kennedy, that sort of thing, it's always aesthetically disappointing; most of the poems are bad. What you admire is the fervor of the poems, the genuineness of their feelings; you are sorry that they are not more substantial as persuasions or as tributes. The poster poem is a special kind of art which only a few people in any culture have practiced with any distinction. I suspect Mayakovsky was a great poster poet. Mostly when we turn to poetry—it seems to me—we don't ask of it that it say "Vote Socialist" or "Get out of Vietnam" or "Kill the Cops" or anything like that. We want poetry to be as nearly as possible a miraculous precipitation of somebody's whole soul, as Coleridge said. We want it to be honest in the sense that it spills the beans totally, that it says whatever it says with all the reservations, all the qualifications which the speaker must feel. My idea of a fine political poem is William Butler Yeats' "Easter 1916." The interesting thing about that poem is that Yeats moves you tremendously about the foolhardy, heroic men who fought at the post office in Dublin; and he persuades you that what they did has transformed the casual comedy of Dublin life into a terrible beauty, into something tragic. He says, "MacDonagh, and MacBride / And Connolly, and Pearse," and you are moved about them. At the same time, he makes it pretty clear that political fanaticism costs the heart something, that about the time he dies in the post office, or is executed for what he did there, a man has lost some portion of his personality, some of the richness of his nature, to a political fever. He says also, "For England may keep faith / For all that is done and said." In the middle of a poem celebrating Irish martyrs he says, "Bear it in mind that what they did was foolish, that it was against the general's orders, that England may keep faith, that it may have been all in vain, and that it may be that any continuation of their kind of spirit would be destructive." It is an extraordinary balancing act— Yeat's poem—and if you went around with a brush and pasted it on the hoardings of a city, it wouldn't move people to one kind of an action or another; it would move them to contemplation. And perhaps it would move them to thank God that somebody had been totally honest.

Panel: What about somebody like Auden? He is a bit more polemic, more political, wouldn't you say?

Wilbur: In his earlier poems, yes. I think that Auden and Day-Lewis and perhaps here and there Spender in the thirties assigned themselves the task of preparing what they regarded as a stuffy, played-out society for necessary social changes. They were doing a rather different kind of thing from what Yeats was doing in writing a poem about a violent situation which has just occurred. They were looking toward the future—until it came, of course, time to write about the Spanish Civil War. So much of their work—I think of Day-Lewis' wonderful, long poem "From Feathers to Iron," in which he tries to get us to feel about factories as if they were women's bodies producing children, tries to humanize the factory—is an effort to try to revolutionize the British sensibility in the direction of a new social economy. I'm not sure how much of that poetry now survives, is really still alive. "From Feathers to Iron" probably is, because it is still, for all of our sensibilities, a big issue.

Hart Crane, way back at the beginning of his career, was saying, "The major job of contemporary poetry is to assimilate the machine." And everybody's been trying to assimilate the machine ever since. Oh, I felt so happy when I put the words *reinforced concrete* into a poem. But it's very hard to make it stick. It's very hard to change people's feelings. Here in the most advanced technology of the world, we still find an aesthetic reluctance on all hands to accept the machine as a thing of beauty, as a human instrument to be celebrated when put to the right uses. You can safely attack the city and praise the country to any poetry-reading audience nowadays, even though many of your hearers will scarcely, if ever, have left the city.

Panel: Mr. Wilbur, I'd like to return to what you said earlier about American poets always looking to the frontier. Could you relate that idea to the emphasis which I see in Walt Whitman, and works like Hart Crane's "The Bridge"—an interest in the things in the real world, in concrete things rather than in abstractions?

Wilbur: There certainly is a strong strain of that in American poetry, and different people have given it different names. I remember Kathleen Raine, the English poet—during a symposium at the YMHA about 15 years ago—calling it "materialism." And then someone jumped up and said "Empiricism!" . . . You've rendered me a little mute.

Panel: A statement of yours I read made me want to ask you that question. Talking about how you came to write "A Baroque Wall-Fountain in the Villa Sciarra," you said that when you lived in Rome you "felt reproached" by the fountain because of your "Puritanical industry." You then went on to say: "I like it when the ideas of a poem seem to be necessary aspects of things or actions which it presents—stretching away and yet always adhering, like shadows. In this case, I may have come near that desideratum" (*Poet's Choice*, ed. Paul England and Joseph Langland). I was thinking about Walt Whitman and what he contributed to imagist poetry, and then about Hart Crane—and generally in the stream of American poetry the interest in things, the things of the world.

Wilbur: It's an extremely strong strain with us. Emerson and Thoreau you think of first—their great delight, particularly in their prose, in the solid and homely and concrete words, and in his essay *Nature*, Emerson's stress on the fact that all abstract words ultimately derive from things—the word *wrong* means *crooked*, and so forth. And you think of Whitman's insistence in his homemade Indian religion on the body and on material things—his insistence, in fact, that revelation can be achieved through bodily ecstasy. I guess there are a few Indians who think that way, but that's not a widespread conception. I suspect that Kathleen Raine's word "materialism"— though it's a bad word—has a little to do with the question. We are a great inventing and manufacturing country, and if we are going to face the facts of American life, we have to face the fact that this is a very "thingy" country, a very practical country. We have to hope, as Hart Crane rather vaguely and gaseously hoped, to unite the spiritual and the material.

Panel: How do you synthesize this strain of the concrete with contemporary language in a traditional form?

Wilbur: Well, I don't think any form in itself means anything, though I've heard people say the contrary. William Carlos Williams used to say that to write a sonnet is to make a curtsey to the court of Queen Elizabeth I. The reason he said that was because, when he rhymed, it sounded that way. He wisely forsook rhyming and other traditional artifice in favor of a kind of poetry in which he could sound like himself. But I think you only have to name a few names like Robert Frost to reflect that the pentameter, for example, doesn't in any sense render the words which it counterpoints old fashioned— or it would do so only to a very limited and prejudiced ear. The question of what is the live language is a touchy one. Beyond a certain point, you obviously can't worry about what someone might misunderstand. You can't worry about the far-outness of a certain allusion, if you absolutely need it to say what you want to say. You have a sense in writing, not of what the public, whoever that is, will understand—you have a sense of what the present state of the language is and what its conversancy with the past is. So you have a sense of what kind of a risk you're taking when you refer, for example—as I did in one poem—to the river Xanthus. Not everybody is going to remember that Xanthus is another name for the river Scamander—and that you're referring to the twenty-first book of the *Iliad*. You make a decision at the moment of writing a poem; you say, "If I say Xanthus, I'm going to say a whole lot in one word." It's going to mean a lot for anybody who gets it out. But I'm running away with your subject.

Panel: I think we need to pursue the subject of form, particularly as you see it in your own poetry. Several essays I've read have referred to you as a very form-conscious poet. Speak a minute about how you consider form in your own work and particularly with reference to the modern expressions of freedom in verse.

Wilbur: As Eliot and Pound both said, as almost any experienced poet knows, free verse is very, very difficult to write. It probably should be attempted only after a long period of exercise in the easier forms, that is to say, in the meters, in the stanzas, in the rhymes. I take no pleasure in mere form, and I've never said to myself, "I think I'll write a sonnet." I've never written a sonnet or even a rondeau except by sort of blundering into it—finding that some material that was washing around in my head wanted to take that form. If you've done a bit of dancing, you know when the band shifts into a polka, and you adjust. And you do the same thing, it seems to me, on the basis of reading and writing experience, with the material that is vaguely developing in your mind and wants to find a form. If, for instance, you have an idea in your mind that seems to want to be said in three ways and then wind up in a brief and epigrammatic manner, then a certain shape of the sonnet might be very useful to you: three quatrains and a couplet and you have it said. Mostly I don't use so-called traditional forms. I just start writing and let the lines break off where they want to break off and, if they seek to rhyme, it's they that are doing the rhyming, not I. I have the feeling that the material chooses the form. I have no quarrel at all with Emerson. He said, "not meter, but meter-making argument makes poetry," and I think that's true. I simply write a kind of free verse that ends by rhyming much of the time. If you do use the greatest strictness with yourself, not allowing the rhyme to run away with you and decide what the poem shall say, it seems to me that you end with a greater freedom, a greater power. Some of the freedom comes in the process itself. This is something I have often rambled on about. Non-rhyming poets don't know it, and so I like to say it. If you take any two words that rhyme, there operates, as Victor Hugo said, between them a kind of obligation to produce metaphor. This could be demonstrated right now with all of us. If I say *hook-book* to you, it's not the same as if I said *brush-stadium*. There's some kind of implicit, magical demand made on you by the fact that *hook* and *book* sound a bit alike, and your mind starts trying to pull them together in some way or other. Actually the movement of the mind is not like that at all—there's much more floundering to it. But all sorts of idiotic things suggest themselves. The mind is actually set loose by this search for a rhyme that will make some kind of sense. Of course, if you don't find a rhyme that will make some kind of sense, that will say what you were going to say or will, as sometimes happens, show you what you want to say—then you have to chuck it. You musn't let the rhyme do the job. But rhyme can be a great liberator of the unconscious. And this is something not understood very much at present; most people think of rhyme as being—oh, "structured"— as something imposed, and the next thing to hypocrisy. But it's really, properly used, a great liberator of the mind.

Panel: You have translated French poetry. In Europe, the French are famous for their rareness of form. Do you think the French have in any way influenced you?

Wilbur: Oh, I expect so. I've translated a couple of plays by Molière, and I'm doing a third one now. I find it very hard at present to think in anything but couplets. You get obsessed by the couplet when you're translating Molière. And I suppose there are other French poets whose use of form has taken a hold of me. Baudelaire, in particular. I think I'm fascinated by the powerful contrast between a kind of lapidary classical style and an explosive dramatic content in him. I'm not much attracted to the rondeau sort of thing—to those doilies of poems. I would only write them if I had to. I woke up in the middle of the night the other night and wrote a rondeau, but I didn't know I was doing it until I was half way through.

Panel: Mr. Wilbur, you spoke of your material's seeking its own form. Did you ever feel that it would seek its own form and expression in a play of your own?

Wilbur: Well, yes, I tried to write a play back in 1952, and it was simply awful. I was trying to write a verse play and—to be blunt about it, to be embarrassing about it—I think I simply didn't know enough about people at the time to bring convincing characters on to the stage. They were all very wooden. That's when I translated my first Molière play. I thought I might learn something about poetic theater by translating *the master.* I've never written a novel and I doubt that I'll ever have the organizational power to do so.

Panel: On the subject of form still, I want to go back to a discussion of free verse. I remember reading Eliot's comments. He said there are three types of free verse. One that uses iambic norms, and another that imitates the rhythms of natural speech, and a third that follows Whitman's idea that the correct emotion will dictate the form. What do you mean when you say that free verse is the most difficult form?

Wilbur: Well, you want, if you are writing out of material that is important to you—material about which you feel passionately—to hit hard. You want, therefore, to be able to give the signals to the reader, or to give the signals in the work, which demand strong response and show strong emphasis. It's very hard to define a rhythm without a metrical paradigm underlying it in such a way that the reader can be absolutely sure of how to say it. There are some things like the Epistle to the Corinthians . . . "Though I speak with the tongues of men and angels"— what a rhythm that is. That's like the rhythms which open Whitman's great poems: "Out of the cradle endlessly rocking." You know where he's going to go from there, and you know that he's going to come back and back and back to that falling rhythm—I guess you'd call it. There's something I often like to quote in connection with this. Take Milton's description of Satan's expulsion from heaven. I forget what the normal expectation for runover lines is in English, but Milton certainly exceeded it in this passage. Here goes Satan: "Him the Almighty Power / Hurled headlong flaming from the

Ethereal sky / With hideous ruin and combustion, down / To bottomless perdition, there to dwell / In adamantine chains and penal fire, /
Who durst defy the Omnipotent to arms" (*Paradise Lost,* Book I,
44ff.) You just couldn't do that in free verse. I hate the word *formal*
verse, because it sounds so ladyschool, you know. But if you use
verse with meters, if you use sound structures of some kind, stanza
patterns of some type, you set up expectations which you can
disappoint. You can make people fall a long and felt distance in
formal verse—you cannot do that kind of powerful thing in free verse.
This is one reason why free verse poets like William Carlos Williams
are full of exclamation points. They have to keep telling you when to
jump.

Panel: So in writing free verse you lose the ability to control your
audience?

Wilbur: There are certain kinds of control that you can't have.
Rhyme gives you certain kinds of dramatic control, too, if it's used
correctly. There's an example—I hope I can quote it properly—a
poem of Gerard Manley Hopkins', one of his terrible sonnets. It
begins, "No worst, there is none. Pitched past pitch of grief; / More
pangs will, schooled at forepangs, wilder wring. / Comforter, where,
where is your comforting? / Mary, mother of us, where is thy relief?"
Notice the relationship between that "wilder wring" in the second line
and that "comforting" in the third. The "wring" is a very hard rhyme,
and "comforting" breaks off, and it tells you to break your voice. It
almost lets your voice crack at the end of the third line. There's the
kind of accurate music that a fine user of rhyme can force. But there
are very great free verse poems.

Panel: There is a development in modern music now, back to
form, back to classical patterns. Do you think anything like that will
happen with poetry—the return to classical patterns and forms?

Wilbur: Well, if I had to play prophet—and I guess I do—I think I
would say that we're about to have a division amongst writers of lyric
poetry. On the one hand we will have, if we're really lucky, an
emergence of really good song lyricists. We haven't yet, for my taste,
discovered anybody who does the rock or pop sort of thing and is, at
the same time, a good poet. But it seems to me that the ground is
being prepared. And somebody much better than Leonard Cohen,
for example, will come along because he now exists. And then on the

other hand, I suspect we will have resurgence of interest in some of
the advantages of the antique discipline. But the sort of thing that the
Williams-Pound school did—and that has been completed by the
best practitioners of the Black Mountain School and people like A. R.
Ammons—is a very genuine kind of poetry, and I should think that it
would continue. We're going to have a division between the poets
who carry guitars and those poets who write for the page. I should
guess that there will be, if for no other reason than fashion, a
recovery of interest in the possibilities of formal means.

Panel: This brings up a subject I think everyone wants to talk
about: the influence of pop culture—which refers not just to pop
music, but to pop art, pop literature, new radicalism, all this sort of
thing—on your poetry and on modern poetry in general.

Wilbur: Well, I think at the moment the kind of stuff I write is
completely divorced from the kind of graphic art and sculpture that is
suggested by such names as Andy Warhol and Roy Lichtenstein and
Oldenburg. I think, although there are still some wonderful painters
and sculptors among us, that sculpture and graphic arts have fallen
on sad days and have fallen into the hands of exploiters, fallen into
the realm of fashion, and that the American public is deserving what
it gets. If they want to pay that much for a coke bottle, that's exactly
what they deserve. But there's no continuity at all between poetry as
I think of it, poetry as my friends write it, and that sort of thing.
Lichtenstein, by blowing up a Flash Gordon panel, can make
thousands and thousands of dollars. There is no way for a poet to do
that. It's because we can't arrange to get corrupted in a big way that
we're preserved from the fate of the other arts. It's also because it's
almost impossible to empty words of their meaning. You can readily
paint a painting that doesn't mean anything in a paraphrasable sense.
You can surely write music which contains no emotional signatures at
all. But words, as Gertrude Stein discovered, incline, no matter what
you do, towards designations and evaluations.

Panel: Speaking of arranging to get corrupted, what about
publishing and about public support for the arts in general and poets
and poetry in particular? I know the National Foundation for the Arts
has given some money to university presses and publishing poets. I
just wondered if you would comment generally on the poet as he
relates to publishing and to the presses.

Wilbur: At the moment it is very easy to get published. There are lots and lots and lots of literary magazines—many of them quite horrible, but at any rate if you want to be published by somebody you have a very good chance. There are, I suppose, many more books of poems published by commercial and university presses annually than there used to be. We at Wesleyan publish about seven volumes per annum, which is more than Harcourt Brace does. Our volumes, although they don't make our poets rich, are now selling—I wish I could give you exact figures. But a quite unknown poet, if he gets published in this series, is likely to be carried and guaranteed a bit by such prestige as the series has, and he will sell 3,000 or 4,000 books. Now a few years ago a sale of 500 volumes was extremely predictable—not good, but predictable. And so the public is larger for books of poems. Now, what else?

Panel: What influence do you think the publishing business has on who gets read, that is, on the direction of American poetry? How do particular things like the Yale Series of Younger Poets encourage the selection of a certain poetry against a certain other?

Wilbur: Yale always has some nameless person doing the first reading and eliminating lots of manuscripts, and then the finalists were submitted to Mr. Auden, to Mr. Fitts—the late Dudley Fitts—or, as at present, Stanley Kunitz. One man's taste prevails there. At Wesleyan we have a board of four who are of very different tastes. We've published poetry, I should think, of every possible, distinguishable school in America, and we're not in the least interested in excluding any kind of poetry. I guess we would all vote against pop poetry, so-called, and I can't imagine any volume of found poetry—that is to say, rearranged advertisement copy—that we would publish.

Panel: Well, what about government sponsorship and foundation sponsorship?

Wilbur: I think that Roger Stevens' outfit, which was dispensing a certain amount of money under Mr. Johnson's administration, has collapsed now—that the money isn't there anymore. In general, the dispensers of big money to the arts like to give the money to ballet companies, theaters, and groups—same way in scholarship. If you can get seventeen social scientists together or a batch of physicists who need some terribly expensive machine, you stand a better chance than if there is just one of you who wants to look at butterflies. There are certain foundations, like the Guggenheim, who continue to be very good to poets. The Ford Foundation has interested itself in poets only—I may be wrong here—but I think only or chiefly in connection with a program for the encouragement of the drama. They gave fellowships to poets on the understanding that the poets would go and hang around theaters, in one or another part of the world, and get themselves more dramatically inclined. Most poets teach school, at present, and the virtues and disadvantages of that are obvious. It would be churlish not to say that there are good things about it; and I think that it depends somewhat on the kind of poet you are, how much harm it's going to do you to be a teacher. If you're the kind of poet who spins his poetry out of his own, private, emotional life, then all this classroom stuff is going to be not to the point and perhaps a little adulterating of the consciousness. But if you're the sort of poet who likes to refer to the river Xanthus, it doesn't do you too much harm.

Panel: Do you feel that, because of poetry's inability to be corrupted, this artificial environment of maintaining poetry by university presses and this encouragement that poets give each other is deemphasizing poetry on a public scale?

Wilbur: A couple of years ago, I reviewed a nice biography of Longfellow by Newton Arvin, and it had a last chapter in it which was very pertinent to what you just said. Arvin distinguished various kinds of popular poetry, and right now I can't recall the names he gave to his several categories. There would be a folk poetry which was pre-literate, or non-literate, and then there would be a newspaper verse classification to which a poet like James Metcalf or Edgar Guest or Rod McKuen would belong. And then there would be a classification which he called high demotic, and to that the really fine poets—people like Longfellow, Whittier, or some other of the so-called fireside poets—might belong. There's a letter of Longfellow's that I came across a while back, and it was simply fascinating. He was writing to somebody saying, "America has instituted a system of universal education; we're going to have universal literacy; people whose parents didn't read are able to read, and they're excited about it. And I'm going to write them some poems." He was very breezy about it too. He said, "I think I'll have them printed up as broadsides

and hawk them on the street." And this led to poems like "Paul
Revere's Ride," which is a very good poem, really. The fact that it
doesn't give us any trouble to read doesn't mean that it isn't good,
and it led to things like Whittier's fine poem "Abraham Davenport."
Now the people of my father's generation and of his father's
generation grew up knowing the poetry of these beloved fireside
poets who sold enormously, who were honored everywhere; after all,
Longfellow is honored in Westminster Abbey. There have been no
poets like that since. Leslie Fiedler is about to come to Wesleyan, and
he told me that he was going to give a lecture called "The New
Longfellows." What he's talking about is the guitar-playing poets, and
it is true that these are the most popular poets, in some sense or
other, to exist in America since the fireside poets in the nineteenth
century. But the difference is enormous. Longfellow didn't hesitate in
his poetry to refer, for example, to the *Aeneid*. Also newly literate
people knew the *Aeneid* only through Longfellow's references to it.
Without being a bore, he was a conscious cultural uplifter and a
transmitter of the literature of other times and places. It was really, if
you compare Longfellow to contemporary pop standards, altogether
highbrow.

Panel: We keep coming back to pop, and I have another question
I want to ask. I suppose one of the most controversial questions
about the status of poetry in relation to pop music is how you judge
pop music. There seem to be two perspectives. One seems to be
that pop music, in order to be accepted as a legitimate art form, must
measure up to standards of literature or poetry. The other perspective
tries to judge it as an art form which sets its own standards and has to
work as an artistic unit in itself. How do you judge it—which way?

Wilbur: I think the thing to do, given the material that we have, is
to make a sharp distinction, as either Simon or Garfunkel did the
other day, between the Wallace Stevens sort of thing, as he said, and
the pop lyric. Which is the lyricist—Simon or Garfunkel?

Panel: Simon.

Wilbur: He said, "I happen to like pop lyrics better than poetry,
but I know what I write is not the same thing as what Wallace Stevens
wrote." I've written some show lyrics for Broadway, and although I'm
not very musical, I have been interested in writing lyrics. And so I
have a certain hope that a new Thomas Campion will come along in

time—someone who really is a good poet and who is at the same time a good musician. Meanwhile I think the sensible thing to do is not to bother to assess Bob Dylan as a poet, because he isn't satisfactory as a writer, but to enjoy him, insofar as one can, as a performer and as a pop musician and lyricist. I've not listened to very much of him; people whose tastes I admire tell me there are some quite fine songs, taken as songs, and as performed by him. But when you read him on the page, he doesn't come to very much.

Panel: This is the question that always comes up. Do you feel that it has primarily to meet standards on the page written, or is it a medium that has to be assessed as a new form?

Wilbur: I think it only has to meet such standards if somebody says it does. I gather that Dylan has sometimes referred to himself as a poet; I suppose someone else in the same category might be more modest.

Panel: He doesn't refer to his songs as poetry, though. He writes poetry, but it's not his songs he calls poetry.

Wilbur: I prefer Edgar Guest—I'm quite serious—because he was an honest, simple man. Robert Frost met him one time in Detroit. The only immodest thing Guest said to Frost was to ask him what kind of car he drove. It turned out that Guest had a Cadillac or something like that. But he was very modest about his art. Frost said, "What do you do when you get an idea for a poem?" And Guest said, "Well, if I'm out on the golf course, I say to that idea, 'Report to my office at eleven o'clock tomorrow morning!' "

Panel: By extension from pop music—you said you'd tried writing a verse play. What about poetry and the theater? How do you think that the two interact?

Wilbur: I think potentially verse theater might do very well with us, because we have a lot of people who come out of Carnegie Tech, and various other places, who know how to deliver a line of verse. The two translations of Molière which I did—*The Misanthrope* and *Tartuffe*—played all over the country and in Ontario and London. People just sat there and put up with rhymed couplets, 1800 lines of rhymed couplets. I think that's quite a test.

Panel: But that was Molière.

Wilbur: Yes, that was Molière. Well, you obviously need good playwrights, but I don't see any reason why good playwrights shouldn't use poetic forms successfully. Of course, as I say, we do have a corps of actors to do it, though they sometimes miscast the people. I saw a Chicago production of my *Misanthrope* translation, and there was just the most charming sort of Marilyn Monroe girl—I won't mention her name—who was cast in the part of Celimene. I went around to say hello to her and the rest of the cast after opening night, and she said, "Boy, I just don't get this new stuff!"

Panel: I'd like you to comment on the possibility that some "good poet" would come along and use the form of the guitar. Do you think this would have a great effect on poetry as it is accepted or read or enjoyed or listened to?

Wilbur: Well, I think it would. We'd still have a sharp distinction between the kind of poetry which is at leisure to be full of nuances and reservations—to use the word "but" liberally—and the song lyric, which is always simple. A song lyric has always got to be simple and repetitive, can be only so subtle, can render only so complete an account of anybody's sensibility. But if the quality of the pop lyric in America were greatly elevated, then it would have a considerable effect on the writing of serious poetry, I think. I guess the main point of Ezra Pound's wonderful book *The ABC of Reading* is that in the seventeenth century, the poet, whether or not he was writing for music, thought of the tones of words as bearing some relation to musical sound. That's something which has been greatly lost in subsequent centuries. I know when I first started writing I had no feeling at all for sound. And it wasn't until I began going around and spouting my poems to audiences that I commenced to see how unpronounceable I was being and how inexpressive some of my noises were.

Panel: You mentioned writing the lyrics for *Candide*. Do you think that had any effect, really, on your poetry in general?

Wilbur: I can't tell about that; I'm not sure. When you are writing lyrics for a show, even when it's a very highbrow show as that one was, you are thinking about the audience; you're thinking how it will hit them. You hypothesize a man from Scarsdale out there and you write *to* him. Of course, your collaborators differ with you as to the capacities of that man from Scarsdale. And you never know who he is. But you are concerned with the audience. It seems to me that in writing poetry you are, as I said before, only obliquely, only through the language and its mirroring of the state of the culture, concerned with an audience. Although, heaven knows, if you didn't ultimately want to be read, you wouldn't write very much. It just has to be a sneaky desire.

Panel: May I return to what you said about the verse play and then the lyrics and then the poetry? Somehow the verse play seems to be somewhere in the middle between the two in terms of the audience and its involvement in the work. Is this true?

Wilbur: Well, I think if I wrote a verse play—I don't detect any talent yet in myself for writing one—I would try to make it have a continual effect on the audience. I'd try to think of that and would try not to indulge myself in great arias. I like in general the modestly poetic character of Eliot's verse plays, although I must say that my favorite among his verse plays is *Murder in the Cathedral,* which is the most poetic of them.

Panel: Besides being a poet, you are a translator, too. I wonder if there can be an adequate translation? Because of the differences in languages, structures, connotations, isn't every translation a complete new creation of a poem insofar as both form and substance go?

Wilbur: Well, it pretty well has to be. It's just a matter of degree, I think. A translator like Ezra Pound or Robert Lowell will call what he does an adaptation, an homage, an imitation; and Pound will be so free as to take a poem of Voltaire's and reduce it to prose and throw away any material he doesn't want to use. Robert Lowell will translate a two-stanza poem of Rilke's and make Rilke a present of a third stanza of Lowell's own composition. Pound and Lowell are both fine poets, so anything they do is interesting and worth reading. But that's not my idea of translating. Obviously you can't translate anybody word for word, even in prose. I try to translate thought by thought, and not to leave out any thoughts. And then I try, insofar as I can, to reproduce the form. It's fairly easy in some cases to reproduce the form: Russian, for example. Although Russian poetry inclines to be more thumpy than ours, it has our meters and the same kind of emphatic character. And so you can duplicate a lot of the noise of a Russian poem. With the French it's obviously very much more difficult. You declare the pentameter to be the equivalent of the Alexandrine, and on the whole the material that was in the twelve syllables of the French line will sort itself out within the ten

syllables of the English line. But you know that there is an initial
formal infidelity there. But I try for the illusion that I've been perfectly
faithful, and when I've done a job that pleases me I can tell it pleases
me because I forget the original.

Panel: I'd like to ask whether, when you began, when you first
decided to be a writer, did you have a vision or dream of where you
were going? Or did you just step into it, and it sort of happened to
you? What happened?

Wilbur: It quite happened to me; I just blundered into it. I was
brought up in the house of a portrait painter. But we were not an arty
household really. It was just a house in which painting, a little music,
anything you might like to do in the way of any of the arts was
approved of. And the guests or visitors to my house were likely to be
bored with specimens of my little drawings, my first poems. I thought
at the time I left college that I was going to be a journalist or perhaps
a cartoonist on a newspaper. There have been many journalists in my
mother's family. And then during World War II (War, as a young sailor
said to me on the plane yesterday, mostly is just sitting around on
your butt), I found myself writing a lot of poems. By the time the war
ended, I had a drawer full of them. My wife once showed them to a
French friend of ours who had some literary connections in New
York. He took them home to his Cambridge apartment, and a few
hours after his departure he came bursting in through the door of our
apartment, kissed me on both cheeks and said, "You're a poet!" He
sent these poems to New York, to the publisher Reynal and Hitchcock, and they most improbably wrote me a letter saying they would
publish them. And so I decided I must be a poet. And I began to
abandon more and more of my ambition to be a scholar. I expect
with most people it's just a matter of having it thrust upon you, of
your being unable not to do it. A woman once said to Robert Frost,
who had actually never seen any of her work, "Should I go on with
my poetry?" He said, "Try and stop and see what happens," which is
kind of brusque, but it's very reasonable, I think. If you don't have to
do it, why do it?

Panel: Is there anything in particular you'd like to leave us with?

Wilbur: Well, you were going to ask me whether poetry had
anything to do with psychedelic experience, and I was going to say
that it didn't.

Panel: Well, I was going to ask you that, but it just didn't seem to fit, so I let it go. Would you like to make a comment about the effect of drugs on creativity?

Wilbur: Well, yes, I think that I wish Coleridge had never taken opium. There are people going around saying Blake took hashish. I don't know. But I deny it all about Edgar Allan Poe. I do think that actually there is nothing more dangerous to the imagination than fantasy. The drug experience is shadow boxing, and the business of the poet is to be confronting, with his imagination, these solid objects here. So I think that there is not only no good relation between drugs and art but that, as somebody told me as long ago as ten years, it's very damaging to whatever creative powers you have to develop too much of a psychic dependency, even on harmless grass.

Panel: Thank you very much, Mr. Wilbur.

Craft Interview with Richard Wilbur
The New York Quarterly/1972

From *The New York Quarterly,* 12 (Autumn 1972), 16-36. Reprinted by permission of *The New York Quarterly.*

Following is the twelfth in a series of craft interviews with outstanding poets on the general subject of style and prosody and technique in writing.

We have tried to keep these interviews as objective as possible, and we are limiting our discussion to those questions which might occur to a practicing writer.

NYQ: How long are you likely to work on a poem?

Richard Wilbur: Long enough. Generally pretty long. The last poem I finished concerned a mind reader whom I met in Rome in 1954. Very shortly after I met him, I commenced to think of writing about him. In the intervening years I've now and then jotted down on an envelope, or in a little book, some phrase that might belong to a poem about this man, but it wasn't until three years ago—that is, fourteen years after I met him—that I actually got going on the poem, and now it's taken me three years to finish it. It is, to be sure, a long poem for me, a hundred and some lines. Occasionally I've had the luck to write a poem in a day, but that's not commonly my experience.

NYQ: When you say, 'in a day,' do you mean first version or completed.

RW: Over and done with. I don't actually revise, or it's very seldom that I revise. What I do is write so leisurely that all the revisions occur in thought or in the margins of the page. It can make for a page which is as dense, graphically, as some men's-room walls. Which is not to say that a poem is like going to the men's room.

NYQ: Is this a recent development, this slow process of writing?

RW: No, I've always been that way. Always extremely slow. And I think perhaps it has something to do with my respect for the written word—even my own. I don't dare set things down, for fear I'll leave them there.

NYQ: But you do take notes.

RW: I take very, very fragmentary, suggestive, or wispy notes. I never write out the matter of a whole poem in prose or in jottings, and then proceed. I'm aware that some august people have done that, but I couldn't do it; I think it would take all of the surprise out of the experience, so that there wouldn't be any carrot to lure me on. Sometimes, to be sure, I've got lost in detail toward the end of a long effort, and have made a little outline so as to discover its argumentative dimension.

NYQ: What you do write down before, it would be a snatch of an image, a word?

RW: A word, yes, or, in a sketchy way, the central idea. Not always do these little notes which I put down (and I don't keep anything in the way of a continuing notebook; I'm not like Ted Roethke), not always do these little jottings actually appear in the final poem. They're just a way of reminding me that there's a poem I might be thinking about.

NYQ: Do you keep these little notes in any organized fashion?

RW: Pretty disorganized. I have a little blank book in which I've been making jottings for perhaps ten years, and I may have used 15 pages of it. And then there are scrawled-on scraps and sullied envelopes here and there—tucked into that blank book, or stuck in the drawers of desks.

NYQ: What form does the 'carrot' take which lures you on? Is it a vision of a completed, crafted work of art? Or some kind of emotion?

RW: Both, I should think. I do aim at making a good thing, working out a poem which shall be well constructed; at the same time I wouldn't be interested in writing a poem if it weren't getting a great deal of me and of humanity off my chest. I believe I'm not expected to feel this way, but I agree with Emerson that it's not meter but meter-making argument that's important. To go back to what we were saying earlier, I probably denied too flatly that I do any revisions; but the revisions are likely to be small and local. I showed this poem just finished to Bill Meredith, who's a fine poet and is also the sterling kind of friend who can look at a poem of yours and discuss it neither in a flattering nor in a malicious way. I pretty well trust him. He's pointed out some four words or phrases which he thinks I might profitably tinker with. And I think perhaps I will, in at least two of the cases. But that's the kind of revision I do: finding a better word for the end of some line in a long poem. If there's too much to be done, I tend to throw the poem out altogether.

NYQ: Do you experience in this process of revision a separate distinct critical faculty?

RW: I don't know that I can be so analytic about my feelings on such occasions. But I'll try. I do know that, like everybody else, I feel that I have to achieve a certain distance from what I've written before I can mess with it. That must imply, then, that one is allowing the critical faculty a little more prominence and isolation than it had during the process of writing. You become, then, two people, the advocate of your poem as you wrote it and the critic of it. That's dangerous, and should be avoided save when necessary. The poet should be wary of the usurping critic in himself, who is capable of concerning himself with ambition, fashion, publication, and book reviewers. The unitary poet, in action, never thinks of such rot.

NYQ: You wouldn't revise, then, after publication.

RW: Very seldom. Once or twice I've found that a poem of mine was needlessly confusing, and that a change which was in no way a disreputable concession could increase the precision of the poem, the intelligibility of the poem. I haven't minded making changes of that kind.

NYQ: You have used words to explain references and allusions. Do you append those after you have written the poem?

RW: Yes, it would always occur afterwards. When you offer notes, it's just a matter of being civil. I don't think of it as a patronizing or show-off gesture. There are a great many things which—although I keep my mind fairly busy and self-respecting in intellectual matters—I just don't know, and need to be told about. I expect my reader to be tolerant of being told this or that which I happen to have stumbled on. I had a note in my last book in which I unburdened myself of much that I had lately learned about the constellations. I'm sure that many of my readers had not just read the little Simon and Schuster astronomy book which I'd picked up in a drugstore.

NYQ: Also by using a note you can keep the explanation out of the poem itself?

RW: Yes, it would be wretched economy to build all one's information into a poem.

NYQ: Do you have a poet who has served you as a model?

RW: No, I don't think I've had any *one*. When I was in high school I read all sorts of poets in an extra-curricular way—it's so often extra-curricularly, I think, that we read the poets who matter to us—and they were as widely separated as Joyce, whose poems are very Elizabethan and conventional, and Eliot, and Hart Crane, and Robert Frost. And I read Wordsworth in class with good will though I found much of him damnably earnest, and still do. All of those would add up to a quite varied set of influences and models. And I think that most of my life I've been in luck in this respect. I've seldom been overwhelmed by the influence of any one writer so that what I wrote myself was too imitative. There's a piece of mine that's probably got too much Yeats in it, and which probably resulted from my having taught a seminar on Yeats at Harvard with John Kelleher. There are one or two poems which show how much I've liked Robert Frost, or Baudelaire. I expect there are some rhythms out of Gerard Manley Hopkins in my first book, and maybe I stole a word or two from Emily Dickinson somewhere. But I've never enlisted under anyone else.

NYQ: You don't mention Auden?

RW: Well, Auden has been a constant delight to me ever since I began to read him. I feel that, at the moment, he's the best presence around—our most civilized, accomplished and heartening poet. I don't know whether at any time I've sounded like him, though Roethke thought my poem "The Undead" showed traces. I can't tell about that. Very often I think we fear that we've been perceptibly influenced by another writer, and yet we're too much ourselves, and too safeguarded by our ineptitudes, for it to be perceptible to others.

NYQ: Or perhaps that influence becomes subconscious.

RW: Yes, that can happen. Once I was composing a poem called "The Death of a Toad," and at the end of the first stanza of it I had an odd feeling of self-approval, the sort of feeling I don't usually have when I start in to write something. That made me self-mistrustful, and after a few minutes' pondering I became aware that I had reproduced a sequence of adjectives out of Edgar Allan Poe's "Dream-Land," and that's why it felt so proper to me. Needless to say, I revised. I suppose every poet ought to be wary of self-approval, it most likely indicates that there's some kind of hidden thievery operating.

NYQ: Do you have periods when you're not writing?

RW: Indeed I do. I suspect that everybody has dry periods. One advantage of getting older is that you have been through it before and before and before: though it doesn't do very *much* good, you can tell yourself that you will come out of it, that you will write again, and therefore you can stay somewhat this side of despair. It's odd, isn't it, that when you have written, and it's mattered to you and to other people, you feel guilty as well as impotent when you're not writing. I don't think this necessarily has anything to do with the parable of the Talents, but you do feel a kind of guilt—or is it shame—as if you were not being quite a man.

NYQ: How long are such dry periods likely to last?

RW: They've lasted for many months with me. Happily, I've never had to go through a whole year without getting my hand in again, however briefly. One thing I do when I find that nothing is coming out of me, is to turn to translation—a risky thing to do, of course, because translation is easier to do than your own work, and it can be a way of distracting yourself from poems of your own which you might do if you left yourself exposed to the pain of your impotence.

NYQ: Do you have a work schedule?

RW: No, I've never had a schedule. I go simply by impulse, whim. What I do try to do is to keep my life uncluttered when I'm not teaching, and therefore be able to harken to the first whisper of any idea. I very much mistrust, for myself at any rate, the idea of sitting down clerkishly every day at a certain hour and making verses. The Trollope regimen won't do for poets. What would happen in my case, I think, is that I would write more poems, but I would write my poem about the mind reader ten years before it was ripe and spoil it. Oh, I may have spoiled it now, but it would have been worse if I had done it back then in the fifties.

NYQ: Could this method of working have to do with the fact that you write short poems?

RW: That's quite true, I think. When you're engaged in a long poem you do have to keep plugging at it, or thinking of plugging at it, because you're waiting not for one inspiration but for a sequence of inspirations. Also because, I think, in any long poem there are going to be non-Crocean stretches, connective tissue. There are going to be architectural problems which you can face and cope with in a state of imperfect frenzy. I remember Robert Frost, one time, talking about the dullness of Wordsworth. He used "dullness" as a term of approval, speaking of Wordsworth's willingness to write prosaically so as to fulfill the structure of his longer poems and make bridges between his more intense passages.

NYQ: Do you find, just averaging things out, that you're more of a day or night writer, more of a summer than a winter writer?

RW: I've never figured it out in a seasonal way. I've got to pay some attention to that and see if Cyril Connolly is right. He said something about the month of October, I think. He said if you're going to write a work of genius you will do it in October. I expect that was a little personal.

NYQ: Probably, Keats wrote his great Odes in the Spring.

RW: I used to be a night person, used to be able to work until three or four in the morning, and now I find that I get sleepy after midnight, and do a little better at other hours of the day. Unfortunately, I'm not old enough yet to be an early morning person. I sleep extremely well in the morning, and can't get up at five as some of my slightly older friends do. I'm stuck with the middle of the day, alas—the period in which the phone rings and people drop in on you.

NYQ: On to less practical subjects. What is the importance, in your mind, of traditional forms of poetry. Are they essential?

RW: If by traditional forms we mean meters, stanzas, rhymes, that kind of thing, I don't think any of those has any meaning in itself or is absolutely essential to poetry. There are some poets who are no good at these things. William Carlos Williams fully proved in his early work that he was no good at writing with the help of such means. He found himself, and began to delight us, when he moved into the use of a kind of controlled free verse. And I have no case whatever against controlled free verse. Yet I think it is absurd to feel that free verse—which has only been with us in America for a little over a hundred years—has definitely "replaced" measure and rhyme and other traditional instruments. Precisely because trimeter, for example, doesn't mean anything, there's no reason why it shouldn't be put to good use now and tomorrow. It's not inherently dated, and, in ways one really needn't go into, meter, rhyme and the like are, or can be, serviceable for people who know how to handle them well.

NYQ: Perhaps their demands put your imagination into places it wouldn't go otherwise?

RW: Yes, that's something which is not always recognized, the freeing effect of a lot of traditional techniques. They are not simply a straitjacket, they can also liberate you from whatever narrow track your own mind is running on, and prompt it to be loose and inventive, to entertain possibilities it hadn't foreseen.

NYQ: Do you ever write a poem just for whimsy, a toy poem of just pure craft and little else?

RW: I have a desire to go for broke, I think, whenever I start writing. I find it hard to do anything which is foredoomed to triviality or to the character of an exercise, although I don't mind at all writing children's poems—I've been doing some of that. That's a conscious step, however, into another genre of poetry in which your expectations change.

NYQ: How about traditional forms, like the elegy?

RW: Well, you're working in such a case with certain expectations of the convention; and, of course, you're working against them. If you can't make it new you won't allow it out of the shop. It is a help to have a form that you're working with and against. I teach Milton here very often, and I suppose the greatest example of working with and against a convention is "Lycidas."

NYQ: Is bad art bad, then, in a contemporary way? That is, it seems that in order to be a trumpet player you at least have to know how to move your fingers to call yourself one, or know how to draw in order to call yourself a painter. What do you have to know in order to call yourself a poet?

RW: There are no widely acknowledged qualifications at present. I'm on the Board of the Wesleyan University Press. Actually, I've been on a year's leave from the Board, because I got sick of reading poetry, and I've just gone back. Rather grudgingly, too, because I don't feel very much attuned to a fair part of the work now being done. I don't feel able to distinguish between the better and the worse of it, because the fashionable aesthetics seem to me so distressing. I don't like, I can't adjust to, simplistic political poetry, the crowd-pleasing sort of anti-Vietnam poem. I can't adjust to the kind of Black poetry that simply cusses and hollers artlessly. And most of all I can't adjust to the sort of poem which is mechanically, prosaically "irrational," which is often self-pitying, which starts all its sentences with 'I,' and which writes constantly out of a limply weird subjective world. There is an awful lot of that being produced. If you are given a box containing twenty manuscripts of verse, and eighteen of them are in that style, it's in the first place depressing, and in the second place you are unable for weariness to say that this is better than that. It's bad to be bored out of exerting one's critical faculty. I imagine that a lot of poetry which is deranged in a mild way, and more silly than funny, is trying to suggest drug experience, trying to borrow something from the excitement that was recently felt about the drug experience. There are even some good poets, writing in other styles, whom I suspect of having been subtly influenced by the drug cult's notion that vision and self-transcendence are easily come by. It's not so, of course; it's hard and rare as hell to get beyond yourself. *Beside* yourself is another matter. I like Robert Frost's saying that before you can be inter-personal you have to be personal. It seems to me that's what Timothy Leary forgot.

NYQ: Would you, then, agree with the statement by Valery that "a man is a poet if his imagination is stimulated by disciplines"? Some kind of discipline.

RW: Yes, I would agree. The idea of letting go is very attractive to people nowadays; for some, fingerpainting and happenings are the norms of the art experience. But I don't think the kind of art you and I like to consume was ever produced in a spirit of simply letting go. One only arrives at a useful precision in spontaneous art if there's been a lot of discipline in one's life earlier. Dr. Johnson said, "what is written without effort is in general read without pleasure." I have trouble with some of my students and some of my friends at the moment about this matter of precision. I always say that art ought to be a trap for the reader to fall into, and that he ought to know when he is caught, and what has caught him. There are some people like Jim Dickey who express a blithe willingness to have the reader's subjectivity collaborate with the poet's in producing a hybrid which will be the reader's experience of the poet's words. I think I'm less generous than he in this matter, and that, given a good reader, a good poet should make him think and feel precisely what he wants to and nothing else. But perhaps I've overstated my case. It is obvious that we all take possession of art as we can, in the light of our own feelings and experience—every statue is going to be different for every beholder, depending on where he stands, but having admitted that I'm all for demanding of the artist a maximum control of his audience. One of the few ways of judging a poem or a painting is to say that it does or does not make you experience it within a certain range of meanings.

NYQ: In a recent interview Jorge Luis Borges suggested he thought the way poetry worked on people's imagination to "trap" them, as you say, was through metaphor. That the poem as a whole was a metaphor which brought the reader from the concrete to the abstract. How do you respond to that?

RW: I think it would be true of some poems I've written, like "The Beacon," which is all one metaphor. The poem is thinking about how much we can know of the world, what the kingdom or province of human thought is, and the poem does its thinking in terms of a lighthouse, and the sea, and night. There are a lot of lesser but connected figures in the poem, mostly having to do with ideas of empire, province, kingdom, domain. I'm sure that I could think of a good many other poems which could be reduced in this manner to a field of thought and a scene or situation in which the thought is embodied. I know that's true, for example, of my more recent poem, "On the Marginal Way." There are certain—I shan't say what all the thoughts of that poem are about—but there are certain thoughts on tap, and they're all connected with the stones of a particular cove off the shore of Maine, and the geological history of those stones, and their changing aspect as the light changes, as the sea rises and falls back. I don't think all poems can be described in this way. It seems to me that there are some quite fine and legitimate poems in which the one really pervasive element is the argument, and the metaphors and other figures appear as illustrations of it, are treated in a subordinated fashion. I think a dramatic poem might well do that.

NYQ: Then the argument would be what would, in a sense, hold the poem together?

RW: Yes. Metaphor, in the small sense and the large, is the main property of poetry. But there are other elements in poetry, and I see no reason why any of these shouldn't be lead dog once in a while. You wouldn't want to blackball certain epigrams for being non-figurative. Much modern French poetry, and some English poetry

written under French inspiration, suffer from being wholly metaphorical, wholly lacking in statement, and thus too difficult to get a
hold of. It's interesting to turn back to the Metaphysicals and discover
how, in spite of what we were once told about them, the figures are
often not sustained and a dramatic argument is the thing most
prominent.

NYQ: On the question of personal style, do you feel your poetry
has been evolving or is evolving into new modes and styles?

RW: I've never tried to initiate blue periods or green periods in my
work, and I've always distrusted self-manipulation. All I can say about
that matter is that, yes, I do feel changes of direction beginning, but
that I can't offer any prognosis. It would seem wrong for me to know
or to guess. I'm getting older, and, as Bill Williams said, age gives as it
takes away, and I'm just going to wait and see what age gives.
Undoubtedly it will give new perspectives.

NYQ: Do you feel that your later work, as in "Walking to Sleep,"
might tend to be less ornate than the earlier poetry? The language
more simplified and direct.

RW: I think that's probably so. Another way of saying it might be
to say that there is less gaiety in the later poems. I do think that, very
often, what may have seemed ornate or decorative in earlier poems
was, for me at any rate, an expression of exuberance. I expect that
progression may continue, but I do hope not to end in a dull
sincerity. I hope to preserve some feeling of exuberance. To lack it is
to lack one access to the truth of the world.

NYQ: You teach classes in literature and in writing? How do you
go about teaching your literature class?

RW: I don't think there's anything peculiar about the way I do it.
The course I was teaching this year started with Anne Bradstreet and
ended in the middle of Williams. It was inevitably somewhat cursory,
but perhaps a little less silly than most survey courses in that almost
our whole business consisted of the study of individual poems—
putting them on the slide, as Ezra Pound said—and understanding,
for example, as well as we could, four poems of Anne Bradstreet
before going on to [Edward] Taylor, and doing four of Taylor before
we went on to Philip Freneau—in some cases, of course, slowing
down and being very careful that we understood what Whitman was
up to in the whole of "Song of Myself." I suppose that I do about ten

or fifteen minutes' worth of generalizing in a class meeting of about an hour and a half, and for the rest I simply talk over with my students—who this year were simply marvelous in their preparation, intelligence and enthusiasm—what's going on in a poem line by line, and, where we can, how this poem might be illuminated by comparison to its neighbor, or why William Carlos Williams' poem "The Catholic Bells" reminds us of Walt Whitman. That kind of thing.

NYQ: When you go line by line are you trying to determine what the poem "means" or how it was made?

RW: I think we do both. We talk about how it got its effects, how it made its points, but also what the general position of the poet seems to be—not so much position as concern; that's what we aim at finding out, what's eating the poet. Of course, every now and then there's a dissenter from the method who would prefer to have a somewhat more swooning and less argumentative relation to the poem. My answer to that is that what we do is what can be done in the classroom, and that while extra-curricular swooning is admirable, we simply cannot swoon profitably in class. I'm probably making it sound too dry. It isn't dry at all, and we always read the poems aloud. And we allow ourselves parenthetical wows.

NYQ: Many teachers try to impose symbols and meanings on a poem, how do you feel about that?

RW: I try to be uncertain even where I feel pretty strongly, not to impose any one way of reading, and to entertain seriously every decent suggestion which comes from the floor. The only time I've stamped my foot this year was when somebody took too seriously the girl-drying-her-hair simile in "Birches" and suggested that the whole poem had to do with climbing girls. I wouldn't have that.

NYQ: How would you scotch that kind of thing?

RW: In this case I simply said no, no, and I wouldn't talk about it because it seemed to me so intolerably untrue. But that was, I think, the only time that I ever played authoritarian this year. It won't do to do that; and I'm not in the least disposed to impose archetypal, Freudian or other patterns on the poems we read. In general my attitude about criticism and about teaching is that you look at the thing and see what it wants you to say about it.

NYQ: You've lived in Europe; could you compare the state of poetry teaching here to that in Europe?

RW: I think we probably do it much better than they do it in Europe. That's my guess. I'm judging mainly from the attitude of foreign students who come here and are astonished by the openness of our discussions. The French student is likely to be extremely docile, and to have been taught to treat the great poetry and drama of his tradition in a very prescribed manner. There are certain things he *is* to find, so that he can answer questions about them on important examinations. I don't think that we feel there are obligatory findings to be made; and indeed I'm glad when people go off on tangents, if they're not perfectly mad. I'm glad to see people take poetry personally—I guess that's what it amounts to.

NYQ: From your experience with your poetry writing class, are there any poets who you detect to be large influences on the present generation of young people?

RW: Oh, I suppose I couldn't produce any names which would surprise you. Any poets in Untermeyer's Anthology are likely to be having a continuing effect. It seems to me that most of my students are interested in Stevens, in Pound, in Williams, in others of that great generation. But the ones who are very strong about poetry, and very concerned with writing their own, also attach themselves to writers of the moment, like Creeley, Snodgrass, Ginsberg—it's a very long list. Most current styles seem to have their adherents, in one year or another. If you'd asked me the question last year, I think I would have said that people who write a kind of trickly confessional poetry were the strongest influences on our students. But this year I noticed in our verse-writing seminar (in which I don't try to coerce people at all into writing this way or that) an astonishing number of voluntary villanelles, sonnets, quatrains and so on.

NYQ: Any foreign poets influencing your students? Baudelaire for instance.

RW: The individual student poet who is also a French major may well catch fire from Baudelaire, as a student of German may learn from Rilke. But there seems to be no foreign poet in fashion, not even Neruda.

NYQ: What do you do in your verse-writing seminar?

RW: I ask them to write an original poem every other week. These poems are printed up, anonymously, and distributed to the class. We criticise them collectively. I also criticise them myself in writing. For the odd weeks, I suggest various well-tried exercises—I'll have them write a riddle, for example. Once in every semester I'll ask that they look through a dictionary of poetic forms, find some form which interests them and write in it. But that's as far as I go in that way. Then I'll suggest things of this sort: I'll say, "It's generally thought enhancing to compare aeroplanes to birds; make a comparison of the reverse nature, comparing something that is presumably exalted to something that is presumably on a lower imaginative plane." Some students will find that such an exercise jars their imaginations in a good way; for others it'll make no difference at all.

NYQ: "The worlds revolve like ancient women gathering fuel in vacant lots"?

RW: That's right, that's exactly the kind of thing I hope to get by that exercise. I have a number of others, all of which are meant simply to shake up the mind a little, to disturb its habits.

NYQ: Wesleyan just recently admitted women. How is it having co-eds in the class?

RW: It's very civilizing. There are qualities of feeling missing from any poetry class if you don't have girls there. And the effect of it is to mature the male students very rapidly. I think they don't linger in their prep school or high school attitudes very long if there are girls with them, raising the tone and legitimizing delicacy.

NYQ: Do you think there are different difficulties with which male and female poets have to contend?

RW: There used to be special difficulties for men, way back when I was first thinking of writing poetry. When I was an undergraduate at Amherst, poetry was associated by some with effeminacy, and I knew one man at Amherst, a poet and teacher, who rather over-stressed his abilities as a boxer in order to reassure the world about his masculinity. There's none of that any more. I'm very sure that it's possible to distinguish between male and female sensibilities—but I should think that there's now no subject matter that you would expect to find in a man's book but not in a woman's. Everyone seems to have access to everything, and the girls seem to have found out how to write about the whole range of masculine topics.

NYQ: You don't think a man might not have the problem of saying things just for their own sake whereas a woman might have more of a problem detaching herself?

RW: I think women have less capacity for nonsense than men do. And so, if I understand you, I agree with what you've said. A man can be a complete abstract-minded ass in a way in which most women can't be.

NYQ: Now, we'd like to talk a little about translation. Hayden Carruth in his recent anthology *The Voice That Is Great Within Us* describes you in terms of the neo-classic French dramatists you have spent so much time translating, and refers to your "courtly tone of respect for order to mask fundamental metaphysical uncertainty." To what extent do you think a poet is attracted to poets in the languages he has translated?

RW: Well, it seems to me that Carruth offers a very good description of something which happens in Racine. In Racine you have the finished and sonorous surface, and underneath that an awareness of violence, irrationality, disorder. However, if I try to apply Carruth's words to myself, as you quote them, it looks as if he's implying some kind of faking or bad faith. Is he? That word "mask" troubles me. Actually, what he seems to be saying was said once before by Theodore Holmes in a review in "Poetry." He said that I had a cheerful, elegant surface and a fundamental despair. Where Mr. Holmes got his information about my fundamental despair, I don't know.

NYQ: You said you felt you were fortunate in not being overwhelmed by any poet enough to imitate him, but what about translation as a kind of imitation?

RW: You write a translation because someone else has written a poem which you love and you want to take possession of it. I think it also is a matter of imposture, too. You want to speak in the voice of that poem, which perhaps you could not do in your own poetic person. I think I've felt myself drawn to certain jobs of translation in that way, feeling that they would be somehow an expansion of me, and might perhaps lead to my coping with a certain area of subject matter, striking a certain kind of attitude, using a certain tone. I detest exercises. I've never done any exercises myself, and I've always sympathized with my students when they've said, "I refuse to do exercises, I'll just write my own stuff, if you don't mind." But doing a job of translation can have some of the benefits, I suppose, of an exercise. It can be an exercise in the use of someone else's palette.

NYQ: Robert Lowell has said, in reference to translating, that poetry is a matter of tone. How do you feel about that?

RW: I think Lowell was right in saying that. It's not the only matter, of course, but it's critical. The translator must catch and convey not only what the poet says but how he means it.

NYQ: Would it be more difficult to translate an ironic tone, do you think?

RW: Perhaps it's a little harder to translate the special ironic dissonances of a language than to translate the pure vowels of some unqualified emotion. Think how hard it would be to render John Crowe Ransom in Afrikaans. Still, I think anything can be done, with luck.

NYQ: You have done both translation from poets in languages you are thoroughly familiar with and translating, with help, from languages you don't know. Could you compare the two?

RW: Translation from languages you don't know works only if poems are well chosen, well assigned, in the first place. And then the linguist must do an extremely good and patient and sustained job of mediation. Working either with Max Hayward or Olga Carlisle, I've asked that the poem be read over and over again in Russian and then, out of my tiny knowledge of Russian, have asked all sorts of detailed questions about the words of the original. I've asked, too, about the meter of the original and its relation to the tone and matter of the poem. I've asked, indeed, almost all of the questions you ask, in a somewhat other way, of yourself while you're composing a poem of your own. Given three days with Max Hayward and a couple of bottles of Scotch, I think you can become quite intimate with two or three Russian poems, and be in a position to take your notes and write something which will be at once faithful and a work of your own.

NYQ: Has Voznesensky seen your translations of his work?

NYQ: Oh, yes. He seems to think well of them, I'm glad to say.

NYQ: Do you ever have a wish to be doing something else to support yourself aside from translating and teaching?

RW: Yes, there are other things I've felt an itch to do. I should like to be a farmer. But that, I suppose, would get altogether in the way of writing poetry, it's so hard a life. I've been drawn to a number of other professions, and, of course, one reason I've felt restless at times is that teaching literature and writing poems are far too much the same thing. I find, especially as one grows older and as one outgrows one's initial infatuation with poetry, it's easier to feel after a hard day's preparation and teaching that one has had enough of poetry for the day and doesn't want to go home and write any. At the moment, I think things are working out pretty well. I enjoy teaching and I very much like my students here. I teach only in the fall, and sometime in December I become a free man and write until September. That's good enough. Indeed, I feel pampered.

NYQ: One final question. Would you recommend poetry as a profession?

RW: Oh, yes. For someone who doesn't mind a bit of discipline.

NYQ: What are its advantages and drawbacks?

RW: There's nothing so wonderful as having constructed something perfectly arbitrary, without any help from anybody else, out of pure delight and self-delight, and then to find that it turns out to be useful to a few others. You have it both ways, if you're lucky: you do exactly as you want to do, you're as lonely and as happy as a child playing with his toy trains, and then it turns out that people are grateful to you for providing them with some sort of emotional machine.

Richard Wilbur
John Graham/1973

Interview excerpted from pp. 76-91 of *The Writer's Voice: Conversations with Contemporary Writers,* edited by George Garrett with interviews conducted by John Graham. Copyright © 1973 by George Garrett, by permission of William Morrow and Company, Inc. The following interview was recorded at the Hollins Conference in Creative Writing and Cinema, which was held from June 15-27, 1970, for John Graham's educational radio program, "The Scholar's Bookshelf."

Dick Wilbur is tall, youthfully handsome, graceful, and slow-moving, almost stately, except when he's on the tennis court, climbing trees or flying kites. He is sturdier than photographs allow him to be, and his voice is always deeper and richer than you expect it to be. Chiefly, moving or in repose, there is an easy, natural, animal elegance about him. Like an eight-point buck. And nothing contrived about it, unless the deer's poise and grace and control is also to be named so. No, it comes with the breath, the rhythm of his breathing. But there is also a sudden childish brightness, a bright and undisguised glint of inner energy that can even mean mischief.

All of which might—and shouldn't—divert attention from the enormous power of his self-control, the lithe but coiled fury of his chosen reticence.

With a wide-brim hat, jeans and boots he could pass for a cowboy if you ever saw one. And it's true, he made the walk in the sun with the Texas infantry.

Graham: Professor Wilbur and I are talking about his latest book of poetry, *Walking to Sleep.* When was that actually published, Dick? That's very recent, isn't it?

Wilbur: It was March, 1969.

Graham: It reflects clearly to me some enduring attitudes,

concerns, and methods of yours. Your first book came out, oh,
twenty-three years ago, wasn't it?

Wilbur: I think it was 1947. I can't substract.

Graham: That's going back a bit. One of the things that fascinates
me, since I've been living in the country and I've always done a lot of
hiking, and that involved nature study, what I would call close
observation—a great number of your poems find their footing in a
very solid sense of sight, touch, a sense of natural growth, often as
"action." I don't think these poems are ever static pictures, but it's
raw observation we first see. And I was wondering—to bring in
another piece, given our urban society—I can remember so clearly a
graduate student with me from Manhattan, in reading Emily
Dickinson with that wonderful little line of a snake wrinkling through
the grass . . .

Wilbur: . . . . "a narrow fellow in the grass . . ."

Graham: This really just didn't mean anything to this man, who
was one of the most intelligent, sensitive readers I've ever known.
The basic question I'm asking is, How are you going to find your
common ground, what do you expect the reader to do with the
details of something like this? Are you trying to *recall* for me what a
little seed growth looks like? Or are you hazarding that maybe I don't
know, maybe I've lived in Manhattan and don't know what happens
when that little lima bean comes punching through?

Wilbur: I find when I read the poem you're referring to, which is
about cotyledons, that it's best—when I say "read," I mean "read to
an audience"—I find that it's best to say a few reminding words
about what happens when a bean seedling comes up out of the
ground. Many urban people, of course, keep backyard gardens and
do know what a bean looks like, and I guess there are people in the
country who have forgotten. I think it's an unanswerable question
how much knowledge of nature one can presume people to possess
nowadays. Writers of the last century presumed a great deal and
probably pretty safely. At present I don't know what one can do,
given the fact that poetry has got to be economical and not too
explanatory, but just hope that one will describe clearly enough so
that the person somewhat ignorant of natural things will divine what
must be the case, what it must be like.

Graham: In one of the poems I like particularly you reverse the

process. This little thing called "Riddle"—it's on page thirty-seven.
Would you mind reading it? It's so short. This is a sort of reverse
temptation in a way, since we've got no title and we don't know what
we're dealing with, and the question is, "Do we know?" at the end,
of course.

Wilbur: The riddle is a fascinating form. It got degraded
considerably, in the last century, into a sort of parlor game for
children—charades and anagrams. The sort of riddle that interests me
is the riddle which describes a concept or a thing without naming it.
It's a serious form of poetry, as the Greeks and the early Anglo-Saxon
poets knew. I think one thing that comes out of the riddle, deriving
from the period of hesitation you undergo before deciding to name
the thing, is a sense of how many properties in the world are shared.
If your riddle is full of something about legs—you know, there's a
riddle that begins "Two legs sat on three legs, and in came four
legs"—well, it takes you a little while to guess that. Before you have
guessed it, you spend a moment in wonder at the infinite "legged-
ness" of things.

Graham: All the envelopes, all the skins that you find in the
world. . . .

Wilbur: Right. And this kind of momentary wonder before you get
the answer is not false to the spirit of poetry; because it seems to me
that the general drift of poetry is through simile and the bolder form
of metaphor to compare things to each other, to liken things to each
other, even to say that things are the same. To get everything
connected. Well, let me read the riddle that you suggested. It goes:

> Where far in forest I am laid,
> In a pace ringed around by stones,
> Look for no melancholy shade,
> And have no thoughts of buried bones;
> For I am bodiless and bright,
> And fill this glade with sudden glow;
> The leaves are washed in under-light;
> Shade lies upon the boughs like snow.

Graham: It seems so obvious to me, after I looked in the back of
the book and got the answer, that I'm depressed, really. The word
"laid," there. One lays a fire when one is camping and . . .

Wilbur: Yes, that's playing fair.

Graham: I don't think you cheated me at all, that's what's depressing.

Wilbur: Of course, it also suggests being buried, doesn't it? It can go. . . .

Graham: But then you warn against that very thing.

Wilbur: But the warnings operate as red herrings.

Graham: Oh really? I'm not familiar enough with the form then.

Wilbur: If I say to you, Don't think of such and such a thing, you find yourself thinking of it. And it seems to me when I say, "Look for no melancholy shade" and "have no thoughts of buried bones," there your thoughts are all filled up with ghosts and bones. And perhaps you don't pay attention to the real clues, which are the "leaves are washed in under-light; Shade lies upon the boughs like snow." How are you going to get the shade on top of the boughs unless there's a fire underneath?

Graham: I'm afraid maybe I am trying to make an "either-or" of this, but having experienced a campfire, one has through this little poem—a campfire. And yet I don't know, I don't know how much "putting together" a reader can do. You know that awful business with Sir Walter Scott, those interminable descriptions of costumes that someone had on. And then Lessing's argument, in fact, can you really reconstruct this picture? He says "no." Scott obviously said "yes." And I think you're saying "yes" here. Rather than *recalling* the painting, the picture à la that "Playboy" poem of yours, you are constructing it.

Wilbur: I suppose people who never had seen a fire under woods before they approach that little riddle may have trouble.

Graham: I'm really interested in this whole problem of the common ground. What I find in so many of your poems—for instance your interest in astronomy—I have a hard time, having never dealt with astronomy at all, of knowing quite how much is my burden and how much is yours. I guess what you already have said is, You have to do the best you can, throw it down, and hope it can be picked up.

Wilbur: I think so, because if you include in such a poem as my poem "In the Field," if you include a full statement of the big bang theory of the creation of the universe, you lose all impetus, and the poem loses its dramatic quality. It's not intended to be informational, really; it's intended to dwell on two opposing feelings one may have living on the surface of the earth.

Graham: You would cut yourself off from your own experience. You couldn't write a little couplet on Berkeley and Dr. Johnson kicking that stone, even though that was very much a part of your knowledge, if you had to sort of back-check with every screaming reader.

Wilbur: I suppose, really, the things I refer to in my poems are things that on the whole can quickly be got in a dictionary if they're not already in the reader's head. Most people, I think, have heard about Dr. Johnson kicking the stone and most people have in mind what is essential about Berkeley's philosophy, and that's all that's needed for the grasping of that poem.

Graham: With your students, do they seem to see nature as important, or are you getting more "urban" poetry? You, clearly, are drawn toward the country.

Wilbur: I do actually use quite a lot of urban imagery. I describe, I concern myself with urban things. I have a poem about the new railway station in the city of Rome in which I try to describe it pretty thoroughly and to get away with using technical and architectural words in the process. And I describe city fountains, things of that sort. I should hate to get the reputation of favoring nature and contending that the urban—indeed, I'd like to think of the city as a part of nature.

Graham: Dick, there are a number of things I am fixed on, almost, in your poetry. I'm excited about your powers of observation and the variety of metrics that I find. I should think, in that little "Aubade" you have "well-chilled wine." That's a beautifully put-together little gathering of consonants. But today, rather than the direct observation, I'd like it if you'd talk with me a little bit about the whole idea of wit and humor, mockery, in poetry. I'm afraid of the word irony. I know that I am trapped somewhat in—was it Matthew Arnold who felt that poetry should be of "high seriousness," even though I know better. I've read too much of Pope, so I know that there can be breathtakingly high seriousness in the joke. We're used to black humor now, especially in our novelists, so that I should not have this bind. Can you tell—what's wrong with me at this point? Because I know I enjoy these very witty poems of yours.

Wilbur: I suppose that it isn't a new discovery that wit is not the reverse of seriousness, but a part of seriousness, a means of being serious. But I think, indeed, it was forgotten by a number of people during the earnest last century. Especially as so many poets in England and America gave themselves the responsibility to reassure and uplift a new, expanded literate audience. I do think that Newton Arvin, in his book on Longfellow, was right in explaining so many phenomena in nineteenth-century English-language poetry in terms of "the new literacy." You're given a new audience, toward which you feel a kind of social responsibility.

Graham: There's that whole nineteenth-century passion for education, which has continued certainly into this century.

Wilbur: Yes, education and Longfellow are related phenomena, I think. But now we have quite a different sense of the audience, I think, and I suppose a greater focus on the work itself and are less constrained by the expectations of any possible reader. So we can return to the truth that a serious poem is stronger if it allows itself to be wild and absurd and potentially ridiculous at times.

Graham: All of these terms suddenly call up, I think, that wonderful poem of yours called "Playboy." Would you mind reading that, it's—I think page thirty-eight—it is a serious poem.

Wilbur: It's finally a serious poem. It's a satirical poem, but not satirical in a grim sense. I'm not trying to wipe anything out, you know.

Graham: The wonderful little image of the boy eating, the sidelong swipe at the sandwich that he takes, right there is a kind of sympathetic . . .

Wilbur: Yes. . . I don't mean to be too superior to him, but it is, finally, meant to be a gently satiric poem. Well, let me read it:

PLAYBOY

High on his stockroom ladder like a dunce
The stock-boy sits, and studies like a sage
The subject matter of one glossy page,
As lost in curves as Archimedes once.

Sometimes, without a glance, he feeds himself.
The left hand, like a mother-bird in flight,
Brings him a sandwich for a sidelong bite,
And then returns it to a dusty shelf.

What so engrosses him? The wild décor
Of this pink-papered alcove into which
A naked girl has stumbled, with its rich
Welter of pelts and pillows on the floor,

Amidst which, kneeling in a supple pose,
She lifts a goblet in her farther hand,
As if about to toast a flower-stand
Above which hovers an exploding rose

Fired from a long-necked crystal vase that rests
Upon a tassled and vermilion cloth
One taste of which would shrivel up a moth?
Or is he pondering her perfect breasts?

Nothing escapes him of her body's grace
Or of her floodlit skin, so sleek and warm
And yet so strangely like a uniform,
But what now grips his fancy is her face,

And how the cunning picture holds her still
At just that smiling instant when her soul,
Grown sweetly faint, and swept beyond control,
Consents to his inexorable will.

Graham: I think that long, long line, that takes the burden of the description of the *Playboy* fold-out and collapses it of its own weight, is an absolute delight.

Wilbur: It's fun, for various purposes, to try to write long sentences in verse. In this case, of course, the trick is to make the sentence so complex as to suggest the mad clutter of that kind of photography.

Graham: The sort of pseudo-Eastern richness of the decor. With this poem you give us so many leads that no one could help but join you at once. But your title poem in *Walking to Sleep* was one that excited me. I've read it and reread it now, and I find shifts of tone in the poem. I think some of the shifts involve a warning almost, through wit or humor. Would you read a bit of it, Dick, and say something about—maybe eight or ten lines—what I'm talking about. It happens very soon.

Wilbur: I think something of what you talk about happens in the first few lines.

Graham: Yes, there's that mechanistic analogy, almost, in the first two analogies in the first two lines.

Wilbur: Well, here goes—"Walking to Sleep." This is—I ought to say, parenthetically, that this is a poem about someone advising someone else on how to get off to sleep.

As a queen sits down, knowing that a chair will be there,
Or a general raises his hand and is given the field-glasses,
Step off assuredly into the blank of your mind.
Something will come to you. Although at first
You nod through nothing like a fogbound prow,
Gravel will breed in the margins of your gaze,
Perhaps with tussocks or a dusty flower,
And, humped like dolphins playing in the bow-wave,
Hills will suggest themselves. All such suggestions
Are yours to take or leave, but hear this warning:

And so on. . . . Yes, I think there are a couple of moments of the kind you're pointing to. For instance, the first line, "As a queen sits down, knowing that a chair will be there," is an encouragement to the sleeper to step off into dreams with confidence, as a queen sits down with confidence. Nevertheless you think of the possibility of the queen sitting down on the floor. And a phrase like "Something will come to you" is very seriously intended, at the same time reflects a very trivial, colloquial—

Graham: —almost vacuous, in a way, possibility. No matter who you are, something happens to anyone's mind. And then the prow, the ship into sleep—and what, gravel grows?

Wilbur: Yes, you shift rather quickly from a sort of marine progress into dreams to a progress along a road.

Graham: And organic, there's the growth of plants, even the growth of gravel, almost, as these things spring up.

Wilbur: The point I was trying to demonstrate, really, what it started off by saying, that as soon as you start to think about something, you furnish it with things, and you furnish any landscape as soon as you start walking along a road, and as soon as you think of a room you start to furnish it.

Graham: As you go on in this poem, you warn, really, that one must not open doors, or must open them with foreknowledge. And then, at some point, you say something like, "What, are you still awake?"

Wilbur: Yes. When I read this long poem aloud to an audience, generally they giggle a little when I say, "What, are you still awake?" because it clearly seems to apply to them, and how well they're taking this hundred-and-forty-line poem.

Graham: Oh, that's bad.

Wilbur: No, I don't mind that at all. I don't mind at all the risk that that line will seem quite simply a gag-line, because by the time we reach it, if my poem is successful, they know that it's serious. And they know that any joke I make will just be a guarantee that there's a whole person talking to them, a whole person who has the sense of balance that's implied in a sense of humor.

Graham: Now this is very interesting. Because another thing I suspect I'm locked in on is admitting or recognizing that there are a number of different kinds of lyrics, not the least being dramatic turns even in lyrics. But this, what you say is very helpful. It is not a single consistent tone like a block of cement, really, but you are revealing the full voice behind this self-aware poet.

Wilbur: I don't trust anybody who isn't capable of nonsense and of moments of collapse into ridiculousness. It seems to be a necessary thing for the serious man or the serious poem, to make these darts, not only into the witty, but into the absurd, into the comic. We don't want art really to be something that's good for us because it's so inexorably disagreeable, you know, like Filboid Studge or rhubarb soda.

Graham: I thought that we might talk a bit about your work in translation. The contribution, Dick, frankly, that you've made to my pleasure—my French is best not talked about—lies in your translations of Molière—*Tartuffe* and—what else?

Wilbur: *The Misanthrope* and I'm working now on *L'École des Femmes, The School for Wives,* and expect to be finished this summer.

Graham: This is good news for me, because I've found the language exciting. Unfortunately, I've seen only amateur productions, but with very good leads who could spring with the language really, and you've given me enormous pleasure. This must be a very curious world for you in a way. Is it confining, or exciting, or puzzling? Do any of these words mean anything?

Wilbur: It's a lot of things both good and bad to be a translator. If you take on a thing so long as Molière's rhymed plays and are trying to get seventeen or eighteen hundred lines out into rhymed couplets, obviously there are going to be periods of drudgery and frustration. I've spent whole days in which I ended by failing to do one couplet, and that can be very, very distressing. After all, there are only so many rhyming possibilities in English. And there are certain lines, in any French play, for which there is no ready equivalent. You have to think a long time before you get it. Almost always, if you are patient enough, you will find something that will allow you to be faithful, if not to every word, to the thought. I think the important thing is to translate thought by thought.

Graham: Do you, in handling a very long project, such as one of Molière's plays, do you try to go through, almost all the way through, if not quickly, exactly, but to try to get an overall structure, with some finished couplets, perhaps?

Wilbur: I wish I could do that. I've never been good at skipping along, either in my own work, or in translations. There are people who are great, who are quick mockers-up of things, but I can't do it. I have to slog along from couplet to couplet, building it very slowly, and hoping that I won't, in the process, lose a full overview of the work.

Graham: With your *School for Wives* that you're working on now, do you read a lot of other Molière at the same time you're working on a specific play, to work tonally with him?

Wilbur: I read some Molière criticism. I may read a play or so in French or in English, just to broaden my sense of what he's up to. But mostly I just settle down to it as a bricklayer settles down to building his wall before he starts.

Graham: Is the French particularly difficult?

Wilbur: It's pretty easy. It's a small vocabulary, with certain key words, which are used again and again, for multiple purposes. One does have to learn the flexibility of the key words in playwrights like Molière or Racine. And, of course, you can't ever find, in English, equally flexible key words; so that for a French word of central importance in a Molière play there are going to be seven or eight equivalents in the English. You just don't aspire to reproduce Molière in the sense that you use his limited language.

Graham: Your work in French is obviously your major commitment toward translation, but what other languages do you find most interesting to work with?

Wilbur: Well, I have a kind of a kitchen knowledge of Italian. And so I've done a few translations from Italian, and mean to do a few more. And I've studied a little bit of Russian, but when I try to translate Russian poets, as I've done in the case of Andrei Voznesensky and Anna Akhmatova, and shall do shortly with Yevtushenko, I need help. I need some kind of a linguistic adviser. Indeed, I need someone to sit down with me, go through the whole poem, read it to me in the Russian, translate it into rough English, and then answer all sorts of questions for me as to what the rhythm's doing and what the overtones of particular words are. Then I can settle down and write it as if it were my own poem.

Graham: Then, with this, it is a form, almost, of forced experiment for you as a poet in English, to exercise your skills—I almost want to say against a foreign object?

Wilbur: Well, I like resistance in art. I think there are some artists who think of art as purely expression, as a kind of explosion of the self. My sensibility is attracted to the sculpture kind of thing, in which you bang at something that resists you and try to arrive, with its opposition, at something in its nature of an attractive compromise.

Graham: Dick, would you mind reading the little "Dead Still" here on page seventy?

Wilbur: Yes, this is a poem of Andrei Voznesensky, a youngish Russian poet who's been over here a couple of times and has made quite a hit in America. The translation is called "Dead Still" and it's a poem about a period, oh, I think about 1963 or 1964, when he was being more or less persecuted by the conservatives, or neo-Stalinists, if you will, in the Russian literary establishment. The poem takes place on the shores of the Black Sea, in the midst of a love affair.

DEAD STILL
Now, with your palms on the blades of my shoulders,
Let us embrace:

Let there be only your lips' breath on my face,
Only, behind our backs, the plunge of rollers.

Our backs, which like two shells in moonlight shine,
Are shut behind us now;
We lie here huddled, listening brow to brow,
Like life's twin formula or double sign.

In folly's world-wide wind
Our shoulders shield from the weather
The calm we now beget together,
Like a flame held between hand and hand.

Does each cell have a soul within it?
If so, fling open all your little doors,
And all your souls shall flutter like the linnet
In the cages of my pores.

Nothing is hidden that shall not be known.
Yet by no storm of scorn shall we
Be pried from this embrace, and left alone
Like muted shells forgetful of the sea.

Meanwhile, O load of stress and bother,
Lie on the shells of our backs in a great heap!
It will but press us closer, one to the other.

We are asleep.

Graham: The things that fascinate me in here, and in terms of the challenge, the difficulty for you as translator—are such things as the very short lines. It seems to me in here, "Our shoulders shield from the weather"—it seems to me that the vowel play, alliteration, and so forth, makes that a fine line. Are these rather precise—I'm picking on meter and vowel—are these fairly close to the original?

Wilbur: Oh, they are, they're as close as I can get. I like to try to have the illusion of perfect fidelity. Of course, that's not to be accomplished, possibly, but I've pretty well maintained here Voznesensky's capricious line lengths and his rhyme system, which is a varying one. And wherever I could find a precise equivalent to his language, I've done so. There was in this poem—let's see if I can remember the word for it—darn it, I can't! There's a word, a Russian word which means small ventilation window, and the fact is that we don't have in America the kind of small ventilation windows they have in Russia, and so we don't have a word for it. Well, what did I say? I said, "Fling open all your little doors," whereas the Russian of it would have been "Fling open all your little small ventilation windows." But that's close enough, I think.

Graham: And it gives, actually—"all your souls shall flutter like the linnet"—it seems to me that the flinging open of the doors, in my experience as an American, gives one the sense of out-going, of the potential joining of all these little cells that the lovers could possibly have. So you've got to worry about everything and more, in these translations.

Wilbur: The fact is that no translator can do it all, no translator can simply take any poem that comes his way and do it justice. I think that the translation I just read you comes off fairly well and is one of my better efforts. And—well the reason it is, is that I feel a considerable sympathy with the attitudes of it, and Max Hayward, the Russian expert, who suggested this poem to me, knew darn well before he suggested it that it was suitable for me.

Graham: This is an interesting terminology—"suitable." It would be madness then, for you simply to take on, let's say in French where you're most easy, simply to take on an "anthology."

Wilbur: That would be very dreary, because I like to do everything I do in the way of translation, for love. And there is, of course, a large puzzle-solving element in any job of translation, but if it's merely puzzle-solving, then it's terribly chilly, and one probably will not convey whatever the emotional content of the original is.

An Interview with Richard Wilbur

Philip Dacey/1974

From *Crazy Horse*, 15 (Fall 1974), 37-44. Reprinted by permission of Philip Dacey.

Crazy Horse: We always begin by having the poet sketch his, or her, life for us. Would you do that?

Richard Wilbur: I am not yet feeble enough to be interested in genealogy, but it may as well be said that I am of the 11th generation from Samuel Wildbore, and am descended from settlers of Massachusetts and Rhode Island. The fact does not seem definitive to me, and I have never visited Little Compton, the Rhode Island town which Samuel is said to have founded. In a time of ethnic and racial self-consciousness, it is of no particular advantage to a writer that he belongs to the Anglo-Saxon minority, which is now felt to lack decided characteristics, and about which, significantly, no jokes are told. Robert Lowell is the only writer of recent years to make much use of such ancestry, and it is by and large people of other provenance who now claim to represent some version of "the American experience."

My father, Lawrence Wilbur, left Omaha for New York City at the age of 16, worked his way through the Art Students League, and has recently retired after successive free-lance careers in commercial art and in portraiture. My mother, an energetic woman who writes a good letter, came of a Baltimore family with a tradition of newspaper-editing: I have on my work-table the city desk shears of my beloved grandfather, C. M. Purdy, who covered the campaigns of Bryan as a reporter and was on the *Baltimore Sun,* in various capacities, for decades. I was born in New York City, but my bringing-up was in New Jersey, where my parents had been invited to live at modest rental in a pre-Revolutionary stone house on the estate of an English millionaire named J. D. Armitage. Mr. Armitage had left England, so he always told us, because of its slighting attitude toward persons "in trade;" here in America he prospered, being for a time Myron Taylor's partner in some textile enterprise, and circa 1920 he bought

115

four-hundred-odd acres in North Caldwell, which he transformed
into the Platonic idea of an English gentleman's farm. His manorial
house stood on the hilltop; beneath it, amidst orchards, pastures,
nurseries, walled gardens and lanes, were barn and pen and dairy,
massively constructed in stone and roofed with tile. And then there
were other houses, in addition to our ancient one, occupied by
people related to "Uncle" (as everyone called Mr. Armitage) by
blood, nationality, business, or some affinity. My younger brother
Lawrence and I, though to us the Farm seemed to have been there
forever, grew up in what amounted to a spontaneous English colony:
all was tea, bowls, tennis, Episcopalianism, gardening, music, and
bridge, with agriculture and commerce in the middle distance and
background. Even my father came to say "Right-o" and "by Jove" in
his honest Nebraska accent. In the years during which the Farm
flourished, the public event which had the greatest and most divisive
impact upon it was the abdication of Edward. It was not, I suppose, a
high culture, and yet the people of that community, most of whom I
called "Aunt" or "Uncle," were surely as decent, attractive, civilized,
kind and gay as we children found them.

The town, since overrun by suburban expansion of New York, was
quite sparsely settled in my younger years; we were aware that
Madam Schumann-Heinck lived over on Grandview Avenue, and
there was a little airfield two miles away at which Frank Hawks
sometimes did daredevil tricks in his Texaco plane, but North
Caldwell was mainly fields, woods, ponds, scattered farms and
residences. There were few other children nearby, and so my brother
and I amused ourselves by hanging around the good-natured
farmhands, riding on the haywagon, attending pig-slaughterings, and
getting into everything. We played many games of our own devising,
and when friends came to visit there were farm-wide, daylong games
of Capture the Flag or football-tag. As we grew older, and went to
excellent but distant public schools in Essex Fells and Montclair, we
found good friends and saw much of them; and we went off to a
camp in Maine during the summers; but still we were more alone
than most boys, and this led in my case to reading, writing, cartooning, and the construction of directional short-wave antennae.

When I went to Amherst, in 1938, I was somewhat odd and
awkward, not having belonged quite enough to any gang of
contemporaries. For some time I tried to acquire an acceptable

character by boxing, clowning, and being dissolute, not without strain and waste. During two summer vacations—once alone, and once with two College friends—I rode the rails and hitchhiked all over America; it was boyish adventure tinged with Depression radicalism and the poetry of others. Various things steadied me, so that I ultimately made good use of Amherst: a superior English department converted me to disciplined reading; my writing and drawing amused people, and I became chairman of the undergraduate newspaper; my fellow students, despite all my proto-Beat posturings, largely put up with me; I fell in love with a Smith girl named Charlotte Ward, who astonished me by agreeing to a June wedding following my graduation in 1942.

My Amherst class has always been very close-knit, partly because it lost so many in the Second World War. Even before our commencement, some had volunteered and had died in action. My own girding for war consisted in taking a government correspondence course in cryptography, barbarously practicing Morse Code transmission on my honeymoon, and joining the Enlisted Reserve Corps immediately thereafter. My wife and I lived in Greenwich Village for six months, she earning our rent as a junior executive at Macy's, while I studied, at an E.R.C. school, radio physics, radio repair, and code operation. Reporting for duty at Fort Dix, I was assigned to cryptographic training, and thereafter sent on to a secret cryptanalytic camp in the woods of Virginia, where (as I later discovered) my progress into cryptanalysis was cut short by adverse security reports from the CIC and FBI. It was quite true that I held leftist views and had radical friends, and that I had been so stupid as to keep a volume of Marx in my footlocker; but then as now I had an uncomplicated love of my country, and I was naively amazed to learn that my service record was stamped "Suspected of Disloyalty." For some reason, the Army then gave me a course in commando techniques, after which I was sent overseas with a company of other undesirables, amiable bookies or bootleggers for the most part. Arriving, by way of Africa, in a replacement depot at Naples, I found myself profiting by another's ill luck: a cryptographer in the 36th Infantry Division had just gone insane, and the divisional signal company was willing to overlook my disloyalty. I served with the 36th at Cassino and Anzio, in the invasion of Southern France, and on through the Siegfried Line . . .

This narrative pace will never do: I am moving through my life too slowly for present purposes, while at the same time I am forever saying "I" and leaving out most of the people and moments by which that "I" was shaped. Since the story now grows more populous and complex, the telling had better be summary from here on. When the war ended, we went with our small daughter to Harvard, where I studied English under the G. I. Bill, spent three fortunate years as a Junior Fellow, and then joined the faculty as an assistant professor. Though I had written some poems in the service, and had always been drawn toward newspaper work, I went to Harvard with the strict intention to become a scholar, most likely in seventeenth century literature. What confused matters for good was my wife's showing a drawer full of my poems to our friend André du Bouchet; he sent them to the New York publishers, Reynal and Hitchcock, who accepted them for publication in 1947. Thus began a process of fragmentation which I do not regret, but which has sometimes been frazzling, owing to the slowness with which I think and work and to my puritanical wish to do things properly. I have continued to teach—at Harvard, Wellesley, and now Wesleyan—though I am hardly the savant I once set out to be. As a spasmodic sort of scholar, I have done some editing and criticism, the best of it doubtless some pieces on Poe which proposed and developed a new conception of him; and then there have been poems, translations, excursions into musical theatre, anthologies, State Department cultural junkets, literary juries, board memberships, children's books, reviewing, lecture tours, fellowship months or years in Paris, New Mexico, Rome and Texas. In short, I have been a thoroughly scattered man of letters, and it has all been further complicated by my enjoyment of my family, of sitting up and talking to all hours, of vegetable growing, of tennis, and of getting lost in the woods. What matters most, in my work life, is the poems, and in my sanguine moments I tell myself that all else has been tributary to them.

CH: Would you talk about some of the considerations that go into choosing (or discovering) a particular form for a poem: For example, in your book *Walking to Sleep,* "The Lilacs" uses Anglo-Saxon metrics, "Fern-Beds in Hampshire County" is written in rhyming couplets, and the title poem employs blank verse. Can you recall the factors that led to the use of those three different forms?

RW: I start out with a partial sense of a poem's tone of voice, theme, and probable length. As the first words of the poem arrive, they seem (if I am well attuned to my half-guessed purpose) to prescribe such matters as rhythm, sonority and line length, and after a provisional line or two they may also seem to suggest rhyme, stanza division, or the like. The process is thus "organic" and spontaneous, as in so-called free verse. I would not—granted—be so responsive to such suggestions if I had not already resorted often to traditional means: "The Lilacs" would probably not have come out in Anglo-Saxon alliterative half-lines if I had not studied Old English with relish, translated a bit of *Beowulf* into modern English, and used the A-S disciplines once before in a poem called "Junk." Some forms, like the sonnet, have obvious logical capabilities, and it is comparatively easy in their case to see why a potential poem has chosen to be fulfilled within them. About "The Lilacs" I can only say that the A-S meters are peculiarly able to express harshness and struggle, while at the same time they may, for brief stretches, be contrastingly rendered soft and fluent. I am not dead sure why "Fern Beds" is rhymed, though the rhyme feels suitable; the varying line lengths were employed, I should think, to stress transitions from simplicity to complexity and from stillness to tidal movement. It may be that one function of the rhymes is to be swept over by an elaborate grammar, thus emphasizing—for example—the intricacy of evolutionary development. It was very likely that a long poem like "Walking to Sleep," which keeps touching down in the flatly colloquial or conversational, would not saddle itself with rhyme and would make use of the most variable meter in English.

CH: Is there any particular form you've tried to master but feel you haven't gotten the better of yet? I don't recall, for example, ever seeing a sestina by you.

RW: From what I have just said, you can see that I think of a poem of mine as discovering, in the process of its writing, the formal means which will back up its statement and increase its precision. I would never, therefore, set out to "master a form." I suppose that I might, if I felt a great fit of mulling repetitiousness coming on, decide to let it come as a sestina; but that has not yet happened to me. Most sestinas impress me as forced and tiresome, though there are happy exceptions—in Elizabeth Bishop, *per esempio.*

CH: In *Walking to Sleep,* you've translated a Charles d'Orleans poem identified in the title as a rondeau. According to Lewis Turco's *Book of Forms,* it's a rondel, not a rondeau. Could you clarify the matter? Also, I was struck recently by the discovery of X. J. Kennedy's earlier version of d'Orleans' poem (also called "Rondeau"). He calls it a "violation" rather than a translation and starts with the line "The world is taking off her clothes," rather than, in your case, "The year has cast its cloak away." Would you comment on the different approaches the two of you took to the d'Orleans poem?

RW: No two authorities—Saintsbury, et al.—appear to agree at all points. However, I should judge that by most contemporary "rules" the poem I translated is a rondel. Charles d'Orleans evidently believed himself to be writing a rondeau, and Babette Deutsch clears him of irregularity by noting that *rondel* and *rondeau* were at one time synonymous. My translation is an effort to be faithful to the original in spirit and letter (save that I could not resist the pleasure and convenience of rendering "Ou'en son jargon ne chante ou crie" as "In cries or chipper tremolos.") X. J. Kennedy's "violation" is a spirited takeoff which surely would have amused the Duke.

CH: I've always wondered if your poem "A Simile for Her Smile" was a kind of tribute to Frost's poem "The Silken Tent." Each is a sentence long, each an extended metaphor, each strives for and achieves a distinctive grace, and your river is a "silken" one. Am I wrong?

RW: I have always cared greatly for Frost, and "The Silken Tent" has always delighted me for all sorts of reasons—one of them being that love of a woman and of a comparison could once move the skeptical Frost to speak of universal love as a possibility. Nevertheless, my poem was not meant as a tribute to his. Your comparison is apt and gratifying.

CH: I particularly admire your poem "Piazza di Spagna, Early Morning." Was it based on an actual incident? If so, would you tell us about it? Also, to what extent does the last line reflect your attitude toward self-consciousness generally?

RW: It was my wife who danced down the Spanish Steps at three in the morning, but actually I was not there; she told me about it. Perhaps, if I had been there, no poem would have come of it. Stevens was right in saying that the imagination is happiest with "the half colors of quarter things"—with the completion of what is partial or partially apprehended. To my wife's telling I added my own imagining of what she told, and some thoughts I was having about the way architectural shapes and volumes enforce certain behaviors. Where there is too much self-consciousness, whether in a ballerina or in a shoe-shine boy, we lose the incidental effect called beauty. A tennis player who is enamored of his strokes, and makes gracefulness the end of his activity, does not for my money play a beautiful game.

CH: Would you care to talk at all about the existence in poetry of two opposing traditions: one of affirmative, praise-poetry, in which the attitude toward the world is that of thanksgiving, and the other of a darker sort, described recently by Helen Trimpi as a poetry concerning itself with "evil in the older sense of privation of being and, hence, with experiences that range from the perception of death to the awareness of personal shortcomings." To what extent do you write with an awareness of needing to navigate between those two traditions?

RW: To be brief about it, I should say that the world is ultimately good and every art an expression of hope and joy. But forced enthusiasm and an exclusive sunniness can put both of those propositions in doubt. What art needs to do, as Milton said, is to reflect how all things "Rising or falling still advance His praise," and in the process to make a full acknowledgement of fallen-ness, doubt, and death. Not all art, of course, will accomplish these things on the scale of the Sistine Chapel; there is nothing wrong with modesty and homeliness. But there is something wrong with poems which lack all redeeming gaiety—and there may be gaiety in art which confronts the most desperate things. I do not enjoy poems which are mean, glum, artless and querulous. Isn't it odd that our American society, the most cosseted in human history, is now so given to petulance and dreary complaint, like the huge sad lady of Auden's "The Duet"? Grousing is not the mood of any art which is doing its job.

CH: You once said in an interview that you believe poetry is not a blurt of emotion and that a poet can be artificial while being absolutely sincere. I'd very much like you to elaborate on that.

RW: There would be no reason to write a poem if one were not aiming at an unusual fullness and accuracy of statement. To achieve that, the poet must use words, rhythms and sounds in subtle, concentrated, deliberate ways, hoping at the same time to give an illusion of offhand delivery. Sincerity, for the poet, lies not merely in meaning something but also in taking the crafty trouble to embody that meaning exactly and coercively. That's what I tell myself, at any rate.

CH: An impressive number of young poets are publishing poems and bringing out books these days. I'm tempted to say that the notion of an apprenticeship has perhaps fallen onto hard times in our poetry culture. Would you agree?

RW: It was harsh of Cyril Connolly to say that "the only true function of a writer is to produce a masterpiece," and it would be oppressive to quote him at the first meeting of a verse-writing seminar. Yet far too many people are emerging from such seminars, sheaves of verse in hand, with no notion of what a masterpiece might be, and no notion of how to make things difficult for themselves. I expect that some of the books to which you refer are published for essentially sociological reasons: they are to be read as dispatches from the Youth culture, graffiti from the Black culture, cries from the Movement. There are, however, some truly good young talents emerging.

CH: I'm struck by what seems to me to be a shying away from intellection in poetry nowadays. To the extent that's an accurate description, I'd trace the situation back to the Imagists and to such familiar notions as "no ideas but in things" (though Williams is of course not responsible for anyone who misinterprets or abuses his principles). Would you comment?

RW: Many of the poems I most value are imagist in character, but I agree with you that such poems may often combine delicacy of image and execution with an over-simplicity of thought, as could happen in Ezra Pound. Simple-mindedness was encouraged, I think, by those anti-war poetry readings of the 1960's in which we all participated, and which concerned themselves not only with the war but with many other causes regarding which the audiences were virtually unanimous. It was good to oppose the war, but the effect of those pep rallies on poetry and poets was stupefying.

CH: What's your feeling about literary wars? Are they something you'd prefer to hold yourself above or out of, to preserve your energies for your poetry? That's my impression, at any rate. Is it a fair one?

RW: Yes.

CH: Here in the 1970's, anything seems to go; I struggle hard to find a pattern and find none. Would you agree, or do you see more of a pattern than I do? Regardless, where do you think poetry will be in 2000? What does your crystal ball tell you?

RW: There are fine poets of all ages now writing, but I see no one powerful style prevailing or developing.

A practical thought occurs to me. Colleges and universities begin to be short of funds, and no doubt this will mean fewer poetry readings, at least for a time. The fast-building popularity of readings over the past twenty-five years has done good things for the poet's ear and for his sense of the dramatic, but I half think that a withering-away of the poetry circuit might now be beneficial. It is not altogether good for us to be crowd-pleasers and show-offs; thinking of our audience, we should imagine something uncertain and ideal, not an auditorium full of adolescents; and we should refresh our sense of the distinction between good poems and those "good reading poems" which so frequently depend for their effect on the poet's presence and legend.

When I squint into the crystal ball, in answering this sort of question, I find myself fruitlessly trying to envision new schools and new aesthetic theories; but when I turn and look at my contemporaries I am reminded that no age can satisfactorily be seen (or foreseen) in terms of notions and groupings. Even in so balanced and intelligent a text as Karl Malkoff's *Handbook of Contemporary Poetry,* one feels that the encyclopaedist's desire for coverage and classification has given Charles Olson's theories, for example, more space than they deserve, and that certain persons are mentioned, or left unmentioned, mostly because they are groupable or not. What we need in any period is strong single talents producing not theories but poems; we have them now, and surely will have them in 2000 A.D.

CH: Do you think there's any particular living poet who's not getting the attention he or she deserves and whom you'd like to recommend to our readers?

RW: I was recently made aware that Geoffrey Hill, an excellent English poet, lacks an American publisher. I hope that omission will soon be repaired. William Meredith's new-and-selected volume *Earth Walk,* one of the best books of recent years, should have made more of a splash than it did. I wish that my students would read more of the likes of Graves, Larkin, and Nemerov. Those people are well known, of course, but it is quite possible, within a certain readership, for authors to be "well known" and comparatively neglected.

An Interview with Richard Wilbur

Irv Broughton/1975

From *Mill Mountain Review,* Vol. II, No. 2 (1975), 92-109. Reprinted by permission of Irv Broughton.

Interviewer: On summer vacations years ago you toured the United States hobo style, riding freight cars and so forth. I was wondering if you considered yourself an early day "Easy Rider"?

Wilbur: Oh, no, I don't think I was "in search of America," except, perhaps, in some old romantic sense. And I certainly wasn't running away from any aspect of America; or trying to find out whether I was courageous. I don't know just what my mission was—part of it, I think, was mere curiosity, restlessness. I had read Hart Crane on the subject of railroads, and I'm sure that I had read some other people. I think there were some good railroad whistles in Muriel Rukeyser, here and there. There was a lot of railroad mysticism in the 1930's, and undoubtedly it was partially that, as well as simply youthful adventure, that set me going. Then, also, I didn't have very much money, Irv, and so I thought that hoboing would be a way to see the forty-eight states; or I guess it was forty-seven of them I saw. I didn't go to. . . .

Interviewer: Which one did you miss?

Wilbur: Well, I didn't go into Georgia because I had heard they would put me on the chain gang if some yard dick caught me.

Interviewer: You're now on a farm here, and I wondered, you grew up [on] a farm. Is this a homecoming?

Wilbur: I do feel comfortable with cows about.

Interviewer: Cue the cows, would you!

Wilbur: Yes, I wish they'd make good background noises for us. (A sound of an airplane passing overhead is audible on tape.) Actually, the farm I was brought up on in New Jersey was not one which my family worked, and so I had the best of everything. I had the pleasure of riding on the haywagon, but I didn't have to make the load, or get up early in the morning and do all those onerous tasks. And often I had the pleasure of playing tennis against a nice campestral background, against the waving corn tassels. We have about the same thing here. Of course, I do work pretty hard at raising vegetables and herbs.

Interviewer: What are your favorites to raise?

Wilbur: The sensible thing to raise is tomatoes, of course. That's where you really make a difference. But I raise all sorts of other things, rather dumb things. I have some okra plants which are only *that* high and will never get higher. That's my experiment for the year. I raise things like rocket, which you can't buy on the market. I have a perverse taste for hot lettuce.

Interviewer: In '61 you traveled to Russia on a foreign exchange program. Do you enjoy such things?

Wilbur: I enjoyed that very well. I was given time in which to prepare myself for it. There wasn't time for me to learn the Russian language, but I could read up on Russia, and I could read a good many novels and whatever poetry was available to me in translation—good or bad. And that trip in 1961 was made at a very fortunate time. Peter Viereck and I went over there, as a two-man team, at a time when Russia was anxious to prove that they could be more liberal than we as hosts. We'd been rather foolish to a delegation of Russian writers who came to America. We wouldn't let the novelist Leonov, for example, look through one of our California telescopes — as if the heavens were secret information; and they weren't allowed to look at Brooklyn Navy Yard, either. Well, the Russians said to Peter and to me that we could see anything or anybody we wanted. We offered them a list of fifty writers we wanted to meet, and not under vodka-toast circumstances, but tête-à-tête and in their homes, if possible. They did play ball with us in 49 instances out of 50. In one case there was a poet who had behaved badly politically, and had been put into the loony bin—a thing they do over there. They didn't give us quite the straight story about him. But we were allowed to go anywhere we liked, and we were not always accompanied by interpreters and Intourist guides. And so I thought it was an extremely fortunate jaunt.

Interviewer: Viereck himself returned to the forms later in his own poetry and so have many others: Borges, Eliot, Pound—many of them returned to the forms later. Do you think this is an affirmation of the poetic form?

Wilbur: By poetic form, do you mean the use of meters, the use of rhymes?

Interviewer: Yes, yes.

Wilbur: Sonnet forms, that kind of thing. I'm really not militant about that at all. I do think it's perfectly possible to write satisfactory poems in free verse. It does, however, depress me to hear good people like Galway Kinnell say that we're beyond all that formal stuff now. . . . We'll have no more use for meters or the trouble of rhyme. It seems to me that traditional means, if you have the ability to use them, can be turned to enormous account; that there are many effects you can get with them that you can't possibly get without them.

Interviewer: Yevtushenko said that there might be one or two unused rhymes somewhere in Argentina. Isn't that a problem?

Wilbur: It is a problem. I can remember talking about cat-rat rhymes at one time with somebody or other—I think it was Jack Sweeney—and saying that nobody again would ever be able to write a poem rhyming "fire" and "desire," and so on. He immediately reminded me of a lyric in one of Eliot's "Four Quartets" which rhymes very freshly on precisely the words I was saying couldn't be used again. It is, I guess, all a matter of how you come up to them, how necessary the words are. Forced rhyme is no good. Unforced rhyme, even if the rhymes have been used a thousand times, can be effective.

Interviewer: If you were a writer in Russia today, do you think your work would be different?

Wilbur: I have no doubt it would be. I think I'd be reacting in some way to the pressure to be edifying, and to encourage the workers in the economy to be orthodox. I imagine nevertheless that my natural inclination to be oblique, and to play, is close to what a lot of the good Russian poets do. They say one thing out of the front of the mouth and another thing, another qualifying thing, out of the corner of the mouth. It makes for poems of great subtlety, sometimes. Also, poems which are awfully hard to translate.

Interviewer: You're doing a good deal of translation now.

Wilbur: Well, I don't do it in bulk really, but whenever I encounter a poem which seems to me an almost-possible utterance for myself, and which offers me a formal challenge, I feel like taking it on. I like to do sonnets, that kind of thing. I'll take such a poem on, partly for fear that somebody else will take it on and wreck it. Most translation at present doesn't try to preserve the meters and other formal aspects of the original. And I do think that in many cases you simply can't bring across the quality of the poet without trying for some of that. Obviously, everything you do will be at best an approximation. But with certain poets I think it's obligatory to try for a formal equivalence. For example, nobody in France could translate the Australian poet A. D. Hope into free verse and convey anything that he's about. I don't suppose anybody ever translated Alexander Pope satisfactorily without a rhyme here and there.

Interviewer: Mrs. Osip Mandelsam says that translation is the exact opposite of verse writing.

Wilbur: Oh, I think they're different, all right. Yes. Because you know how it's going to come out, if you're a translator. You don't if you're a poet. Nevertheless, I think if you take time enough on any job of translation, ask enough hard questions about what every word in the original means, and what relation the rhythm of the original has to the subject matter, and so on, you'll finally end by taking possession of it, which isn't to say it'll sound like you. But it *is* to say that you'll have asked of the original many of the kinds of questions you ask of your own work when it's in process.

Interviewer: She says further, "A real poet should beware translation, that it may deter the birth of real poetry."

Wilbur: It's undoubtedly true that translation can be a dodge for the lazy poet, or the tired poet. It's a way of seeming to have an output when you can't think of any notions of your own. Yet it can have great advantages for your own writing, I think. As I've said in a written piece recently, to translate someone is often an act of imposture in which you say something which you're not quite prepared to say in your own person, or take a tone which is not quite your own. Yet you'd like to have that latitude in your own work before you're through. And this gives you a little practice. I'm sure that all of Ezra Pound's translations had some effect upon the central Ezra Pound, wherever that was; sometimes I think it's hard to find.

Interviewer: Do you think verse translations enrich the language in which they are translated?

Wilbur: Oh, very often, yes. Each language does have a particular kind of genius, and it also has its particular individual geniuses. The bringing over of anything that's like the original, into English, is going to make changes, is going to offer people alternative ways of saying it. I suppose the clearest example of this would be the effect of Japanese and Chinese translation with us. The condensation, obliqueness and impersonality of Japanese poetry has been very suggestive for a lot of our people.

Interviewer: Doesn't it occur that at some point translation corrupts and is detrimental to the original language?

Wilbur: I think we damage the English language, and damage poetry in the English language, by producing bad translation in it. I can't think of an example right now—if I could, perhaps I wouldn't want to give it—but I think there are poets who have done a lot of translations and have fallen into the habit of talking like a book of translation, and lost track of their own voices. It's a little bit like living abroad. Expatriates find themselves using the slang of 1927, or saying "actually" instead of "currently."

Interviewer: Doesn't this do irreparable damage to our concept of foreign literature?

Wilbur: Certainly so. I believe that when Harvard University began messing around with humanities programs, they rather hoped that students reading the great books in translation would be moved to go into the classics department and read them in the originals—or into the modern languages departments. And I don't think that's happened, really. And so, in some cases we've done a kind of public dishonor to some fine book or fine poem by knowing it unnecessarily through bad English versions. I'm sorry about that. Yet, I suppose, in almost every case something is better than nothing. In the case of Goethe, it's hard to say. I don't read Goethe in the original; in such English and American translations as I've read, he sounds awful. I'm not sure it's a favor to anybody that there are English and American translations of Goethe.

Interviewer: If you were to be done abroad—and done poorly— how would you think about it? Would you prefer not to have been done at all? "'Tis better not to have been done than to have been done."

Wilbur: It would depend, I suppose, on my guesses as to my future reputation. If I thought I was going to stick around for awhile, then I could be confident that people would say, "Oh, that doesn't render him. Let me do a good translation." However, if I'm going to fade very soon, I'd rather be represented very well or not at all.

Interviewer: What do you think about writing for eternity and similar things?

Wilbur: I don't think it's a consideration.

Interviewer: Andrew Sarris considers most film criticism as Puritanical. Do you think this could be said of poetry criticism? . . . I think he means that in the broadest sense.

Wilbur: Puritanical. Well, there *are* ways that criticism can be Puritanical. There was a lot of social-minded criticism in the 30's which imposed political duties on the poet, and for those who were going to perform such duties anyway, I suppose it did no harm. For others, it really may have been harmful for the critics to keep saying to them, "The poet *must,* the poet owes it to his society," and so on. And then there's that "theological" kind of criticism which used to talk about the heresy of this and the fallacy of that. I think that such language is a little strong, a little arm-twisting, and is likely to be dampening to the original sort of poet who's out of step with the fashions of his time.

Interviewer: Your poems have been criticized from the standpoint that "How can this artist be so likeable in this horrendous world?"— that's a paraphrase of one man's statement.

Wilbur: Uh hm.

Interviewer: How can you be so likeable . . .?

Wilbur: Thank heavens, I'm not aware of being likeable. If somebody finds me so, I'll pardon him, but I have no desire at all, in my poetry, to be ingratiating. I don't have any consciousness of talking directly to people when I write—as would be required for such an intention. I don't write to please, except to please myself, and to please a group of now nameless people who've established themselves as my superego. Once I've written a poem, of course, I'm very pleased if it pleases.

Interviewer: You talked about carrying a poem around like it was a precious possession and that you didn't show it to anyone until that final moment when it was done.

Wilbur: Yes.

Interviewer: Why is that?

Wilbur: Well, I don't want to stop worrying about it. I should hate it if somebody approved of me prematurely, before I achieved the poem, got through to the last line. And I wouldn't want the contrary to happen either. I did that recently—made the mistake of showing someone a long poem which was in process. I had been working on it for a year and a half, and I suppose I was impatient for a pat on the back. And it didn't make out too well with that critic. Took me some months to work up heart to go on with it. I do think it's foolishness to seek approval before you've pleased yourself.

Interviewer: Louise Bogan feels that you have the exact moment of timing with your poems. She says you let them drop at the exact right time, sort of, I suppose, like fruit, out here amongst the apple trees.

Wilbur: Yes, well, I hope so. I do think timing is very important in poetry, as in talk. When you get to the end, you should stop. And your ending, I suppose, is something which, if you have certain effects in mind, you should build toward. Not every discourse, however, need have a crescendo. There are other shapes.

Interviewer: Is it possible to write major poetry in two languages?

Wilbur: I suppose that someone like Nabokov, if he put poetry first, would be capable of writing an extremely fine and witty poetry in more than one language. Perhaps more than two. But he's exceptional, isn't he? I doubt that there are many people who could do it, because in poetry, especially, you write out of such intimate and, in some degree, unexamined feelings about words. You know the words of your own language as you know your brothers and sisters and your wife and your children—which is to say very deeply, and yet not altogether clearly. However good your feeling is for another language, it's always got to be comparatively superficial, narrowly clear in a dictionary sense.

Interviewer: You wrote the lyrics to the comic opera *Candide*. Could you have written the limericks to *Hair?*

Wilbur: No, no. I'm not attracted to the youth culture or its enthusiasms, and so I don't believe I could have done that. It would have been a technical challenge, I expect, but I'd have flunked it. It's not that I'm agin the young, but I really don't care for rock music and I don't care for the kind of language which goes with most rock lyrics.

I think it's very good that the rock lyric has broken the frame of the old Musical Comedy number, and has included a lot of material, a lot of kinds of language which for a long time were not used. That's the good thing about it. But I really don't feel that anything terribly worth listening to has occurred in the rock lyric so far. I know my children would detest me for saying this, but for my sins, I had to read all the lyrics of Bob Dylan some time ago—because some students of mine accepted a challenge of mine, or took advantage of a tolerance of mine, and wrote term papers on him. He may be good with guitar accompaniment, but the words simply aren't much.

Interviewer: Alan Pryce-Jones, some time ago, referred to Bernstein's music for *Candide* as some of Bernstein's most outstanding work and hastened to add, though, that as outstanding as Bernstein's music was, it was overshadowed by the dance.

Wilbur: No, I don't think that's true. It seems to me that we really didn't have quite as much dance as we meant to in that show. Are you speaking of another show, perhaps? Something like *On The Town?* In *Candide* we had only one or two numbers in which there was much balletic motion and, of those, one was quite short. And we didn't, until the last minute, have a choreographer. The director, Tyrone Guthrie, had merely been moving people around the stage in crisscrossing masses prior to that last-minute effort to put a little more choreography into it. No, I don't think what Pryce-Jones says was so. I don't think the music, though it was very kinetic music—that's what Bernstein's best at, really, very kinetic music—was overshadowed by such dancing as we had.

Interviewer: Is this a problem sometimes, in your own frame of reference, in doing a collaboration; I mean, here you're working with a group of people and hopefully you're working as a unit.

Wilbur: Well, I came into that show, *Candide,* five years after others—that is to say, Bernstein, Lillian Hellman—had started working on it, and there had been five other people working on the lyrics. So I was really asked in to do, initially, a mopping-up action, to rewrite a lot of lyrics which were unsatisfactory or which, in view of changes in the book, were going to have to be tinkered with. Then we started to change the book so much, and made so many cuts, that there were a number of new lyrics to be done. But, as I think I was going to say, I came into something in which other people had

had a long-standing investment, and their imaginations of the project were pretty stubborn. And so I had my times in collaborating with Leonard Bernstein. We tended to butt heads quite a lot. Sometimes I got my way, sometimes he got his way. Once or twice we did it just like Mickey Rooney in the movies, and produced something satisfactory—rapidly, sleeplessly, and in perfect harmony, freely giving in to each other. He would let me knock out a note and I'd let him knock out a word.

Interviewer: Which poems affect you the most?

Wilbur: Many poems have taken my head off. Oh, I don't think I can go through all my reading experience, and say which poems have most excited me. There really are too many. There are a couple of tercets of Dante which overwhelm me with their simplicity every time I come back to them. The exciting poems I like best are the ones which are absolutely inexhaustible. There's a little poem of Coventry Patmore's I keep saying which has as yet shown me no points of weakness.

Interviewer: Would you say it?

Wilbur: I think I can say it from memory. I don't remember the title of it.

Interviewer: That's all right.

Wilbur: But, as I remember, I didn't like the title of it. It was some dreadful, abstract word ["Magna est veritas"]. It's better to just start with the first line, in a concrete scene. Coventry Patmore's poem goes:

> Here, in this little bay,
> Full of tumultuous life and great repose,
> Where, twice a day,
> The purposeless, glad ocean comes and goes,
> Under high cliffs, and far from the huge town,
> I sit me down.
> For want of me the world's course will not fail:
> When all its work is done, the lie shall rot;
> The truth is great, and shall prevail,
> When none cares whether it prevail or not.

Interviewer: Great, very nice.

Wilbur: The next to the last line is from one of the apocryphal books, I think it's *Tobit,* but I forget the context, in any case. It is a Biblical allusion. "The truth is great, and shall prevail."

Interviewer: Those words are very close to you, special.

Wilbur: Well, I like the last two lines, taken together. The truth is great, and shall prevail, *when* (which I think means *though)* none cares whether it prevail or not. I read that poem at a service at the local church the other day. And I read it as an example of trustfulness in God. It seems to me that Coventry Patmore is saying, with the greatest blitheness, that no matter what he does, no matter what anybody does or does not do, or wish, the truth is great and shall prevail. The world is good and will turn out so.

Interviewer: Are most of the lines that stick with you like that, are they affirmative?

Wilbur: I'm not necessarily stuck on affirmations. I think I simply like the voice to be true. I like, for example, a lot of the real hard nastiness of François Villon, because it seems to me authentic. Limited, perhaps, but genuine.

Interviewer: James Dickey said, "It's not possible to know, nobody will ever know what is poetry."

Wilbur: Well, if you stepped that question down a little and said, "What is a poem?" then you could start to name different kinds of poems, different particular poems. You could start saying whether this or that bit of writing worked as a poem works. Probably that's where to start: where Aristotle starts—saying, What does it do to you when you are in the presence of a poem? You discover how what you regard as a poem, what you choose to call a poem, works on you. Then if something else doesn't, you declare it not to be a poem. . . . I was saying about the Johnson sonnet that I'm really not satisfied with the last line of it, but I don't think I'd go back now and try to improve it. A poem of scorn, or whatever that is, is not to be revised some years later. You might go back and revise a love poem, but not scorn poems.

Interviewer: Do you think the reading public is intellectually adolescent?

Wilbur: Well, I don't know. They used to say that about the radio public—that it was really eight years old. I don't know how they went about discovering that. The reading public for poetry is chiefly, I think, so far as sales are concerned, a bright student public. I have no objection to that at all. It's very pleasant to think of being read by a lot of such people. It's true that I don't admire all of their excitements, and I suppose that the institution of the poetry reading has led to a certain amount of currying favor with the student audience one way or another. It's a good audience to have. But I suppose you put it as simply as that because it's hard to state the whole truth. I don't think anybody would write poems, or I think people would write very few poems, if there were not readers. So there has got to be some kind of thought of the reader in a poet's head. And yet, as he writes, no real poet says to himself, "How is my reader going to like this? Is he smiling now?"

Interviewer: Louise Bogan also said of you that Wilbur points to a time when tenderness will be not so rare.

Wilbur: She must have said that about my first book. Well, that's something nobody can know about himself. You can't know if you give a tender impression or not. I'm glad she thought so; I think that's a good quality to have.

Interviewer: Do you read other translations of work you're working on, translating?

Wilbur: Generally not. When I've worked on whole plays of Molière—I've done three of those now—I've sometimes looked at prose translations of plays I was rendering in heroic couplets. But only when I was really stuck for a word. And of course, I would never look at a rhyming translation of anything I was doing into rhyme. That would absolutely cut my thought processes off, I suppose. I would be embarrassed to adopt the rhyme another translator had used.

Interviewer: What happens later when you find you may have used the same rhyme?

Wilbur: Oh, that doesn't matter. If I've arrived at it independently, that's perfectly all right. About that, one can be as self-respecting as that fellow who thought of evolution at the time Darwin did. Curiously enough, the same rhymes don't occur too often—at any rate in translations of Molière. There's a Columbia professor who's done a certain number of translations of Molière into rhymed verse recently—though I guess I was the person who started it. He did one of *The School for Wives,* and he did his before I did mine. I simply didn't look at his till I was all through with my own. And then, I admit, I was rather strenuously hopeful that there wouldn't be too many of the same rhyming solutions. The first two rhymes in his translation and mine were the same, as it turned out. But after that we diverged considerably.

Interviewer: Do you know any poets who use a dictionary, a rhyming dictionary?

Wilbur: No. I guess the only time I've ever used one was in the course of a job of translation, when I felt myself controlled by what the original had to say, and wanted to say that at all costs, in language as close as possible to the original. And so I looked now and then into a rhyming dictionary, almost always in a vain hope of finding a word I hadn't thought of. I work so slowly that, when it comes to rhymes, I usually think of them all. It's very bad to use a rhyming dictionary, in my experience at any rate, because it means that the words you should think of at leisure, and mull over, and discover possibilities in, are given to you too suddenly, too easily, and you experience their possibilities superficially.

Interviewer: It's been said that the use of "I" or "you" in terms of the persons in the poem is actually an impersonalization. Is this valid?

Wilbur: I suppose that the "I" in anybody's poem is never merely the poet. It's some aspect of the poet, or someone he is trying to be. I suspect there are Browningesque poems in which the speaker of the poem, the "I" of the poem, is someone the poet would damn well not wish to be. And surely the same is true of the "you." The "you" is the construct of the poet's imagination or a necessity of his dramatic strategy.

Interviewer: Who would you like to be?

Wilbur: Where? When? In a poem?

Interviewer: Yes.

Wilbur: I don't think I have ever approached a poem that way—trying to project an ideal self. Partly, I imagine, because, from the very beginning, I've thought of poetry as getting one's various selves to quarrel intelligibly in public. And to be ideal, to be an ideal persona, would be to foreclose the possibilities of the poem.

Interviewer: Your sonnet for LBJ is a sort of an adventure into the political realm, though you attack him on slightly different grounds.

Wilbur: It's a pretty oblique attack. I'm really angry at him, of course, because of the Vietnam war, but the poem presumes to be attacking him because he refused Peter Hurd's commissioned portrait. I wrote the poem at a time when I hadn't seen Peter Hurd's commissioned portrait. Now that I've seen it, I don't think it is anywhere near as good as most of Hurd's work; in particular, his landscapes.

Interviewer: Would you still damn LBJ on that?

Wilbur: Well, I would certainly object to his reasons for refusing it, and I would object to the churlishness with which he refused it.

Interviewer: What were the reasons?

Wilbur: I think he rejected it because he said (in the painter's presence) that it was the ugliest thing he had ever seen. Whereas he could have found that in a mirror. Enough; I'm being nasty.

Interviewer: Among poets, Elizabeth Bishop wanted to be a painter. You're very concerned [with] and interested in painting. Your father, I believe, was a painter.

Wilbur: Yes, still is.

Interviewer: What is this, speaking in regard to poets? Their interest in painting and yours?

Wilbur: Well there is a great deal. I don't know whether I can explain it. There must be some poets who have very little visual imagination, even though the eye is the primary sense. Everybody's agreed on that. Since the Middle Ages, I think. Even D. H. Lawrence, who made out a strong case against the primacy of vision, was a painter. Well, I just can't say. I think I can say why there are more painter poets, or poets who are would-be painters, than there are poets who have to do with music. It strikes me that music is infinitely more abstract than painting or poetry. That you can't make any precise statements as to what music is up to. Poetry simply has to be exact and concrete or it bores us to death. And on the whole, I think—despite some successes in abstract painting—that it's the same with painting.

Interviewer: Brion Gyson made the comment that writing is fifty years behind painting.

Wilbur: What should I do with that? It seems to me that painting is not altogether in good health. There are some fine paintings being done by particular persons, but I should say that the world of the New York galleries was involved in a very sorry way with the fashion world. There's a terrible turnover in styles, and a terrible modishness, falsifying the work of a lot of people who otherwise might be good. I don't think we have any such situation in writing. As for who's ahead in terms of time, I certainly don't know what it's going to be fifty years from now and I don't think the writing of poetry is fifty years behind the present. I don't believe really in the avant-garde, do you?

Interviewer: No, not too much.

Wilbur: For years, anybody writing an imitation of William Carlos Williams has felt that he was in the avant-garde. I suppose that's been so for thirty or forty years. Funny how "modern" seems to mark time. If a little magazine comes out with a title in lower case, it feels modern. Does your magazine have a title in lower case? No.

Interviewer: No, it doesn't.

Wilbur: But you know what I mean. That's been modern since 1920. And so much that is regarded as experimental is a repetition of the Imagistic experiments of the 'teens and twenties. I really think it's much more experimental at the moment to see what you can do with the fresh use of traditional means.

Interviewer: There's nothing new under the sun.

Wilbur: Well, every poem had better be new, but I don't suppose that there are likely to be any new poetic means, new combinations, new ways of handling them. I like that thing that Robert Frost said when someone asked him why he wrote poetry: he gave one of his sassy answers and said, "To see if I can make them all different." Of course, he didn't. Nobody does. But every poet aspires to that, I think, and relishes that in other poets. It keeps happening.

Interviewer: Do you feel anything of Frost out here in the countryside? You've got birch trees out there, a wall. . . .

Wilbur: Oh, yes, we have a lot of props here. I don't think I have too many of Robert Frost's attitudes, though I was terribly fond of him personally, and think very highly of his poems. I think that Frost is often misunderstood as a nature poet. I recall his saying, one time, that he'd only written one nature poem in his life. I thought about it for awhile and realized which one he meant. It was an early poem called "In a Vale," in which he lays claim, in a kind of puckish way, to mystic insights into nature. It's a poem which really denies what it's claiming by the playfulness of its tone. Elsewhere, it seems to me, Frost makes almost no statements about nature—about what it is, about what it means.

Interviewer: What about, is there a puckishness in your work?

Wilbur: Everybody has playfulness in his poetry.

Interviewer: Do you value wit?

Wilbur: Yes, I think that when one is making a serious statement, a little playfulness is, if it's done well, a kind of earnest of one's earnestness. If a poem can't stand to be locally amusing, then I suspect it's really not very serious; not as serious as it thinks it is.

Interviewer: If there was a Richard Wilbur *Hamlet,* what would it be like?

Wilbur: Heavens, I don't know. You mean, what sort of tortured personality would I like to project?

Interviewer: No, if you were to shape *Hamlet.*

Wilbur: I haven't thought about rewriting *Hamlet.*

Interviewer: Do you think it's good, good enough?

Wilbur: I think it'll do, though to tell the truth I've never thought to a conclusion about *Hamlet.* It's always been a puzzling play. I have never known, as Mr. Eliot didn't know, everything that was bothering Hamlet. What was making him so whole-hog disgusted.

Interviewer: Do you like films?

Wilbur: Yes, I like films a good deal, though I must say I treat them badly. I treat them whorishly. I turn on the television and look at the late movie, or I go to a new film without religiously reading all of the critics and seeing whether or not I should. I don't really like to talk about film as an art. Yet I love it, as a medium. I detest, really, a great deal of what's being done now in the films. I made the mistake of seeing, last Spring, *The Godfather* and *The French Connection* within a couple of weeks and I felt that I'd had enough of that kind of nastiness for a lifetime. I propose to look now and see whether films are labeled "violent." I gather they are proposing to label violent films as "violent."

Interviewer: Well, you seem to get . . . something visceral about films. I mean, isn't this fundamental to art?

Wilbur: A visceral feeling for the medium?

Interviewer: Yes, yes.

Wilbur: I simply delight in it. I can sit and watch quite uninterest-ing films, quite inartistic films, because, after all, they're showing me pictures of things. I can watch Antonioni, who seems to me the most boring director in the modern world. When he concentrates irrelevantly on a doorknob it is, after all, a doorknob.

Interviewer: Do you like Bergman?

Wilbur: Very much, very much. I haven't seen a great quantity of Bergman. I haven't seen any of his newer films, but I remember staggering out of his movie, *The Magician,* in tears, and I almost never weep over anything. His movie *The Virgin Spring* destroyed me.

Interviewer: Isn't that what art should do, set you to weeping?

Wilbur: Nothing wrong with weeping. I'd never cared for the behavior of an old friend of the family who, when Tschaikovsky's Fifth was put on the what do you call it—what did we call it—gramophone, used to take out his handkerchief in advance. I suspect that he didn't need to listen to it, that the very thought of it was sufficient to make him cry. I'm just objecting to emotionalism. But true feeling, in response to a fine work of art, should certainly extend to weeping if it's called for.

Interviewer: What do you like about Bergman?

Wilbur: I suppose I like his areas of concern, which are religion, morals, and the arts. I like the fact that he can be thoroughly mysterious without hokum, though I gather he's been charged with hokum in some of his films which I haven't seen.

Interviewer: You talked about a baroque wall fountain, saying that this was relating to your Puritanical nature.

Wilbur: That was a very pleasant fountain, but when I lived in Rome and walked past that fountain every day on my way to work, I always felt tempted by it, tempted to linger; and reproached by it, I suppose, because I was driving myself so humorlessly to go and get an eight-hour day done. That statement about Puritanical industry is meant to be a little playful, but it's also true that I had, even in the city of Rome, a tendency to work eight hours a day when I could. That's a rather stupid thing to do with poetry, though not so stupid with translation. I suspect nobody has more than about two or three hours of poetry in him a day.

Interviewer: Do you usually use up those two or three hours?

Wilbur: Not always. I'm awfully capricious, really. At present, I suppose I'm losing some of my Puritanism.

Interviewer: When did you first notice this loss?

Wilbur: Well, I can't tell you. I'm not so introspective as that, so self-noticing. Perhaps when we moved up here to Cummington, and

I found myself living in an environment so attractive. It's very hard, given those woods out there, with the ponds and streams in them, not to go for a walk. And I suppose anyone who uses natural imagery rather frequently, as I do, can feel that he's working when he's out there.

Interviewer: Has there been a change, do you feel a change in the intensity and so on of your poems as you spend more time here in the country?

Wilbur: I can't tell about that. I doubt that there has been. At any rate, I haven't set about intentionally altering myself, either in the mood of my work or in its means. I don't really believe in that kind of manhandling of one's self. Some poets whom I admire greatly have given themselves orders, as it were, have set about to change their styles. And have rather willfully constructed books. W. B. Yeats, I think, was a poet who set out to make each book a constellation, with intelligible relationships between all the poems, and I think very often he wrote poems to fill in the pattern. Well, since Yeats did it so well, it must have been desirable for him, but it's not anything I could do for myself. It would be a violation of myself not to be a little more whimsical, self-indulgent—maybe there's a nice word for it.

Interviewer: If you were living in New York, do you think you'd write different ones? I mean, that's the extreme.

Wilbur: I'm sure that I would. I have lived in New York, was born there. I've lived there at various times for longer or shorter periods. I'm one of the great majority of ex-New Yorkers who now feel that not under any circumstances could they go back. It's simply too disagreeable a city at present. I can't consent to Robert Lowell's saying that it's the center of American culture. That doesn't seem to me to be the fact at all. I should say that American culture was remarkably dispersed, and that some of our best writing, some of our best everything, is being done in what, to the New Yorker, would seem faraway and backward places. A theatre person can't think that way, I suppose, but if you're in the writing business you can.

Interviewer: That's getting down to the people, grass roots, then, in America?

Wilbur: Oh, I'm not talking regionalism or anything like that. I suppose I'm simply saying that you don't have to be in New York. There are certain people you don't have to know, certain connections you don't have to have, certain shows you don't have to see, in order to be fully alive as a writer.

Interviewer: Dan Berrigan said that after he had gotten recognition on the strength of his Lamont prize, that he knew publishers would accept most anything and he had to guard against it.

Wilbur: I expect most people find that to be true. There are so few editors who have any taste about poetry. Most of our major magazines, I think, don't even have poetry editors. And your chances of getting published, and in some sense published well, are very good, once you've been approved of once or twice. That's too bad, of course. You don't get whatever kind of criticism a rejection slip amounts to. For the other kind of criticism, you have to depend not on editors, but on your friends. On a few friends who, without malice, can be quite honest and tell you, "Don't publish that," or "Do fix that."

Interviewer: Who have been your friends in that regard?

Wilbur: One of my best friendly critics is William Meredith. I show him about everything I write, and he's one of the few people on whose say-so I've made changes. He feels that my diction is a little bit intolerably antique. And so when I say "yet," he wants me to say "still." Sometimes I say "still" just to please him. And there are a number of other people. One of the best pieces of friendly criticism I ever had was from Archibald MacLeish. Again, that was a matter of one word. He looked at a poem I had sent him, and said, "The poem buckles a little at precisely this point. Can't you find a better word for that?" Happily, I could. I call that terribly good criticism, when someone can put his finger on *the* weak word in a poem which otherwise is not too bad.

Interviewer: William Jay Smith spoke of seeing one of your poems early in its life.

Wilbur: Oh, yes, yes. I've often shown poems to Bill Smith, and as a matter of fact, he took my disorderly sheaf of poems, the poems which made up my last book, *Walking to Sleep,* and put them into order, and I thought very artfully. That's the kind of thing I can't begin to do. When I organize a book, since the poems are all—as I say—one-shots, and don't amount to variations on a theme, I use the crudest possible methods of organization. I'll say, well, that was a long poem; let's rest them with a short one. Or, that was a heavy poem;

let's have something trivial. Those really are the principles on which
I've put all books together except the last one which, as I say, was
delivered into Bill Smith's hands.

Interviewer: You refer to the baroque wall fountain as the very
symbol of concretion of pleasure. Can you explain that?

Wilbur: Well, we all have a general sense of what pleasure is,
before somebody asks us to define it. One way to define it would be
to decide on certain words. Another way would be simply to point.
And if I could point, I'd point at that fountain, with all its marvelous
splashing water, and its scallop shells, and its geese, and its fauns.

Interviewer: You once said that one does not use poetry for its
major purpose as a means of organizing one's self in the world until
one's world gets out of hand. When did your world get out of hand?

Wilbur: Well, I think what I was referring to was World War II. Of
course, everybody's world gets out of hand in peacetime, but mine
spectacularly did in wartime—for all sorts of external reasons and, I
think, on account of a corresponding internal confusion. Out of that
shakeup, poetry is likely to come as a means of achieving some kind
of security.

Interviewer: You've written several poems about war.

Wilbur: Well, I didn't write as many poems—as many printable,
usable, bearable poems—out of the war as I thought I might. Even
now I think of turning back and using some of my experiences in
World War II, but I don't know whether I could manage to do it. I
don't know whether I could recover the experiences authentically.

Interviewer: How long does it take to translate an experience into
a poem ordinarily? Is there a waiting period or something?

Wilbur: I should think so. The last large poem I wrote—it was
called "The Mind-Reader"—is based on an experience I had in the
Fall of 1954 in Rome, and I've been thinking about that experience
for, how many years is it?—seventeen, eighteen? And making
occasional notes about it on the backs of envelopes, or in one or
another little scribbling book I have. But it wasn't, I suppose, until
three years ago that I got around to setting down a few lines about it,
and it took me, on and off, three years to get it done. That's a longer
period of waiting than has generally been the case with me, and I
must say I can recall occasions in which something happened to me
and I sat plump down and wrote about it.

Interviewer: Which of your "plump down and wrote about 'em" poems has become most recognized?

Wilbur: There's one called "The Death of a Toad," which I wrote immediately after killing a toad with a power mower. I suppose what happened was that the experience jelled a lot of feelings I'd already had, because the poem isn't, in fact, simply about a toad. I was ready for something like that to happen, to which I might instantly respond by writing.

Interviewer: Would you say that's responding out of inspiration, or do you believe in that word?

Wilbur: Well, inspiration is a word forever out of fashion. I think everybody's always embarrassed by it, though I can't think of a better. Yes, I think you have to be somehow mysteriously ready to go, things have to fall into place, and there's no willing that to happen.

Interviewer: No conditions that would help?

Wilbur: None that I can think of. That is, there's no right room in which to write, no correct time of day, no proper meal to have had, no drink to have avoided. I really can't think of any sure-fire arrangements, and I try not to worry too much about such things. If you do, of course, you can find all kinds of handsome excuses for not writing.

Interviewer: Do you sometimes have a drought—a few weeks or months?

Wilbur: Oh, yes. I have long ones—and, as a matter of fact, what happens during such periods is that I lose the habit of converting things as they come into poems. It's hard to get that habit started again. I wish my dry periods were briefer, so that the habit would be more readily recovered.

Interviewer: Then, do you discover oases in your writing, also?

Wilbur: Oases? What would those be?

Interviewer: Those would be the opposite of droughts.

Wilbur: Oh, spates, spates! I never have much of one, because— well—to write two poems in a couple of weeks would be going pretty fast for me. One reason for that, I think, is that I've never had the habit some people have of writing in poem sequences. That sort of note poem that Bill Williams used to write could become a very long poem, accomplished in a series of fragmentary inspirations. Wallace

Stevens, in a somewhat more formal way, did the same kind of thing. What I seem to do when I have a hunch or a notion for a poem is to collect ideas and images that belong to it and write about them very slowly, and try to kill the subject once and for all in one poem. Once you've done that you have to pause awhile before you go on to something else.

Interviewer: Say you had a time machine. What period of history would you pick to visit?

Wilbur: I'd like to visit—not for all reasons, I assure you, but for some—Italy during the age of Leonardo or Alberti. The period when the sense of human possibility was enormous. What other periods, I wonder? I don't do much longing for other periods, actually. Maybe that's the only one I can come up with at this moment.

Interviewer: What's the most poetic experience you've ever had?

Wilbur: I don't really think of experiences as being poetic. I suppose that's an evasive and half-true thing to say. A poem amounts to rendering an experience, and other ideas and experiences which you associate with it, as fully-stated as possible. Very seldom, I think, do you accomplish in life that kind of fullness of consciousness. Life isn't that concentrated. Mostly it's "splendid waste," as Henry James said. I suppose if I thought of "poetic" as signifying intensely emotional, I could give all sorts of answers, but that really isn't the way I think about it. Poetry is, to be sure, emotional, but it's emotion at its most precise and understanding. Nothing to which you would say "Wow!" in ordinary experience seems to me to resemble a poem.

Interview: Richard Wilbur

Christopher Bogan and Carl Kaplan/1975

From *The Amherst Student Review*, Vol. CIV, No. 37 (March 17, 1975), 4-5, 13-14. Reprinted by permission of *The Amherst Student Review.*

While at Amherst, [Richard] Wilbur was a Chairman of the STUDENT and wrote a weekly column, "The Mock Turtle," for its editorial page. He also found time to contribute to the campus humor magazine, the Amherst TOUCHSTONE. After graduating, he entered the war where he served with the 36th Infantry Division. Upon the war's end, he returned to the U.S. and attended Harvard as a graduate fellow. He later taught at Harvard, and then Wellesley, and is presently a member of the English Department at Wesleyan.

The thought came to us several months back that we might talk with Richard Wilbur for the REVIEW, and consequently we wrote him inquiring into the possibility of such a conversation. Quite promptly we received a reply thanking us for our letter and saying that "it would be a pleasure to hear from you," in order that a time might be arranged. This kind of graciousness proved not to be uncharacteristic of Wilbur himself.

We finally met him on a crisp Saturday morning in the beginning of February, and, from the first, he was genuinely friendly and relaxed. When we arrived at his house, he came out to meet us wearing corduroy pants, Clark Treks, and a yellow shirt opened at the collar. Immediately he was talking casually with us. Indeed, it was never really an interview, but rather a pleasant afternoon conversation.

We walked into his house and sat down in the living room, inconspicuously trying to locate an electrical outlet for the tape recorder. He leaned back in his chair and rested his head against the glass of a large picture window, and, with a pipe in his hand and icicles slowly dripping from the roof ledge outside, began to talk freely, with characteristic good humor.

Perhaps his own words, worked out in a Baudelaire translation, describe him better than anything we might think to write: "There, there is nothing else but grace and

measure,/Richness, quietness, and pleasure." From the
first to the last it was our pleasure to talk with Richard
Wilbur.

*Who was the young man who wrote the "Mock Turtle" and what was
he like?*

I guess I did write that column. What was I like then? I think that I
was like most people in my family, a late maturer; so that I came to
Amherst quite gawky, unadjusted and unsmooth. I wasted a lot of my
time trying to adjust in one way or another. My chief strategy, I
suppose, was an attempt to capitalize on my gaucherie by turning it
into a style. (He laughs.) A lot of my classmates now describe me as
having been proto-hippie. But that wasn't it at all. Hippies are herd
animals, and I was making up my squalor for myself. It was not an
invention of which I am proud. I suppose what I am telling you is
that I ran around in horrible clothing, drinking more beer than was
good for me, and leading in general a disorderly existence. I did so
for the first two years, at any rate, of my Amherst life. And I never
reformed altogether.

What teachers do you remember?

Quantities of teachers. I do particularly remember Armour Craig. I
took the first course he ever gave: It was in seventeenth century
prose. It was at 7:50 in the morning, and it kept me more nearly
awake than anything else I could have done at that hour.

7:50?

Yes! It was very taxing. The course was very taxing in a good way,
and so I slept in it very little. I think that Armour Craig was such a
quirky and interesting teacher that he, more than anybody else, gave
me the idea of going on and being a teacher myself.

*You attended Amherst during a very difficult time in our history.
Pearl Harbor was bombed by the Japanese while you were a senior,
and before that, of course, Amherst and many other colleges and
universities actively debated the role the United States should play
vis-a-vis the war in Europe. The editorial pages of the Amherst
STUDENT during your tenure as Chairman took a strong isolationist
stand toward the War before December 7, 1942. The Williams
RECORD, on the other hand, was staunchly anti-isolationist, and a*

great deal of friction was generated between you and the Williams editor.

To begin with, what was it like going to classes during that time and how would you describe the atmosphere of the college then?

We weren't terribly distracted, I think, by the fact that the War was going on, because our views and expectations were fairly simple. Some of our classmates volunteered early; some of them were dead before we ever graduated. Regardless of those isolationist editorials I wrote, with which there may have been some student agreement, I suspect that we all felt we were going to get into it, and that it would probably prove on reflection to be a just war. Our consciences were easy about it. We were certainly not inclined to set ourselves up against the state, once war was declared, though as I recall we were all respectful of the few people who decided to be conscientious objectors. They were not, of course, initially objecting to any peculiar injustice of World War II, but to war itself. I think we respected that, even as we trotted off to enlist.

My skirmish with the Williams RECORD was, I'm afraid, a little bit smarty on my part. I think that I believed myself to believe what I was saying, but that I was also playing the boy debater and seeing if a little yellow-journalism sensation couldn't be got out of our quarrel.

I don't think I was a very good Chairman of the STUDENT. There were things I was quite serious about in those days, but what you might call public issues were not the things I took very seriously or brought any great understanding to. I've improved in that respect, but not much. I know, for example, that inflation and recession are very serious matters right now. However, as soon as anybody says either word my eyes begin to grow hooded, my memory evacuates, and I can't think to any purpose. I never could. I couldn't when I was Chairman of the STUDENT, and so my efforts to say something about matters which other people considered serious were often really trivial or simply exercises in verbal facility. An editor can find himself having to do that because he's gone and got himself elected editor. I have just never been good at seeing the world which, to take the very best example, Walter Lippman managed to see for so long, with the kind of survey an essentially political mind has, and with all the inclusions and omissions of such a mind. I quickly tire of the rhetoric of it even from the best, and it's not where my mind, such as it is, can manage to be.

I think probably the editorial I wrote which made the most legitimate stir was one which said then what I believe now: Youth are consistently over-valued in our society. Much too much is expected of people merely because they are young. I believe that the piece was published about the time I was graduating, and I remember that the baccalaureate sermon was preached upon it. And someone else referred to it from another platform during my graduation week. Very heady for me.

Don't you think there is something in that—that too much virtue always is ascribed to college students merely because they haven't done anything very bad? So often during the troubles in the sixties, a kind of high-minded honesty was attributed to college students, which didn't necessarily characterize them. Students were contrasted to their "hypocritical elders," until students began to believe it. Meanwhile a lot of them were rioting, protesting, and making non-negotiable demands in rather bad faith. One can tell this because, now that college students are no longer threatened by service in the Vietnam war, they've ceased to protest it. But American napalm is still being dropped on the same people about whom there was so much indignation a few years ago. The ascription of special virtue to youth was very noticeable during the sixties, but of course it was going on when I was at Amherst too, and my little editorial was an objection to so much hope being reposed in the young. I thought that some hope ought to be reposed in the proven old, and that it ought to be recognized that so much that's considered originality in the young merely consists in the parroting of this or that older person. At any rate, whenever I thought that I was being original as a young man, it seems to me that I was imitating the thought of elders by whom I had been energized, and whom I idealized. There's nothing wrong with that; I think that's the way it works. It's part of everybody's education not merely to respond intellectually to the ideas of his seniors but to become selectively apostolic.

Shortly after you left Amherst, you went into the Army and then later joined the 36th Infantry. Did you really carry a copy of Finnegan's Wake *in your barracks bag all that time?*

Yes, I did. I had *Finnegan's Wake;* I had some of the poems of
Dylan Thomas; I had all of the Poets of the Month published by
James Laughlin at New Directions, and I had a subscription to the
overseas edition of *The New Yorker.* I never threw out any copies. I
also had the poems of Gerard Manley Hopkins, and a volume of
Tennyson, I think, and a paperback of Edgar Allen Poe. I can
remember that during one long week in which I scarcely got out of
my foxhole at Monte Cassino, I read that whole paperback of Poe.
     For the first time I began to have a sense that there was something
besides spookery in Poe, that there might be some kind of allegorical
depth to his fiction. Why did I have such an insight there and then? It
wasn't, I think, because I was scared, though I was. Perhaps it was
because, under circumstances where one did very little save sleep
and wake, one's attention was drawn to all of the semi-states which
lie between full waking and deep slumber. I began to perceive that in
Poe's fiction some effort was being made to represent the stages or
stations of the mind.
     You began to write your first poetry then, when you were—
     Well, I had written poems before. There were a couple of poems of
mine, serious ones, unsigned I think, in the Amherst TOUCHSTONE. I
had written poems, on and off, for the consumption of friends, of my
wife-to-be, of my parents and teachers, for a long time; but I began
to write rather constantly once I got abroad in the service. It was one
of the few things one could do, under what were chiefly boring
circumstances, to keep sane.
     *It must have been more than a question of boredom, though, that
motivated you to write.*
     Yes, I think it was a question of confusion, or a desire to make
order of confusion, to give words to one's fears and uncertainties and
so tame them a little. I've written a few paragraphs about this here or
there, arguing that too serene a condition of life doesn't conduce to
writing poetry. You have to have some experiences of danger,
lostness and mess. The bottom has to fall out of your thoughts
periodically before you feel the need to be clear and orderly in
words. There may be artistic peril in living in such a pleasant house
as this, in such a pleasant part of the country. I must say I have very
little awareness of the sort of unpleasantness that goes on every night

in the streets of Newark, New Jersey. I know that it exists, but I don't come up against it very often and so I don't write about it.

After the War you returned to the U.S. and then went to Harvard, is that correct?

Yes.

Is this when you began your formal work on Poe?

It wasn't long before I did. I was lucky enough to be taken into the Society of Fellows for three years, and during those years I did start to work on Poe as well as a number of other things. I wrote almost an entire book on Poe, and then set it aside because I hadn't yet found the vocabulary with which to describe him.

Did that book stem from the perceptions which you had on Poe during the War?

Yes. However cloudy, those were true intuitions. I had seen that Poe was concerned with states of the psyche, transitions between those states, and the possible meanings and implications that such states might have. I think I had guessed quite early in the game that Poe associated certain kinds of dreaming, especially very abstract dreams not to be explained away in terms of what happened the day before, with visions of the beyond. Such dreams were proof of the soul's previous pure state, and glimpses of the state to which it might pass after this one.

This is very interesting in view of a piece you once wrote called "On My Own Work." There you said that "a good part of my own work could, I suppose, be understood as a public quarrel with the aesthetics of Edgar Allen Poe." Does this still seem true to you?

Yes, I think so. The trouble with Poe's aesthetic is that he's a world-denier, a denier of the body, and a denier of matter. Where he places value, therefore, is in whatever is not earthly, whatever is not material, whatever is not bodily. Unfortunately, these things are very difficult for an artist to indicate, to present to us. I don't think Poe was in any position to offer the reader a vision of the immaterial. So inevitably, therefore, Poe's subject matter became the depicted process of negating this world, and his more exciting techniques are techniques of erasure, of explosion, of uncreation.

I can see the sensational attractiveness of that, and I suppose that is why I have to resist it. I simply cannot finally stomach any kind of idealism or spirituality which is contemptuous toward the body or what we call the material. I'm for bringing the body and the spirit to terms, rather than annulling the body. That's one way of stating my quarrel with Poe. I find myself fascinated with him and opposed to him all down the line.

A kind of anti-self?

Yes. I never really knew until a few years ago whether I thought very much of Poe as an artist. Now I've decided that I think he's rather a junky poet, but that his fiction is exceptional art. It's too bad he lived a life of driven hack-work, because we might have gotten even better prose from him. The language of his stories is, of course, ordinarily a very unnatural language, a very artificial and hopped-up language. But you come to be aware, if you re-read him as much as I have, that every word has been carefully chosen and that there is an intention to mean something precisely, or to affect the reader in a precise way, in almost all of Poe's word choices. That's what I mean when I say he is a good writer.

We would like to talk about your poetry now, but we know from past essays and interviews that you are reluctant to discuss your "body of work." You once said that each of your poems can best be understood as being autonomous in itself. Do you still feel this way?

Yes, I still do feel that way. I know that if I were to play the critic to my own work I would probably come up with some kind of statement as to my basic concerns, and I could probably make some judgments as to which are my best answerings of the basic questions which disturb me. I feel that I could do that for my own poems because I've managed to write some criticism as well as poems, and I have done thematic shakedowns of certain poets like Yeats and Graves. I have come to feel that I understand quite intimately what it is that's eating them and how each of their poems belongs to their lifelong dealing with one or two matters.

But I wouldn't want to be a successful critic of myself, because that would involve too much self-consciousness. I think that writing a poem is a highly conscious business, and awareness of the relation of what you are writing to the body of your work is likely to be too distracting. The poem is likely to be falsified.

I try to put all my attention on the poem I am writing, when I'm writing. Anything else I may have said I try to put out of my mind. Of course this means that I somewhat repeat myself from time to time, but I've noticed all the poets who are worth a damn repeat themselves. Perhaps not verbatim, but they all have their special subjects which they take terribly seriously and can't get away from.

It struck me a few years back, when John Kelleher and I were teaching a course on Yeats at Harvard, that, wildly different as Yeats' late poems may seem from his early ones, he's really saying much the same things over again, and playing the same old tricks, under cover of a change of rhetoric. I think this can be said about almost everybody. Though if challenged to apply it to Auden, I'd be in trouble, I expect. I would have to retire to my cabin and think up a couple of pretty slick sentences for getting out of it. Well, I suppose what I'd do would be to say that "Auden was, for all his playfulness, first and last a very earnest person morally, full of social imperatives. Therefore moving from a concern with political-cultural revolution to a concern with Anglicanism wasn't so great a jump, in view of that fundamental set of his nature." Those sentences are fairly persuasive to me, but I mentioned Auden, of course, because he is not the clearest case of a man responding to the same challenges all through his life. Someone like Wallace Stevens is conspicuously talking about the same thing from the beginning of his life to the end. At the beginning of his poetic life he finds himself rhyming at times and writing in regular meters. He also finds himself attracted to the Baroque grammar of Milton, maybe, or the sonorities of Tennyson. After *Harmonium* the technique greatly relaxes, and Stevens operates much of the time, as somebody said, on "a reminiscence of the pentameter." Nevertheless, from the very beginning he's talking with noble inconclusiveness about the commerce of the imagination with the world. I think he changes considerably less in the course of his life's work than somebody like Auden.

Frost, I think, first and last has the same concerns, even though there are a few surprises in his very last work, *In the Clearing*.

What are your concerns?

Well, I shy away from saying. I think what we were just discussing about me and my anti-self, Edgar Allan Poe, is fairly close to it. There must be other things I think about, but I know that I keep coming back to a feeling that the impulse of the spirit or soul to refine itself too far, to escape too well, must be resisted. As one of my poems says, in effect, the angels have got to come down and dwell among us, be useful to us. I don't suppose I would like to codify myself into a theology. There's probably not a sensible one to be got out of my poems.

I don't think that I finally object at all to the idea of hierarchy: it seems to me that some things are higher and purer than others. I suppose what worries me about Edgar Allan Poe is what worried Allen Tate about him. Allen Tate wrote a nice essay on Dante's imagination versus Poe's imagination, in which he points out that Dante proceeds towards the invisible always through the visible. He proceeds without any slighting of the sensible, and approaches the transcendent through the order of nature. Poe, however, tends to destroy the objects of nature. He destroys all that is not transcendent on his way to a kind of invisible communion with the supernal. It doesn't seem to me a very trustworthy program, and of course it's a version of spirituality which is absolutely stripped of human emotion and of concern for earthly order or moral good.

Even though you ultimately come to reject Poe, there must be some kind of deep attraction to him or you would not have been able to sustain your interest in him for so long. Does this attraction ever find expression in your poetry?

I think so. I don't know that I have ever been able to bring myself purely to express that in me which tempts me toward Edgar Poe or which tempts me toward the kind of mysticism which I finally dis-approve of, but I have in recent years written more and more poems in which voices not my own are allowed to have their say. When you start doing that, what you're really doing of course is allowing parts of yourself which ordinarily are put down, which lose out in inner symposia, to speak for a bit. I'm sure that in psychology, as in other fields, there is a kind of identity or at least complimentarity allowed of opposites. What you feel opposed to is what you in heart belong to or are most tempted toward.

Could you tell us a little about your habits of writing?

It all depends on what I'm writing. If it's poems, I haven't any discipline about that at all. I try to fight free of busy work. I try to get away from unsatisfying work I need not do, or to get away from the sort of work we do in order to feel temporarily comfortable: cleaning up one's study and that kind of thing. You can spend your life sharpening your pencils and saying, "There now." I try not to do too much of that, and I try not to spend too much time on correspondence, so that if a poem wants to report to me, I'll be able to say "at ease."

If it's something like a job of scholarship, of editing, or of criticism, then I work on it as anybody else does—as fast as I can, consulting books in the library and doing drafts, a thing I don't do at all in writing poems.

When I'm translating I find that I don't have to be in any special state of mind. I just plug ahead and try to get from line one hundred forty-two to line one hundred forty-six in a day. I'm thinking now of translations of Molière's plays. I've done three of those, and they tend to be about sixteen hundred to eighteen hundred lines long. One clearly can't translate so many French Alexandrines into English rhymed couplets in a state of continual inspiraton. I hope to do four, six, eight decent lines in a day.

But with poetry, I suppose that I really do fit the Romantic stereotype. It's not that I like to compose while sitting on a rock in a high wind with an eagle hovering above me, but I do mean to say that I won't force myself to knock out verses. I guess the most unromantic thing about the way I write poetry is that I'll make myself sit in a chair for six hours straight and not do anything else. I may not come up with a line, I may not come up with a word, but I can be patient. I've never been able to give myself orders to report to that silo at eight in the morning and write 'til twelve. A novelist can do that, I think, with good results. I really don't think a poet can; I can't.

You've done several major verse translations of Molière now and you've also translated quite a few shorter poems from several different languages. When do you work on them?

I do them whenever I've overcome my fatigue from doing the last one, because they take so long. It's a joy but a real drudgery too. It's a hell of a thing to spend a whole day of one's short life getting two lines of Molière, two lines which aren't even of your own full conceiving. For if you're a good translator, what you've done is bring across his thought. And so one hesitates to embark on a huge project like that yet again. I've done three of those plays now, as I said. There really remains just one which I'm tempted to try, and that is *Les Femmes Savantes*. I guess we translate that as "The Learned Ladies," usually. One reason I'm tempted to try it is because it's hard to figure out whether Molière is or is not intolerably unfair and patronizing to women in that late play of his. I looked into it about a year ago and thought "Oh, no." I'm not a women's libber; I'm far from being in the Movement in any sense; but the play's apparent contempt for the desire of women to be educated is offensive to me, and would produce riots in the theaters. And so I thought, let's forget about it. But since then, a few people whose grasp of Molière is better than mine have said they thought I may have read the play a little crudely, and that it might be possible to translate the piece in such a way as to convey something approaching the complexity and balance of the earlier plays.

Aside from personal satisfaction, do you translate from any sense of cultural obligation? That is, do you feel personally obliged to make the literature of another language accessible in your own?

I think so; yes. I don't pretend that my first impulse is benevolence or a feeling of responsibility to the culture, but I'm at all times aware that that's important. I think it's important to have versions of Molière, of Cervantes, of all sorts of things which will make it possible for the common reader, by whom I mean somebody who really is a reader and who is to be respected, to commune with the past in a lively way. Most translations are pretty depressing, I think. So when somebody like Walter Arndt comes along and does Pushkin, we have to be very glad that he's done so. He probably hasn't done so to be nice to us, but there's a very good side effect to it; it's very useful to the culture.

Another aspect of your work involves the writing of children's books, such as Opposites *and* Loudmouse. *Were they originally written for your children?*

(Mrs. Wilbur enters the room.)

No, although I don't think I'd have taken those assignments if I hadn't always told a lot of stories to my children. For awhile there, there were three of our children who, though not terribly close together in age, were all interested in being told a story at night. It used to be something to work all day at Wesleyan and then come home to "Hello, Daddy, can we have a story?" I would have to lie down on the couch in the living room and think for about half an hour. Then I'd say "All right" and tell the story, which would take another half hour. And then I was really ready for the evening's cocktail. Many of these stories took the form of sagas. My character Loudmouse was really a figure in twenty or thirty stories, I expect.

Mrs. Wilbur: Are you sure?

Mr. Wilbur: Yes, he appeared in a number of stories—

Mrs. Wilbur: That you told the children?

Mr. Wilbur: Yes.

Mrs. Wilbur: Well, I never heard of that before in my life.

Mr. Wilbur: Well, you were out of the room during those sessions. You were getting dinner or something.

Mrs. Wilbur: I used to listen to your stories, and you always told them after dinner.

Mr. Wilbur: Is that right?

Mrs. Wilbur: I'd better get out of here . . . goodbye.

Mr. Wilbur: I told them after dinner?

Mrs. Wilbur: Always. (exit)

All right. Then we'll have to correct the order of things. The drink came before dinner, which came before the stories . . . What an awful memory I have.

Seriously, I did tell a fair number of stories in which the figure of Loudmouse appeared. I had, over a period of years, a lot of training in telling stories to children and finding out what pleases them; violence being a large part of it. And so I responded when Louis Untermeyer asked me to write a children's book for a series he was creating for Collier books. I think it was called "Modern Masters Books for Children," or something like that.

You once wrote an essay in which you used the metaphor of a genie in a bottle to describe poetry, your poetry, that conforms to strict verse rules. We were wondering what goes through your mind when you read poets such as Ginsberg and Olson? Poets who choose not to use the "bottle."

Yes. Well, I like a lot of people who do not use the bottle. I think the form of Walt Whitman, for example, is completely adequate for his purposes. I'm very glad he didn't give us more "O Captain! My Captain!" I don't think he could have given us what he had to give in anything but that cadenced and incantatory near-prose that he uses. Rhythmically its character is strong enough, when Whitman is at his best, to be a delight when read aloud. I find that the swells and emphases come at the right places, and so there's nothing really to complain about.

I also haven't anything to complain of in the poetry of William Carlos Williams. I guess what I'm getting around to saying, in my sneaky way, is that Whitman, in whose name so much ill has been done, is himself (in "Song of Myself" for example) a highly disciplined writer with wonderful, accurate, operatic enthusiasms geared for rhythm and sound. Dr. Williams is a highly disciplined writer who can be figured out as normative in terms of the number of stresses per line. His self-discipline can be sensed by any reader, whether he chooses to count it out or not.

Slovenly free verse, it seems to me, is not enough of a bottle—and there's a great deal of it nowadays. There's a great deal of stuff offered to us as poetry that does not have the discipline of a Baudelaire prose poem. I suppose I do feel that in such cases the language is insufficiently honed and heightened to be called poetic. Poetic language, however simple, must have a special kind of a charge on it. Word for word, it does more work than the words of prose.

I don't try to get my students at Wesleyan to write in formal patterns, or count their syllables, or anything like that. I do, on the first day of our meeting, remind them that such things exist. And I find that, more and more, nobody needs to be reminded. It's interesting; in the last couple of years there's been a spontaneous revival of playful interest in poetic forms among my students, not prompted by me at all. They come into class that way. It makes for more failures, of course, but it also makes for a better spirit of play in the writing. It makes too for successes from which I can take more enjoyment.

Mr. Wilbur, we ask your indulgence for the remainder of the interview. We have a series of what we call "pot luck" questions. Some of these have nothing to do with anything remotely literary, but you see, that's the idea. You may respond as briefly as you wish to any question, or indeed not respond at all.

The first one goes like this—If you were ruler of the world, what book would you have everyone read?

That's very tough. I think it would have to be a book that has proven to further cultural cohesion. Ezra Pound would say Confucius, perhaps, but I think I would prescribe the *Book of Common Prayer.*

You certainly have met a great many people who would generally be considered prominent. Have you ever met anyone whom you thought to be truly great?

Yes, I think I've met a number. Some of the great are not prominent, of course, but very obscure. However, speaking at random, I should say that I found the quality of greatness in I. A. Richards, under whom I worked for awhile at Harvard. This greatness seemed to me to lie not necessarily in his ideas, or in any system of ideas he had come up with, but in the extraordinary verve and adventurousness of his mind. You had a perfect uncertainty as to where he would go next. He had an absolute readiness to take on whatever problematical thing arose in his path. Richards' great delight is mountain climbing, and the operations of his mind have the same type of daring that you associate with that sport.

What do you think of Amherst's decision to go coed?

I'm not bloody-minded about it. I'm not violently partisan; but I was opposed to it. The decision, it seemed to me, was made at the end of a sorry decade in which there had been a great deal of mob activity, not only on the part of students, but also on the part of caved-in administrators and faculty members hungry for popularity. I was happy that Amherst had got through the ugliness of the sixties as handsomely as it did. It seems to me that the people at Amherst had behaved rather sensibly. I was sorry to see them decide, just as things were quieting down, to do something so trendy as to become coeducational. I realize that there are advantages to it, especially for the shy young man. (Smile.) I think the presence of women anywhere is civilizing. Yet it strikes me that Amherst, which was getting along pretty well without the change, has lost an opportunity to be distinctive, has lost an opportunity for a kind of continuity which is rare in our society.

We'd like to sound you out on liberal arts curriculum. At the present time Amherst College is considering reinstituting some kind of core curriculum. What educational advice do you give your students at Wesleyan? Were you facetious when you said before that all undergraduates should be made to take Latin for four years?

I really do mean that. I think that Wesleyan is now moving back—at any rate, our English department is now moving back—toward requiring more courses. That's a natural reflex from the sort of foolishness we were doing six or seven years ago, when we were allowing our students to think up courses on their own and teach them to each other for credit. I think we've become more and more aware at Wesleyan—though some of our students, given their heads, have thought up marvelous curricula for themselves—that the majority of people are not ready to do that. One of my best English majors of a few years ago, in his senior year, was of the opinion that Coleridge was a twentieth century author. I think we had failed him in some way if he really thought so. I'm for increasing the requirements, especially in the first and second years, so that we can be sure that students will have had a look at some of the texts which most people would consider to be fundamental.

I'm strongly for demanding language study, because speaking as a person of fifty-odd whose command of languages is unsatisfactory, I wish the whip had been laid on me when I was younger, when my mind was better able to learn languages than it is now.

Let me add just one more thing here. I think my fundamental position on all this is that universities and colleges ought to be very flexible whenever sensible, original programs of study are proposed to them by students. If the student works up his own program and it makes some kind of sense, then I think he ought to be allowed to take it. But I'd like to leave the initiative with the student. For the majority I think a "normal" program is called for, one which it will take ingenuity and imagination to violate.

If you could choose, what poem in all of literature would you like to have written.

Short poem or long poem?

You have your choice.

Well, obviously I'd want to have written the *Divine Comedy.*

That's not fair, we didn't mean that long.

All right, but I was being quite sincere. I have enough Italian so that I can read the original with fair competence, using a dictionary, and I should like enormously to have written the *Divine Comedy.* On the other hand, if you want me to talk sense, I should like to have written "Lycidas." And then there's Tennyson's "Ulysses." I think that's a fine poem. And there are poems of Campion's, poems of Marvell's. There are a few poems of Robert Frost's which I would like to have written . . . Small and perfect lyrics like "Spring Pools" . . . Oh heavens, there are lots I wish I had written.

Do you go to church at all?

Yes.

When you pray, whom do you pray to?

Oh boy, I wish I had an easy answer for that. I think I waver between praying to a better self, to a better version of myself, and waiting to hear from something that is altogether not me.

In other words, I waver between the Emersonian and the strictly Christian in my behavior. When I get a clear message from something absolutely other, I'll let you know.

How would you like to be remembered one hundred years from now?

Well, I don't care about being remembered personally. I think— simply because I put so much sweat into those Molière translations— that I'd like people in the theater to be turning to them still for purposes of production, now and then.

I should like to be thought of as someone who wrote two or three poems which, as Robert Frost said, have been "hard to get rid of."

Mr. Wilbur, thank you for a very pleasant afternoon.

A Conversation with Richard Wilbur
Edwin Honig/1976

From *Modern Language Notes,* Vol. 91 (October 1976), 1084-98. Reprinted by permission of The Johns Hopkins University Press.

October 15, 1975 in Middletown, Connecticut.

EH: I was reading the introduction to your translations of *The Misanthrope* and *Tartuffe,* and I noticed you said about the necessity of using the couplet that *The Misanthrope* required it because the work is so epigrammatic, although *Tartuffe* is less so.

RW: Yes. I think there are fewer moments of deliberate wit in *Tartuffe,* and so the requirement that one keep rhyme and meter for the sake of epigrammatic snap is a little less. Still, there's a good deal of that quality in anything that Molière wrote, so I wouldn't think of putting any of his verse plays into prose.

EH: Even though he was not a poet outside of the plays?

RW: Very little, I think. He did (I believe) write a number of lyrics and some little verses, but no, he wasn't really a poet outside of the plays, and inside the poetic plays he's a very prosaic poet in many respects. I guess I said in one of the introductions that, by contrast to someone like Racine, he's almost free of figurative language; he also doesn't use key words, thematic words, in the vigorous way that Racine does, although some mistaken critic, I suppose, might want to argue about that with me. In any case, it makes Molière much easier to translate than Racine would be, not merely because he's comedy (and somehow rhyme consorts more readily with comedy than with tragedy) but also because you don't have to wrestle with difficult figures and key words quite so much.

EH: There are many interesting things about those translations that I would like to come back to a little later. Meanwhile, may I ask what your original contact with the idea of translation was? That is, how you conceived of it when you started. Not necessarily with Molière, but earlier. I know you did other things earlier.

162

RW: I think my first experience with translation was when André du Bouchet, who's now a rather well-established French poet, and I were fellow graduate students at Harvard. I had picked up enough French from basic courses, and reading, and being in France during World War II, so that I felt able to make a start on most French poems. So I would sit around with André, trying to translate his poems into English, and he sat around trying to translate mine into French. And it was a nice way to begin one's career as a translator. Not that I did anything that was any good, but knowing André I was able to begin the translation of any one of his poems with a sense that I knew his tones of voice and his preoccupations.

EH: What you say immediately strikes a chord because now, almost every time I've spoken with a poet who's translated there has been an experience of working with someone at the beginning, whether a friend or an inciting informant. In the case of Ben Belitt, who began with Wallace Fowlie, the challenge was to please his informant who was interested in the early modern poets—Rimbaud particularly—who hadn't been translated very well. So that the relationship was the immediate instigation not only to do the translations but also to do them very well.

RW: I suppose that, Fowlie being a translator of the French himself, they must have been vying a little bit. They were having a *concours,* weren't they?

EH: Well, I don't know what the circumstances were. I had the impression that Fowlie wanted verse translations which stood up on their own. Whether he had done Rimbaud in verse or prose, I don't know. Later on Belitt worked on other poets, but in this connection he got to know some of them personally. This was the stimulus for him to do Neruda, for example.

RW: He got to know Neruda personally? Yes, I think that's terribly important. I couldn't imagine beginning to translate anybody living or dead without at least having the illusion of some kind of personal understanding—some understanding of the range of his feelings beyond the particular work. That's hard, of course, in the case of someone like Du Bellay, one of whose poems I recently translated. But even in his case I did develop an adequate sense of background and of the emotional set in which the poem was made.

EH: Does that mean that you almost always translate from poets you have a sense of identity with?

RW: Yes, I think so. I suspect I have to like the poem pretty well in the first place. This keeps me, I think, from being a professional translator—doing things wholesale. I have to like the poem and feel it has something to do with my feelings—that I understand the feelings which went into it. Perhaps, also, I like it and am particularly well motivated when I feel the poem represents, as it were, an extension or stretching of my own emotional possibilities.

EH: You emphasize something which Belitt also suggested as a prime motivation for doing the poem—pleasure, pleasure in doing it, rather than gain, but gain as it might happen through pleasure.

RW: Monetary gain is always unexpected, I suppose, in the translation business, though I imagine it's better paid now than it used to be, isn't it?

EH: I don't know.

RW: But you don't think of pay . . . at any rate, someone like me who translates individual poems by different people out of various languages is obviously not proceeding in a businesslike manner. I'm just responding to things which catch my eye or which have been brought to my attention. Sometimes people who have a feeling for what I'm like, or what my work is like, are fairly accurate about prescribing what I should attempt. For example, Simon Karlinsky wrote me a while back about doing a number of poems by the exiled Russian poet Nikolai Morshen, since he saw some affinities between Morshen and me. And as soon as the poems arrived I saw those affinities too; Karlinsky is a very good finger man. I found Max Hayward to be similarly gifted in matching the translator to the poem. The Voznesensky poems which he and Pat Blake once picked out for me to do were pretty much the right ones.

EH: I see. Well, that goes along with other incidents of the same kind I know about. I want to go back now to your beginnings as a translator. Your first experience translating had to do with the poems of a friend, the French poet, du Bouchet. Then, after that, what happened?

RW: I think my early efforts at translation had largely to do with the French, because that was the only foreign language of which I possessed anything; though of that I had a very faulty knowledge, and still do.

EH: It was school French?

RW: School French fortified by the French which a soldier picks up during a war experience. I remember translating some little poems of Villiers de l'Isle-Adam, an author to whom du Bouchet had directed my attention. I had an anthology of great old chestnuts of the French tradition, and found in it an ode of La Fontaine's which appealed to me a good deal and . . .

EH: You just picked these out, as you were looking through.

RW: . . . just picked them out. As they say—they grabbed me. Having done La Fontaine's "Ode to Pleasure," I asked Harry Levin to see if I'd gotten the words right. He kindly helped me as he had helped Marianne Moore . . . or perhaps was to help; I forget at what time he began to help her with her French translations. He was always generous with that kind of aid. I tried to do a little Catullus around about 1949 or so, but I had no luck with it. I can't stand the mincing and evasive translations of his tougher poems that one has in the Loeb Library; at the same time I couldn't find a way to be nasty in a language which was poetically effective.

EH: Why did you want to translate Catullus?

RW: I'd always been fascinated by particular tones of his. He does not seem to me to be a terribly broad sensibility, but a great deal of personality transpires from his poetry as it does, say, from Villon— another example of a person who is not very broad but is very strong.

EH: Yes, Villon and Catullus together would make a very strong *team.* Then the kind of interest you developed in translation came from similar desultory lookings into books and advice from people who wrote you or asked you to do it.

RW: Well, the askings came later after I'd done a certain number of poems, more or less by accident. That is, through falling in love with them myself or through having someone say, Have a look at this. I suppose I began to be invited to do poems in translation after I had done *The Misanthrope* translation, which was published in 1955. People began to think of me as an available translator—someone who, with a little linguistic aid, might do things out of languages he didn't know.

EH: So that was the first significant translation you did.

RW: Yes. There are translations sprinkled through my second book, *Ceremony,* and my third book, *Things of This World.* But there aren't too many of them, really. I suppose I began to be thought of as a laborer in that vineyard when *The Misanthrope* came out . . . I must qualify that. I do remember now that when I was living out in the town of Corrales, New Mexico, which we both know so well, Jackson Mathews wrote me and said he was putting together for New Directions a collection of *The Flowers of Evil* of Baudelaire, and that he wasn't quite satisfied with the existing versions of the great chestnut poems, the "Invitation to the Voyage," "Correspondences," and "The Albatross." He asked me to try them. So I tried them. That was 1952.

EH: Did you feel that you had *done* the job—that is, was he satisfied with them?

RW: He was satisfied with them, though I remember Jack saying that my reaching for a rhyme in the "Correspondences" poem had obliged me to refer to a "child's caress" in a way that would have offended Baudelaire's fastidiousness. But he liked them all right and used them in that anthology. And I was satisfied with "L'Invitation au Voyage." Though I thought, "Of course, it's a failure," I thought that it was a less ludicrous failure than the attempts of others.

EH: Yes, one has to measure one's success by the failures of others, even of one's own. One of the things which interest me (and I think you fit this description) is the way a very scrupulous translator who has a strong poetic voice of his own (I'm only speaking of the translation of poetry here) cannot escape merging his voice with that of the poet he is translating. What do you feel? Do you deliberately try to suppress your own style in translating?

RW: I think that I do try to avoid putting into anyone else's poem, as I bring it across into English, mannerisms of my own, and I certainly try to efface myself as much as possible. I shouldn't like to seem to be demonstrating that Voznesensky could write like Wilbur if he'd only try. What I say to myself—not too dishonestly, I hope—is that I'm putting whatever abilities I have at the service of the person I'm translating, and that because I feel some kind of affinity with him, or at least with the particular work I'm rendering, I *can* use such words as readily come to me without imposing myself on the work. I can give an example of this. I can contrast myself with Ezra Pound in this respect. Ezra Pound translated Voltaire's poem to Madame du Châtelet, turning it into a kind of imagistic prose poem. Some of the effects are quite brilliant and charming. He takes everything that is abstract and makes it concrete. When there's a reference to love, for example, capitalized love (and Voltaire is really thinking of statues of Eros in a garden), Pound puts lovers on the grass.

EH: Where they belong.

RW: Yes. I translated the same poem, trying—without using antique language, without sounding eighteenth-century—to transmit it purely, both regarding the language and regarding the form. I discovered in the process that he kept shifting his rhyme pattern in the quatrain he was using, and where he was unfaithful to his own precedent I followed him; even went that far. Faithful to his infidelities.

EH: You were conscious of Pound's translation when doing yours.

RW: I had seen it, but it was so different an effort from mine that it couldn't possibly have influenced me. At the same time I wasn't writing a rebuke to Pound—he was doing an Imagist exercise upon the basis of a Voltaire poem.

EH: Yes.

RW: I was trying to persuade myself that I was bringing the poem alive into English with no additions of my own. I know that any such belief is an illusion, but the pursuit of the illusion can bring one closer to the fact, I think. I know that when I first tried to do some poems from the Spanish, which I don't really understand—I'm particularly prone to error when I'm doing Spanish, because I know some Italian and get betrayed by cognates. What was I saying? I once tried some poems of Jorge Guillén, and though of course I had some linguistic assistance, I still managed to make blunders. When I found that I had made mistakes, I did my best to iron them out, in the light of criticism. But when the first Guillén translation was published I can remember friends saying, That's a nice Wilbur poem, strongly influenced by Jorge Guillén. I had no such sense of it, and was distressed.

EH: It might be that when you translate a contemporary this is more likely to happen. Perhaps when you translate du Bellay or Voltaire, where the language is not contemporary, the effect is different. But I wanted to ask you, in connection with what you said about Pound regarding his translation as an exercise in imagist writing, do you regard individual translations of single poems as exercises of a sort? I don't mean translations of plays now.

RW: I find that I feel a kind of abhorrence for the word "exercise," even though in teaching poetry I ask my students, if they feel like it, to do this or that kind of exercise which I propose. No, I have a feeling that though I am not writing a poem of my own, I am not merely lubricating my muscles, as it were, when I bring somebody else's poem into English. I feel as though I were doing something complete, the purpose of which lies within itself.

EH: You don't feel that sense of substitution for doing your own work that Lowell talks about in his apologia for his *Imitations.*

RW: One or two things I've said have betrayed an awareness that I'm drawn to a poem because it's partly me and partly not me. Because to write it in English will seem to extend me emotionally. In that sense I have a personal interest in what is being done, and I am in that sense writing another poem of my own. Since I am following as carefully as I can the thoughts and feelings of someone close yet different, it's very likely going to have consequences for the next poem I write.

EH: You sense that?

RW: Yes.

EH: As you're working or afterwards?

RW: Oh, afterwards. I don't think that I would ever undertake a job of translation out of an expectation of what it would do for me as a writer, or for the purpose of keeping my hand in. But I do know, in retrospect, that by Englishing 1,800 lines of a Molière play I've doomed myself for some months thereafter to cast my thoughts in couplets—at least initially. For better or worse, ideas propose themselves in couplets for quite a while after I've done such a job.

EH: Well, this then is a kind of fate—after translation. Working off a high. I spoke to John Hollander about his experiences as a translator and he mentioned the Yiddish poets with whom he had to work. Because he didn't actually know Yiddish, he had to learn some and check with Irving Howe, on a poet of Russian origin named Halpern. He said this was a very significant experience for him because in doing the work he found he was able to extend his voice in such way that after doing Halpern his own work changed— expanded in its possibilities, I take it.

RW: I'm sure it's that way. Think of it on the children's playground level, where some little classmate says to you, I dare you to say such and such a forbidden word, and you say it at once. At *his* urging. You're more capable of saying it on your own impulse thereafter.

EH: So there is an extension and expansion, at least potentially, in one's work as a translator. It isn't only that one does it for pleasure, but the pleasure is really the potentiality of growing in one's own work.

RW: Though I think, speaking for myself, that I would always hide any such motive from myself in the process of writing, I know that it's one of the rewards of translating.

EH: Very good. I'm very interested in that. I think we should go back to the Molière plays. You did three of them.

RW: Yes, and I'm now working on a fourth. I didn't think I was going to do four, but I've gotten drawn into *Les Femmes Savantes,* and am now approaching the end of the first act. So I suppose I'll go on to the end.

EH: Are you doing this one in the same way you did the others?

RW: Yes, and of course by now it does go faster. I know how to do it, much more surely than when I began with *The Misanthrope,* around 1952. At the same time, there are a few obstacles which arise when one is doing a fourth Molière play. Though Molière shamelessly reproduced his own rhymes and situations, I feel hesitant to use once again the same rhymes by which I solved the couplets of the other three plays I have done. That's silly, but I nevertheless feel it.

EH: Are only certain rhymes possible or ideally any number of them?

RW: Given a coercive text which wants you to reproduce it as exactly as possible, and given what amount to repeated vaudeville situations, one finds that the poverty of rhyme in English becomes painful; and even though Molière has, in dealing with the same comic situations, used the same words, I find myself wishing that in my own role I didn't have to. That lengthens the task.

EH: It's a fine psychological matter. I wonder if it has to do with your being a modern poet who doesn't like to repeat himself . . .

RW: I think that's it.

EH: . . . or whether it has to do with your not being essentially a professional playwright, in the way Molière was, who would know the value of stock and type things at work in theatre.

RW: I'm sure that both of those things would be true. I expect that most poets who choose to rhyme, nowadays, are troubled about using easy rhymes and are embarrassed about using their own rhymes more than once.

EH: Yes.

RW: It extends also, I suppose, to the whole vocabulary. I can remember Dick Eberhart saying to me once about a poem of mine which satisfied me very much, "You've used that word before!"

EH: Oh, God. Like a member of the family who knows all your bad habits.

RW: Yes.

EH: Well, rhyme is the essence of your translations of Molière. In some ways it's what makes for the dramatic element as well as keeps the poetry going. I'm not sure I'm able to explain what I mean when I say, "It makes for the dramatic element," because one would think that rhyme would *stop* dramatic happening or would be an artifice that was too transparent.

RW: I think the transparency and prosaic quality of so much of the language keeps the rhyme from seeming too artificial. And also, the flow of Molière's speech, his tendency not to close every couplet, makes it possible for rhyme to attain its chief effect as provider of poetic emphasis. And also as a sign of the stages of an argument: one of the things I've noticed is that, in the very best prose translations of these verse plays of Molière, the long speeches seem infinitely too long. That is because the steps and the stages are not in the prose demarcated by measures and rhymes.

EH: He has a number of long speeches.

RW: Lots of *tirades,* yes.

EH: I suppose that one of the things that strikes an English reader about rhyme in verse plays, where our tradition is unrhymed iambic pentameter, is the fact that in other traditions one can get so much out of a simple and very basic kind of rhyme—I mean in foreign language plays. In Spanish, for example, almost any playwright writing in Molière's time would be engaged in doing a play where there are about eight or ten different verse forms possible, and each used formulaically according to the kind of emotion or the kind of situation, usually quite stock, that is being prepared.

RW: So there would be a rough analogy to grand opera.

EH: Yes. But of course it's impossible to reproduce in translation, though it's been attempted in the nineteenth century. That kind of variety . . . one would expect to find a greater variety in such drama, just as, I suppose, one wonders that a musical tune, a complicated one, can be played on a simple stringed instrument, which may have only one string, like the *gusle,* say. There must be something there having to do with the way the form is traditionally manoeuvered.

RW: You mean that the couplet, as Molière uses it, must be a very supple form.

EH: Yes.

RW: I think it is. As he uses it, very often he will produce the equivalent of an aria. Then there will be the long speeches, recognizable as *tirades;* very often there will be stichomythia, the trading-off of couplets or of individual lines; then often there will be patterns in which people will exchange speeches of six lines in length. Very often when there is a six-line speech, it will break down into three couplets paralleling each other, repeating the thought in very much the way that the divisions of the sonnet often do. And, of course, many Molière plays break briefly into prose. A letter, for example, will be in prose.

EH: So you're pointing to the ways in which the standard couplet could be made various enough to accommodate certain changes.

RW: There are, additionally, songs and poems produced by the characters of the plays. M. Trissotin produces a horrible poem in *The Learned Ladies.*

EH: You chose to translate all four plays. You were not assigned to them.

RW: No. I got the idea of doing *The Misanthrope* from having seen it done by the Comédie Française in 1948, and from having associations with The Poets Theatre in Cambridge, and from applying to the Guggenheims for an award which would enable me to write a poetic play. I did try to write one in New Mexico, but had no luck. It occurred to me that translating *The Misanthrope* would be a good thing to do in itself, and might teach me something about poetry in the theatre. I don't think that I had any thoughts of performance when I started out. I was simply producing, I hoped, a finished reading version. And I was rather surprised, when The Poets Theatre did it in 1955, to find how satisfactorily it worked on the stage, since I had practically no experience in the theatre and didn't know how to write for actors. I know that my later translations of Molière are better paced and articulated for the voices of actors and actresses than *The Misanthrope* is.

EH: So that after having stumbled on a way to make voices viable in translation, you found yourself listening to what you were doing with that consciousness, knowing that the work would be performed.

RW: Yes, as soon as The Poets Theatre started producing *The Misanthrope*—and then afterwards, when it was done in New York and began to be done in other places—I found myself hanging around the theatre listening to people wrestling with what I'd written.

EH: And then discovering surprising things, no doubt.

RW: Yes, finding in some cases that I'd wrought better than I knew, and in some cases that I'd produced conjunctions of sounds which were difficult to articulate—or had, in choosing between two possible renderings of a line, taken the less dramatic way. Now I always say the lines aloud and imagine the thing in production.

EH: You think that has changed the way you write?

RW: Yes.

EH: So that in some ways you've become a dramatist despite yourself.

RW: Yes. And then, of course, all of this has had an effect upon my own poetry, which in a very general sense of the word has become more dramatic.

EH: The feeling you have about the writing of your own poetry is not a stable thing—it's modified all the time by the things you want to put into it, ways you want to get them into the poetry. And translation is an avenue that's always open in some way to provide you with certain alternatives to the ways you'd been writing before. Or is that putting it too . . .

RW: Yes. It proves to be so. At the same time, as I've said, I'd never consciously use translation, as a means to something else.

EH: Well, there's more to what one does than just producing something that works, isn't there? Some views of the translator and his product have it that all that counts is not any theory at all or even whether the translator knows the language he's translating out of. All that matters is whether it works or not, and I have a feeling that's too blunt a view of what really is involved.

RW: I couldn't possibly translate if I thought—what may well be true of one or two of my efforts—that the product was justified merely by its *working*. It has to work in a faithful way. There wouldn't otherwise seem to me to be any reason not to have written one's own poem, and there wouldn't seem to me any reason to put the name of the victimized author of the original text on the translation.

EH: I know you've written about this in an issue of *Translation 2,* the periodical published at Columbia, but I don't recall if you said anything there about this aspect of the subject. Poets who have translated and then have themselves been subjected to translation by others, must face a unique double process of transformation. I wonder if your feelings match those of other poets I've spoken to— that the translator should produce not a slavish imitation of the work but a readable poem in his own language, based on your work.

RW: Well, I think there must come moments in the most faithfully intended translation when you have a choice between reproducing what is apparently, in the dictionary sense of the term, the exact meaning of the original, and falling below the aesthetic level of the rest, or providing what seems to you a close equivalent. I think that I would always go for the close equivalent in such a case. I like something that Jack Mathews once said, when he was speaking well of my translation of *Tartuffe*. Instead of describing it as word-for-word faithful, he said that it was thought-for-thought faithful. Now if you propose to be thought-for-thought faithful, which means not leaving out any of the thoughts of the original, you can chuck particular words which don't have handsome equivalents in you own language.

EH: Well, it's clear translation can never be word-for-word.

RW: Even when one is translating Molière, who really *is* close to us. There are a lot of things in the English and American traditions through which you can reach out to Molière, and you can put him into a form which is oddly familiar to us, even though rhymed drama isn't part of our recent tradition.

EH: How do you feel about translating from languages you don't know, like Russian, Spanish, and Hungarian? I mean, if you have a view that you must be more faithful than not to the original text, then you must have to trust to the fact that your informant in the language you don't know, is faithful.

RW: Well, for one thing, I always get a lot of information out of my informant. I spent, oh, a couple of days sitting and drinking scotch

with Max Hayward while we talked over three poems only of
Voznesensky's. He read over the poems to me in Russian, and he
gave me, with admirable restraint, strictly prosaic translations of them,
not pushing me toward one or another word choice, and I asked him
questions about the appropriateness of the meters to the subject, and
I asked questions about the individual Russian words—what their
flavors were, whether they were high or low—that sort of thing. I took
notes all the time about what he told me. By the time I was through, I
really had done about as much thinking (though not in the same
order) as I would do in producing a poem of my own. About as
much thinking, or researching, or recognizing, or questioning. I've
just translated two poems from Hungarian, using literal versions sent
me by the editors of the *New Hungarian Quarterly,* to which were
appended comments on the characters and tones of the poems, and
which were accompanied also by the originals. I would never try to
translate anything without the original there—even where I do not
understand the language. Looking at the originals of these Hungarian
poems, I was able to catch something of their rhythm. I recognized
certain words, and so drew closer, or felt I was drawing closer, to the
poem themselves. And I've done the same with Spanish. Of course,
Spanish is not so forbidding a language to someone who has French
or Italian, as Hungarian would be. Yet I have asked an intolerable lot
of questions of the people who were helping me with Spanish. In the
case of Russian, I've boned up in a kind of elementary way on the
language, so that at least I have leapt the hedge of the Cyrillic
alphabet and can sound the lines to myself.

EH: Do you get much from sound in Russian? Does it help in any
way?

RW: A good deal. And it helps me a good deal that I've heard
many people declaim Russian poetry.

EH: Do you think if English were declaimed, in the way that
Russian conventionally is declaimed, that would similarly affect, let's
say some hypothetical translator of Poe?

RW: It has to be Poe, doesn't it?

EH: Well, maybe Vachel Lindsay would do.

RW: Maybe Vachel Lindsay, Sidney Lanier's "Marshes of Glynn,"
maybe certain English poems. Some of Dowson or Yeats might do
well if translated by someone accustomed to the declamatory.

EH: I recall a reading where Voznesensky had worked up a way, which is very familiar now to his audiences here, of declaiming his poems, perhaps starting with a translation in English from a reader who accompanied him on the podium, then waving the translator away at the last poem, and saying, "You aren't necessary now," and then speaking that poem about the bells so the sounds came through on their own in the best unadulterated Russian manner. Which brings up a question about the degree of one's knowledge of, or fluency in, a foreign language. If one knows, say, French well, it's still not knowing it as well as any native knows it, even if he's bilingual, as Nabokov is, or Beckett, or Borges. What is so utterly familiar to him, especially if he's a writer, seems to channel itself into one place, which is what he can get out of it as a literary trove, rather than the idiom as it flows and flows ordinarily, when one is native to the language. I'm not sure this is clear. What I'm trying to say is that perhaps there isn't finally a knowledge of a language satisfactory enough to any translator so that he can always feel certain that he knows the right thing to know.

RW: I'm sure that's true. I rather suspect that if there's an exception to your rule it would be Nabokov.

EH: Perhaps so.

RW: I remember a sentence or so in a letter of Ezra Pound's to Iris Barry. He tells her that for purposes of translation, you don't have to know all those languages. You only have to know the words in the best poems in those languages. He's being preposterous, I think. He's probably aware of a certain bravado in what he's saying, and yet there's also a certain truth in it too. He's saying what it is you are in fact likely to be working with when you do a job of translation. I suppose for someone like Borges, who speaks a very easy English, the English of Robert Louis Stevenson is more central than it is for me, say. However good his English is, it's slightly odd—it's connected with, centered in, specific literary enjoyments of his past. My knowledge of any foreign language, even if I worked harder on it than I've ever done, would continue to be so limited—it would continue to be much more literary than that of a native.

EH: One conclusion you could come to, then, about a poet translating from a foreign language is that he is crafting a thing, an object, that becomes a poem, rather than using the language as a means of communication in the usual sense. The poet-translator is creating an object apparently that will stand in place, as say, in the original French, a poem of Baudelaire's does. The communication exists in terms of the object rather than a linguistic exchange inviting an immediate interpersonal response, as in a conversation.

RW: That's right. It's the making of an object rather than the getting of something off one's chest, or of addressing a conjectural audience out there. I think I was confessing as much a few minutes ago when I said that when I translate I am putting such abilities as I have at the service of someone else's poem in another language. Now when I write a poem of my own, I don't think I'm putting my abilities at the service of anything—I don't think that way then. I think in a quite strictly Emersonian way about how a poem of my own comes about. What matters is what I'm saying and the form which the poem takes is simply a part of what I'm saying. If I approach a sonnet, for example of Borges, as I dared to do several times, I have to start with a consciousness that the sonnet form must be *coped* with. I do not *elect* it.

EH: As these things go, the realization is often surprising after one has done the work. Sometimes I wonder if one isn't translating all the time—even in writing one's own poems, in a sense. I don't mean in a general way, from experience and so on, but in using a language that's totally free flowing, the idiomatic English that one speaks, that we're speaking now . . .

RW: Yes.

EH: . . . suddenly becoming something else, transforming itself . . .

RW: Yes, into something more condensed and precise.

EH: Yes.

RW: And then there's the translation from the preverbal. I happen to think, in the teeth of certain philosophers, that there are preverbal thoughts from which we fumblingly begin. Don't we often, well before the "idea" of a poem has begun to clarify, feel an odd certainty about the proportions of what is coming on, about its tenor, savor, stance, or mode—about the channels of logic or feeling in which it is going to run? I think of Yeats' statement that a poem often came to him first as a phrase of music. And there's a passage in Mallarmé somewhere which I may have misunderstood, but which comes to mind, in which the poet senses the awakening of a voice perhaps his own, *"Encore dans les plis jaunes de la pensée."** I wonder if Aristotle, in deriving the formulae of the tragic and other emotions, may not have pointed in the direction of that speech-before-speech I'm talking about. I don't mean, for God's sake, that one makes an unconscious, abstract resolve to write a tragedy or a ballad—subject always comes first. What I mean is that the subject, before we fully know it, seems often to have done a good deal of occult marshalling.

*Again within the yellow folds of thought. *Editor.*

The Art of Poetry: Richard Wilbur

Peter Stitt, Ellessa Clay High, and Helen McCloy Ellison/1977

From *The Paris Review*, 72 (Winter 1977), 68-105. Reprinted by permission of *The Paris Review* and Peter Stitt.

Note: Two interviews were done with Richard Wilbur. Because of the different nature of the questioning, the interviews have been kept separate. The first is by Peter Stitt, the second by Ellessa Clay High and Helen McCloy Ellison.

This interview took place at Richard Wilbur's home in the Berkshire Mountains near Cummington, Massachusetts, on a Saturday afternoon in March of 1977. Mr. Wilbur's house sits on a hillside surrounded by New England hill-country farms; there are no wheatfields, but plenty of trees and dairy cows. The room we talked in had a large window through which we could see the remnants of a winter of heavy snow.

Wilbur is a tall man who doesn't look his age—he leads an active life and takes good care of himself. He teaches during the fall semester and usually goes south for the winter. Recently he left Wesleyan University and became a Writer in Residence at Smith College, which is much closer to his home.

Interviewer: When did you begin writing poetry?

Wilbur: I began writing poetry as a small child, and became a hired poet at the age of eight when my first poem was published in *John Martin's Magazine*. As I remember it, it was a horrible little poem about nightingales, which I never could have seen or heard as an American child. Of course, I wasn't thinking of poetry as my chief activity or even chief avocation at that age. I was drawing pictures, playing the piano vilely, thinking of being a cartoonist or a painter, and imagining that I might be a journalist. Poetry was just one of the many products, and I can't be said to have done anything very prodigious.

Interviewer: Were you paid for the poem?

178

Wilbur: Yes, a dollar. I still have the dollar somewhere. Over there in that silo, which I cannot unlock because I've mislaid the key, there are all sorts of brown boxes full of memorabilia, and I think one of them contains the dollar.

Interviewer: What eventually made you decide on a career as a poet?

Wilbur: I really drifted into it. When I was at Amherst College, I was Editor, or Chairman as they called it, of the college newspaper, and I did a lot of writing and drawing for the college humor magazine, *Touchstone*. At the same time, I felt a sort of vocation for the study of English literature and thought I might want to be a scholar. During World War II, I wrote poems to calm my own nerves and to send to my wife and a few friends, a few teachers at Amherst. Then when I came back after the war and went to Harvard on the G.I. Bill to get an M.A. in English, there was a friend we made there, a well-known French poet now, named André du Bouchet. He was involved with a little magazine called *Foreground,* which was being backed by Reynal and Hitchcock as a means of discovering new talent. André heard from my wife one evening that I had a secret cache of poems in my study desk. He asked to see them, then took them away to read. When he came back about an hour later, he kissed me on both cheeks and declared me to be a poet. He sent these poems off to Reynal and Hitchcock, and they also declared me to be a poet, saying that they would like to publish them, and others if I had them, as a book.

Interviewer: How do you compose your poems? Do you write in longhand or on the typewriter? Do you write in bursts or long stretches, quickly or laboriously?

Wilbur: With pencil and paper and laboriously, very slowly on the whole. I do envy people who can compose on the typewriter, though I reject as preposterous Charles Olson's ideas about the relation of the typewriter to poetic form. I don't approach the typewriter until the thing is completely done, and whatever margins the typewriter might offer have nothing to do with the form of a poem as I conceive it. I write poems line by line, very slowly; I sometimes scribble alternative words in the margins rather densely, but I don't go forward with anything unless I am fairly satisfied that what I have set down sounds printable, sayable. I proceed as Dylan Thomas once told me he proceeded—it is a matter of going to one's study, or to the chair in the sun, and starting a new sheet of paper. On it you put what you've already got of a poem you are trying to write. Then you sit and stare at it, hoping that the impetus of writing out the lines that you already have will get you a few lines farther before the day is done. I often don't write more than a couple of lines in a day of, let's say, six hours of staring at the sheet of paper. Composition for me is, externally at least, scarcely distinguishable from catatonia.

Interviewer: What is it that gets you started on a poem? Is it an idea, an image, a rhythm, or something else?

Wilbur: It seems to me that there has to be a sudden, confident sense that there is an exploitable and interesting relationship between something perceived out there and something in the way of incipient meaning within you. And what you see out there has to be seen freshly, or the process is not going to be provoked. Noting a likeness or resemblance between two things in nature can provide this freshness, but I think there must be more. For example, to perceive that the behavior of certain tree leaves is like the behavior of birds' wings is not, so far as I am concerned, enough to justify the sharpening of the pencil. There has to be a feeling that some kind of idea is implicit within that resemblance. It is strange how confident one can be about this. I always detest it when artists and writers marvel at their own creativity, but I think this is a very strange thing which most practiced artists would have in common, the certainty which accompanies these initial, provocative impressions. I am almost always right in feeling that there is a poem in something if it hits me hard enough. You can spoil your material, of course, but that doesn't mean the original feeling was false.

Interviewer: You have been a teacher for many years. Does teaching complement your work as a poet?

Wilbur: I think the best part of teaching from the point of view of the teacher-writer, writer-teacher, is that it makes you read a good deal and makes you be articulate about what you read. You can't read passively because you have to be prepared to move other people to recognitions and acts of analysis. I know a few writers who don't teach and who, in consequence, do very little reading. This doesn't mean that they are bad writers, but in some cases I think they might be better writers if they read more. As for the experience of the

classroom, I enjoy it; I am very depressed by classes which don't
work, and rather elated by classes which do. I like to see if I can
express myself clearly enough to stick an idea in somebody's head.
Of course there are also disadvantages, one of which is that the time
one spends teaching could be spent writing. Another involves this
very articulateness of which I've been speaking. It uses the same gray
cells, pretty much, that writing does, and so one can come to the job
of writing with too little of a sense of rediscovery of the language.
That is one reason I like to live out here in the country and lead a
fairly physical life—play a lot of tennis, raise a lot of vegetables, go on
a lot of long walks. I do things which are non-verbal so that I can
return to language with excitement and move toward language from
kinds of strong awareness for which I haven't instantly found facile
words. It is good for a writer to move into words out of the silence, as
much as he can.

Interviewer: As a young man, did you ever do what John
Berryman did so consciously—visit older poets, to learn from them
or to sit at their feet?

Wilbur: Not as a very young man, though I knew Robert Frost
rather well when I was in my latter twenties and thereafter. My *entrée*
was not so much my own merits as my wife's. Her grandfather,
William Hayes Ward, was the first person to publish Robert Frost. He
edited *The Independent,* a journal of literature and opinion which
later turned into *The Outlook,* which later still became *The Literary
Digest.* So Frost was very fond of my wife's family. He was also
responsive to the fact that I knew most of his poems by heart. And
then I had the luck to please him with a few of my own poems. So
there is someone at whose feet I have sat, although after a while I got
up off the floor and we were just friends. And let's see—I have never
made pilgrimages, though I've always been delighted to meet people
about whose work I cared. I loved meeting people like Stevens and
Williams and Marianne Moore, usually at performances which they
gave. I introduced Stevens one time when he gave a splendid reading
at Sanders Theatre at Harvard. Unfortunately, I am the only person
who heard the reading because the sound equipment was not
working. I was sitting on the stage next to him, and it sounded
wonderful, but the acoustics in that building are so bad that everyone
else was forced to sit through an hour of silence. And they respected

him so much that they did it gratefully. Luckily, the tape recorder was working, so we have a record of that occasion.

Interviewer: Did Frost seem to you the kind of man that Lawrance Thompson says he was in his biography?

Wilbur: I think most of Thompson's evidence is undoubtedly true. But since I take a more positive view of Frost's character than Thompson, I don't find those books agreeable to read. I think Thompson is reacting against the phony picture—the mellow old New England fellow—which Frost gave of himself and which his admirers so often gave. He was, as I well knew, a much more dark and dangerous person than that. There was paranoia in him, and a savage competitiveness. But that is not what you felt when you were with him. Personally, he was extremely warm. You could occasionally put him off, because in eighty-odd years he never lost his original touchiness. But he would come back; perhaps he would even like you better for having braced him a little. I can remember putting him off several times. Once I said to him in Cambridge that he ought to go down to Washington and get Ezra Pound out of the madhouse, that he shouldn't allow his old bitterness and envies against Pound to detain him. I said, "You don't want to be a Brutus, and I don't mean the Brutus in Shakespeare, I mean that other Brutus who was so perfect a Roman judge that he sentenced his own sons to death." Having said that, of course, I winced, because I remembered that Frost's son had committed suicide and that many people, Frost included, had felt that he bore some responsibility in the matter. Well, Frost winced too, and glared at me for a bit, but he finally felt that I and other people who urged him in that manner were right, and acted on it. Another time, as I was leaving his cabin in Ripton, he called me back, and said, with a very youthful diffidence, that he hoped it was understood that we were friends. There wasn't any question of our being enemies, of course; he was just saying that we had had a good talk and he was sorry I was going, something like that. It came very close to being tenderness, and it also came out of, as did so much that he spoke, a very deep loneliness. I was tremendously touched. It seems to me that this kind of thing is not frequent enough in the Thompson biography—what I've read of it. People were always saying, around Bread Loaf and Ripton, that the world did not know the real Robert Frost. I suppose Thompson is telling the world what it never knew. Perhaps he has lost his balance and is over-telling them. So often, I think, a biographical study is likely to be written in a corrective spirit, as was John Brinnin's *Dylan Thomas in America.* There were so many damn fools who thought that Dylan was a healthy, bouncing, priapic figure, rebuking us all for our stuffiness, whereas, although he had been a delight to be with, he had also been a sick man drinking himself to death. Brinnin, as Thomas's closest associate in America, had seen that horror, and had seen the almost willful incomprehension of the many people who adored Dylan and tagged along after him and drank with him. So he had to write the book to correct a false impression, to put the horror on record, and many people didn't understand what had moved him.

Interviewer: You have said that "the work of every good poet may be seen in one way or another as an exploration and declaration of the self." Is this true in your own case?

Wilbur: I don't think that I explore myself in poetry in the way in which some so-called confessional poets do, although I must say I am writing many more poems out of my actual experience and my relationships. But I usually have a certain sense of distance from my material, feeling that I am not spilling my guts but arranging some materials and trying to find out the truth about them. If, in the process, I also find out something about myself, I think it is indirectly done. It is the thing, and not myself, which I set out to explore. But then, having chosen my subject and explored it, and having seen what I can say, I suppose one result of the poem is that I know myself a little better. There are certain things I find that I will not say, and there are certain matters to which I keep coming back. I would rather not name them because I think they are clear enough in the poems. The funny thing is that I often won't know that I have reapproached a subject until a new poem has been finished. Then I will say, oh yes, this turned out to be that question again. My process of self-explora-tion is almost as strangely indirect as that of Beau Brummell in a story that I remember hearing told about him. Somebody asked Brummell which one of the northern lakes he preferred. He turned to his valet and said, "Which one of the northern lakes do I prefer?" "I believe it is Windermere, sir," the valet replied. So Brummell said to his questioner, "Apparently it is Windermere." I see some resemblance between that process and the process by which I make discoveries about myself. I ask some poem to write itself, and once I am through supervising that process, I have discovered whether I like Windermere or not.

I do feel that the truth, especially the truth about oneself, is hard to report, and that if you set out to confess, what you are likely to do is tell lies in addition to reporting some of the truth. And the fact that you are consciously part of the material of the poem may lead you to falsify in ways that are not good. There are good fictions and bad fictions. The kind of fiction which glamorizes you is not good either for your sake or for the reader's, and I think that very often the confessional poet is drawn to glamorize himself, whether he is aware of it or not.

Interviewer: One reviewer of your work has written: "in many of his new poems, Wilbur still addresses us as if he were the only one alive." How do you feel reading something like that?

Wilbur: I remember seeing that somewhere. I think the critic is reacting to the personality which he feels behind the poems he has read. We all do this, of course, but I am sorry that my critic does not like what he has seen in or through my work. Perhaps his idea of humanity in speech and in art involves a greater directness and a higher degree of blurting than he finds in me. I don't like the kind of poetry which seems to harangue the reader. D. H. Lawrence, for example, some of whose work I think is marvelous, can be a dreadful haranguer. Perhaps that reviewer would like the instancy and the insistence of Lawrence, who is indeed dealing directly with his reader, though he is also dealing carelessly with his lines in the process. Lawrence always writes at his worst when he is hectoring an imagined reader. But maybe my critic doesn't like Lawrence either. It is hard to know why these reactions happen. I remember a case that may be similar to this one. Toward the end of World War II, I had a friend—we really did like one another—who came out of a kind of ethnic, urban world. He was periodically exasperated by what he felt was my WASP cool. He would come and stand next to my cot in the barracks and say: "Wilbur, why don't you join the human race?" I would ask him what I could do in order to join the human race, but he never made any specific suggestions—he'd just tell me to loosen up, that sort of thing. I think it is possible that there are some critics for whom one's poetry just cannot work because of temperamental differences and distances.

Interviewer: You have said, "I do think that there is nothing more dangerous to the imagination than fantasy." Many people would equate the two things. Could you elaborate on that?

Wilbur: To me, the imagination is a faculty which fuses things, takes hold of the physical and ideal worlds and makes them one, provisionally. Fantasy, in my mind, is a poetic or artistic activity which leaves something out—it ignores the concrete and the actual in order to create a purely abstract, unreal realm. If we think of fantasy at its least dignified, non-artistic level, this becomes obvious. Sexual reverie very clearly leaves something out, and that something is the physical object of one's desire.

Interviewer: Edgar Allan Poe is a writer who relies a good deal on fantasy; his work and his theory of art both seem very different from yours. What, then, is the basis of your fascination with him?

Wilbur: I first read Poe sensitively during World War II, in a foxhole at Monte Cassino. The extreme isolation of my situation made for a great power to concentrate. I felt a tremendous symbolic or allegorical depth beneath Poe's prose, and this excited my curiosity. I have been reading him ever since, and find myself continually discovering new things. I tried to write a book on him when I was a Junior Fellow at Harvard, between 1947 and 1950, but it didn't quite pan out. I hadn't yet found a language sufficient to describe the operation of his work as I saw it. So I began to write short pieces on him. I think I have said a certain number of things about him which are true, and it is fun to have been a discoverer. Now as for our conflict, Edgar's and mine, I object to him simply because he is far too much a fantasist. Or, as Allen Tate put it, the trouble with him is that his imagination does not proceed upward through the order of nature, moving toward the invisible through the visible. Instead, he tries to destroy the visible world on the assumption that if you do that, then the invisible world will rush in to take its place. Well, I question that formula, but I think it is an exciting mistake and resulted in a number of remarkable works.

Interviewer: But you don't seem to care much for his poetry.

Wilbur: I have a strong weakness for certain of the poems—"To

One in Paradise," for example. But too much of the poetry is virtually pure incantation, its substance being cloudy or predestroyed. The fiction, for my money, is far more accessible and far more defensible aesthetically. Poe's stories have a neo-Platonic or gnostic myth for their frame, but within that frame we're also given wonderful pictures of the states and motions and conflicts of the psyche. Modern studies of the dream-process are just catching up with some things which Poe noticed and, in his own way, set down.

Interviewer: Certain critics describe your poetry as rigid in its formality, old-fashioned. Perhaps in an age of loose forms—of free verse, the prose poem and the plain style—your practice strikes them as odd.

Wilbur: It is true that I have used a metrical basis in almost every poem that I have written, and it is true that more than half of my poems rhyme. At the same time, we must recognize that meter in itself is not rigid—it depends on how you use it. I hope that in my best poems I have used meter flexibly, so that the rhythm of a given poem is appropriate to its mood and its subject. Robert Lowell wrote me a friendly note when "Walking to Sleep" came out in the *New Yorker,* praising among other things the looseness of my pentameters. I didn't know what to make of that at first; I didn't think my pentameters were especially loose. But his remark led me to see that they sometimes were and are—that in contrast to many poets I pay little heed to the decasyllabic norm. Most of my poems are put together in the way in which free verse comes about. That is to say, I start talking the poem to myself, and I wait to see what rhythmic lengths the poem naturally wants to fall into. Having let the poem have its head for five or six lines, I decide whether or not I have a stanza. By that time I also probably have discovered whether the poem wants to rhyme, whether it wants to emphasize itself or deepen its sound by rhyming. This seems to me a perfectly organic way to proceed with a poem. Very seldom has this approach gotten me into a formal strait-jacket in which it was impossible to develop the thought as the thought wanted to develop. That can happen. I think one could start out in a very difficult form, like terza rima, and find that the natural drift of the thoughts and perceptions was being impeded, was being falsified, by the technical difficulties. What you do at that point is to start over, maybe, or eliminate some of your rhymes. So I would say that I approach a poem in just the way a free-verse writer does. What matters is the subject and the words which are going to be found for conveying and exploring the subject. The only difference is that I include meters and rhymes in my free-verse proceeding.

Interviewer: James Wright talks of formalism liberating the imagination rather than confining it. Does this make sense to you?

Wilbur: Oh, yes. I have argued that for years. I think it is perfectly true that if you put yourself in a position where you have to pay attention to all sorts of wild suggestions which come to you through the sound contract you have made, it can be liberating. If you are a silly person, it will ruin your poem because you will let the rhyme twist your thought, take your mind off where you were going. But if you are not silly, it can be very enriching and instructive. I don't really take an Apollonian approach to poetry. I think you have to be using your brains all the time, yes, but your brains have to be very attentive to the stupid part of you. I trust the stupid part at least as much. And one way of extorting suggestions from that part of you is through the use of formal devices such as rhyme and stanzaic patterns.

Interviewer: A reviewer, referring to your use of formalism, has called you "a bell too conscious of its clapper, clapper-happy."

Wilbur: I guess that means that I am self-conscious about the sound of my own voice, and I think I would have to plead guilty in some measure. Every line that I set down is considerably pondered, and while I try to have a colloquial and dashing movement in my poems, it does not satisfy me if they are not of a more than colloquial density or import. Now I always find self-consciousness annoying in other people—carefulness I don't. I find gaudiness annoying, richness not. All I can say in answer to that criticism is that I hope that some people find me more careful and rich than clapper-happy.

Interviewer: There is a good deal of attention being paid today to the poem sequence and even to the long poem, as in Warren and Berryman, for example. Do you have any inclination to work along those lines?

Wilbur: I'm not sure any of my poems could qualify as long. I write so slowly that anything which is, let's say, a hundred and fifty lines long seems to me like a long poem. I haven't recently counted the lines of my longer poems, like "The Agent" or "Walking to Sleep" or "The Mind-Reader," but I do know that "Walking to Sleep" takes eight minutes to read aloud. And that is about as long as I believe I am likely to get. "Walking to Sleep" has the density of any of my lyrics—every line has a certain amount of trouble in it—and I think that if I were to write a sixteen-minute poem of that same density, it would be very hard for the reader to consume. If I were to write a longer poem, I think I would have to become more open, plainer, more prosaic, for considerable stretches. Who can tell what he will do? I must say the idea is attractive to me, the idea of seeing how simple I could be and still get away with it. I believe I have been getting simpler as I have gone along. In my last book, in fact, there are some lines—I don't think I have any poems which are simple in toto—which are so simple that an unfriendly reviewer in the *Times* was able to extract them and say, look how dull Wilbur can be. But when I was putting down those simple lines—lines like "It is always a matter, my darling, / Of life or death, as I had forgotten"—I was excited by their very simplicity. They occur within poems which, taken as a whole, are not altogether simple, which you might have to read two or three times to consume. Every time I encounter a good translation of a Chinese poem, I am teased by the thought that it would be nice to try that sort of thing. A good Chinese poem, as Witter Bynner says in his *Jade Mountain,* makes most of our poetry look over-dressed and self-important. And a good Chinese poem is so much the poem of its moment—it is attractive in that way too.

Well, all I can say is that such things attract me, but I don't have any notion of what I am going to do next. I have written almost no poetry for about a year now, though I have translated a play of Molière's—*The Learned Ladies.* That is part of my excuse. The rest of my excuse is that I really did say to myself recently that I must escape altogether from the impulse to over-achieve, which can possess you once you get into the business of producing books of poetry. I called up Stanley Kunitz the day John Berryman killed himself. We consoled one another and talked about whether his act had been predictable. One thing we agreed upon was this, that whereas Stanley and I do many things apart from poetry—we both love gardening, for example—John Berryman was such a very hard worker that he lived almost entirely within his profession. Some of the dream songs seem to drag in a good deal of the world, but they do it mainly through books and *Time* magazine and the daily newspaper.

The impression one is left with is of a man who is working desperately hard at his job. Well, I admire that, but I think it can break your health and destroy your joy in life and art. I haven't got any clever hypotheses about why John killed himself, but a statement of Stanley's during that telephone conversation has stuck in my mind. He said: "In this country it is not enough just to publish a book of good poems and forever after be thanked for it. It should be possible, but it's not." As soon as you publish a book of poems, people begin to say, when is your next book coming out? And if you don't publish books at intervals of three years, they say, why are you so slow? I have been reproached in the *Times Literary Supplement* for taking seven years to get out a book, you know. That kind of pressure is not good for you and isn't good for your work. Stanley said: "As soon as you publish a book of poems in this country, you are in the poetry prison." I think John felt himself to be in the poetry prison, and that may have been contributory to his death.

Interviewer: You once said—and here is another quotation for you—"there's always some impulse in the American writer to set out for the frontier in some sense, to head for the savage, the original, the uncivilized, to stand loose from whatever actual coherences people may try to thrust upon him." Have you felt this impulse, and do you think it shows up in your poetry?

Wilbur: Yes, I feel the impulse. I think that, like most Americans, I have considerable respect for the actual and physical. We are all kickers of stones, you know, and we are not as likely to get enchanted with abstract thought systems as some Europeans, especially the French, are. The French are always coming up with enormously boring notions which they consider *très très très interessantes*. A man like Sartre can get a whole book out of a proposition which is, on the face of it, untrue, the proposition that Jean Genet, because he is masochistic, has the humility of a saint. There isn't any point in saying that even once, but a French intellectual can get a whole book out of it. I suppose we Americans are at fault in the other direction, that we are too primitive and have too much respect for the voiceless and the unvoiceable. Maybe it is just that we are closer to the frontier than they are, and therefore are less capable of getting lost in our minds—we are surer that there is something out there.

Interviewer: I take it that you would not then agree with the critic who said: "Wilbur does not really care for things. For Wilbur, the call to things is equivalent to 'the punctual rape of every blessed day.'"

Wilbur: That is not true at all. The critic is entitled to his insight—we all have to make guesses like this about what we are reading. But that is not how I feel. I feel intensely drawn to things, I think more drawn to things than to thoughts. Since the world has to pass through thought in order to come out as poetry, it may not be immediately obvious that I am drawn to things. But I sure am.

Interviewer: Could I ask which of your books and which of your poems are your favorites?

Wilbur: I'm not sure about that. There is always the coy answer in which you say that your most recent work is your favorite because you hope so desperately that it is not a decline. I think it is possible that my best book is *Things of This World*. I have not tired of most of the poems in it, and I don't find any conspicuous failures there, whereas there are a couple of poems in *Advice to a Prophet* which I wish had never happened. Usually when I feel that way about a poem, I think it has to do with a lack of originality—sounding too much like somebody else. As for my favorite poems, I like "Walking to Sleep" very much. And I haven't gotten tired of "Love Calls Us to the Things of this World." Since I have read that so often to audiences, it seems to me that I have given it the acid test—it must for me have a lasting strength. And then I like the new poem to my daughter, the one called "The Writer." But I enjoyed that also as a formal departure; I enjoyed not rhyming for a change.

Interviewer: Let me conclude by asking your reaction to a comment which William Meredith made about you. He said that you "obviously believe that the universe is decent, in the lovely, derivative sense of that word."

Wilbur: Well, yes. To put it simply, I feel that the universe is full of glorious energy, that the energy tends to take pattern and shape, and that the ultimate character of things is comely and good. I am perfectly aware that I say this in the teeth of all sorts of contrary evidence, and that I must be basing it partly on temperament and partly on faith, but that is my attitude. My feeling is that when you discover order and goodness in the world, it is not something you are imposing—it is something which is likely really to be there, whatever crumminess and evil and disorder there may also be. I don't take

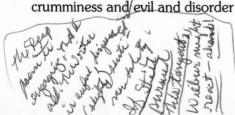

disorder or meaninglessness to be the basic character of things. I don't know where I get my information, but that is how I feel.

This interview with Richard Wilbur took place in Louisville, Kentucky.

Interviewer: Do you see being more personal as an evolution in your work? Have you been holding back from the personal?

Wilbur: Yes, I think so. I think I've held back from the personal, perhaps out of reserve. Lately, however, I've begun to crumble a bit, and write more shamelessly of what is near to me. Also, I think, getting older is a process of getting gradually more and more soft-hearted. And you do begin to draw in a little as you get older. I think of Auden's book *About the House,* which is just a book about *his* house; the different rooms in it, the things he does there, the friends who come to dinner. It's the book of a man who's—maybe he's a little tired of writing about grand subjects and just wants to print some puttering poems, the way a retired man putters around the house.

Interviewer: Over the years some critics have accused your poetry of detachment. It sounds as if you are agreeing with them for the first time.

Wilbur: Well, I think it's inevitable that there be some detachment, and that whoever speaks in the poem is going to be a contrived self. And whatever is said is going to be said because—well, an opportunity to write a good poem presented itself. Sometimes very strong feelings don't get written up because the interesting metaphor or dramatic situation doesn't suggest itself. So much of one's life goes unused.

I remember out in San Francisco in 1956 I spent an afternoon with Lawrence Ferlinghetti and Robert Duncan, and we had a party that evening. I'm not going to be able to remember all these names, but there were a lot of people there; and the big, exciting thing was that Allen Ginsberg had just read "Howl." I don't know whether the poem had even been published as yet by City Lights, but he'd read it in San Francisco, and people had tape recordings of it. There was a lot of hurrah about it. I don't know whether the word "Beat" was yet being used, but the style was certainly evolving there. There was a roomful of young followers of Allen and of others who were wearing what was beginning to be the prescribed clothing—the jeans, bare

feet or desert boots—and they were all full of romance about riding
the rods. Everyone was talking about railroads, and at one point I
said: "What one must never jump on, of course, is an oil car, since
what you have to hold onto is a very hot pipe which is situated at a
bad position and requires you to lean out from the car in the shape of
an L." And somebody said: "Mr. Wilbur, did I hear you rightly? Have
you ridden the rods? Have you been a knight of the road?" And I
said: "Yes." He said: "Why didn't it get into your poetry?" I couldn't
tell him then, but I think I know now. I believe that I did my hoboing
in so romantic a spirit that I was operating within the poetry of others.

Interviewer: It would be like being in Pamplona, thinking of
Hemingway, and not writing.

Wilbur: Of course; that's right. Run with the bulls at Pamplona
and somehow it is not an action entirely of your own.

Interviewer: The Ginsberg reading you mentioned makes me
think of Gary Snyder. Is he more than a "knight of the road" in your
opinion?

Wilbur: Yes. I like his early book *Riprap.* I guess my reservation
about him would have to do with its being too easy to predict what
he's going to say about anything . . . his too-reflexive primitivism.

Interviewer: I'm not sure what you mean.

Wilbur: Well, admiration for the life of the woods, for the Indian,
for unspoiled land; and rejection of cities. Of course, such attitudes
are fairly easy to share, but it seems to me that he doesn't explore
them, he doesn't criticize them, he doesn't sophisticate them quite
enough. . . . It's more complicated than he lets it be by simply
heading for the mountains or the monastery. John Frederick Nims
once said about the *Selected Poems* of Snyder's that it was "Polaroid
poetry." Too much of it follows William Carlos Williams' weaker
poems, I think, in simply telling you some things that are there, in a
tone of breathless simplicity—the cloud stands above the mountain—
so what?! That's the reservation I have about some of his work, but I
do think he's one of the most talented of that whole group, don't
you?

Interviewer: Along these lines, you said in your essay on Emily
Dickinson that poets write about what vexes them. What vexes you?

Wilbur: I'd rather testify about other people, I suppose. I'm wary
of that kind of self-analysis. I know that I have poems in which I set

two voices going against each other. One is a kind of lofty and angelic voice, the other is a slob voice, and these are two parts of myself quarreling in public. I suppose the quarrel is fundamentally of a religious nature, and that the slob, in whom I trust a great deal, is saying to the angelic part: "Come off it. Get down here where you belong." I suppose I've written a lot of poems which relate to that kind of tug-of-war going on in me. Then there'd be other ways, no doubt, which I don't want to explore, of figuring out what it is that gets under my skin. *[handwritten: yes! Tell us?]*

Interviewer: You're saying that you *are* the speaker in your poems?

Wilbur: Any poem that divides into two parts projects two aspects of me, debating. Self-projection, in a general sense, is inescapable. I don't think I would try to express anything in a poem which was absolutely not myself. On the other hand, I don't know of anything which is absolutely not myself, including Adolf Hitler. *[handwritten: Don't Snodgrass did?]*

Interviewer: In the context of this balance which you like to keep in your own work, in "Cottage Street, 1953," you call Sylvia Plath's poetry "unjust." Are you referring to what you see as her poetry's onesidedness?

Wilbur: Its helpless onesidedness. I tried to sprinkle a whole lot of words around there which would add up to a kind of just estimate of her. That, together with the picture I had given of her as a slumped, pale, drowning person. Let the record show that I said *brilliant:* "her brilliant negative / In poems free and helpless and unjust." I suppose she was freed by the onset of her desperate condition of mind to be brilliant in the way the poems of *Ariel* are brilliant. At the same time, she was helpless because it required that condition of mind to bring on those poems. She was unjust because a sick and prejudiced perception of things is—well, that's the limitation on the usefulness of her poetry to any reader, I think. It gives you some insights into a desperate condition of mind which is *not absolutely foreign* to the rest of us, but which goes farther towards morbidity than I've ever gone, thank God. At the same time there's a lot she can't tell you. She's all wrapped up in herself and her feelings about her children, and herself as a writer, and her fantasies about her dead father, and her arbitrary connections between her dead father and her husband. I don't suppose we need to know that her father was not a Nazi in

[handwritten margin notes: Oh, well, Sylvia ...]

order to read that poem ["Daddy"] rightly, or do we? In any case, she's rather unjust to him. She's certainly unjust to her mother.

Interviewer: Diane Wakoski has said she thinks confessional poetry is misnamed—that Plath and Lowell and Sexton are not confessing anything, but are writing out of feelings, like pain, that most of us don't find acceptable as material.

Wilbur: Well, I really think Sylvia Plath's latter poems, when unfortunately she was at her best, were crazy, and that, whatever virtues they have, they have that limitation. I don't think Lowell's best work is to be described in that way. I think whenever he's been emotionally ill it hasn't enabled him to write. He hasn't written out of illness, but in spite of it. The same story with Roethke, and I'm sure the same with Anne Sexton, whom I didn't know as well. As for pain, it's acceptable and necessary material. One of the jobs of poetry is to make the unbearable bearable, not by falsehood but by clear, precise confrontation. Even the most cheerful poet has to cope with pain as part of the human lot; what he shouldn't do is to complain, and dwell on his personal mischance.

Interviewer: You once said: "You write a translation because someone else has written a poem which you love and you want to take possession of it." How did you go about translation, for instance, of Brodsky's poem, "The Funeral of Bobò," in *The Mind-Reader*?

Wilbur: It took me all one month of January to work out its forty-eight lines, because Brodsky, whom I like very much, is very fussy about accuracy. I gather he's been very accurate when he's translated me, doing the rhymes and meters. There isn't any use doing it otherwise, I think. And so when I did "Bobò" I had to do it with something approaching absolute fidelity. I sent my translation to Carl Proffer, his friend at Ann Arbor, with fear and trembling, because in the last stanza I had in fact put in three words that were not in Joseph's original but, I thought, were in keeping with the drift of it. I damned well needed them for a rhyme, too! And I said: "Please clear this with Joseph." And Joseph said they were all right.

Interviewer: Brodsky complained at a reading here in Louisville that Akhmatova's poems had been poorly translated. They had not been rhymed.

Wilbur: He was objecting, I think, to Stanley Kunitz's translation of Akhmatova, which is probably the best book of Akhmatova around in English. But I guess what Joseph minds is that Stanley didn't work hard enough to get the meters and get the rhymes. Maybe Stanley's reply would be, "It wasn't a matter of working hard or not working hard. I felt that some of her poems could be translated into more relaxed English forms." I noticed recently that Denise Levertov and Joseph were tilting at each other in the pages of *The American Poetry Review*: Denise said, if I remember rightly, that Joseph, as a Russian, was much more used to an emphatic use of strict meter than English poets are, and that for him, therefore, the absence of meter and rhyme in a translation from a Russian poet would seem an appalling deprivation; but that for the American reader, for whom presumably the translation was intended, a more-relaxed rendering might be the more enabling sort of treatment. I think that's what Denise said—I still don't agree with it, except in the particular case.

Interviewer: You once said that you do translations only when you're not working on your own poetry. Why is this?

Wilbur: It would require a mad degree of self-knowledge to know exactly when you are capable of doing your own work and when you're not. But there are some circumstances under which it is easier to translate than to try to go ahead with a poem of your own. I think that in order to work on your own poem you need to baby yourself sort of totally, not to have the telephone ring, not otherwise to be vulnerable. I somehow can't work on poetry, which is the most important thing in my life, until I've taken care of all the unimportant things: written that silly letter, marked the class papers, *mowed the lawn!* At any rate, I've gotten into that fussy frame of mind now, whereas I can translate Molière riding on a plane, sitting in a motel. I have with me on this trip a translation of *The Learned Ladies,* which has almost reached the end of the second act, and in a frustrating recent day full of flights, limousines and buses I got four lines done to my satisfaction. And that's a fair average even if one were sitting in a living room. Some days you get sixteen lines done, some days none.

Interviewer: You've written that World War II was instrumental in starting you in poetry, that it gave you a need to organize your world. Can you tell us about that?

Wilbur: I think it was no different for me than for anybody else in that regard. War is an uprooting experience—that's at the very least what it is. It sends you to other places, puts you in other clothes, gives you another name and a serial number. And it also fills your head with doubts as to what the world will become, an accelerated sense of change. And then, of course, if you're in a line company it fills your ears with "Bang! Bang!" and your heart with fear. And there's all of this to be allayed as best one can. There are letters from home, or you can drink: there are all kinds of ways to forget how frightened and disoriented you are. But I think one of the best is to take pencil and paper—which is all you need, thank heavens, to be a poet and which makes it possible to practice poetry in a foxhole—and organize, not the whole of it, because of course you cannot put the world in order, but make some little pattern—make an experience. That is to say, jell things into an experience which will be a poem.

Interviewer: Your first book, *The Beautiful Changes*, contains many war poems, and your Vietnam-era books contain very few. Didn't Vietnam suggest fresh combinations to you?

Wilbur: Not very many. I have one poem called "On the Marginal Way," in the background of which you strongly feel the Vietnam War; and the poem explicitly states that I regard it as a dirty war. I also wrote what I called "A Miltonic Sonnet for Mr. Johnson," abusing him roundly and comparing him unfavorably to the founder of his party, Thomas Jefferson. But I had a distance from the Vietnam War. My physical involvement with it was limited to peace parades and those poetic-protest read-ins which got to be rather tiresome on the poetic side, but which, I suppose, were politically virtuous. So, heavens, I didn't have concrete material to deal with as I did in such poems as I got out of World War II. In World War II I'm talking about the gun that's strapped on your shoulder, and the mine detectors that you're observing as they sweep back and forth across the ground— all kinds of details.

Interviewer: The status of female poets, or of our consciousness of them, has changed considerably in the past few years. Thinking of that, we wanted to ask about a view you expressed in an interview in *The New York Quarterly* in 1972. You said you believed that men and women have different sensibilities.

Wilbur: Yes, I know I'm on dangerous ground in saying that, but I still think it's true. I do think that men are capable of greater emptiness and abstraction. I don't believe in the possibility of a female Hegel, for example, and I have a feeling that women have their feet

on the ground, on the average, a little more than men do, even
though men tend to etherealize women in their imaginations, through
their affection. It's therefore a continuous surprise to notice how
women know where they are, and know what's around, and men
are, by comparison, less practical and less concerned with the
concrete. That may be a big lie, but it is an impression of mine.

Interviewer: Do you think the difference is biologically based,
innate?

Wilbur: I suppose it may have some biological foundation. Some
feminist friends of mine disallow almost all efforts to discover
biological differences between men and women. One of them was
telling me sternly the other day that women could throw baseballs
just as well as men, if they weren't told that they couldn't throw
baseballs, and that may very well be true.

Interviewer: Do you think there are male/female topics anymore?
Or ever were?

Wilbur: No. I think perhaps there were, but I don't think there are
now. I really don't. I suppose that we're all still sufficiently condi-
tioned so that we feel that some materials are *slightly* more the
province of men than of women: a woman being obscene is slightly
obscener than a man being obscene, I think, and attracts more
attention.

Interviewer: How do you relate what you say about men,
women, and abstraction to poetry?

Wilbur: I think of the great describers of the twentieth century and
they'd be people like Marianne Moore and Elizabeth Bishop—and
D.H. Lawrence, who had, whatever I mean by this, a very strong
feminine element in his nature, so that he was able to write poems
about men from the woman's point of view which both men and
women can read with a sense of belief. He's also a great describer of
objects, whereas I think there's considerably less vivid description in
Eliot, in Pound, in all sorts of male poets I might name. Now you're
going to give me trouble by naming William Carlos Williams, who's
an extremely masculine person and a great describer. All I can say is
that my theory doesn't entirely hold water,

Interviewer: You almost seem to be saying that women have a
more natural disposition to be poets.

Wilbur: I don't know about that. I think of poetry in terms of the

compressed expression of the whole of one's experience, all at once;
the combining of things; the bringing together of all those things
which we variously call sensation, and thought, and passion, by
whatever names we call them; and any poetry which isn't concrete is
going to be a flawed poetry. So, in that respect, such women poets as
I've mentioned, and such men poets as are like them, have one
capability without which: nothing. Or—I'll have to take that back,
because I do think that there are some poems which have no
concreteness in them and, nevertheless, are successful. But in the
long run, one would not be satisfied with poetry which didn't seem to
touch down in the mundane, in the actual.

Interviewer: That was one of your criticisms of Poe's poetry,
wasn't it, that it wasn't grounded enough in the concrete.

Wilbur: Yes. He is hurrying away from it as fast as he can go. He
has to mention it in order to destroy it! Otherwise, you'd see nothing
but the smoke. He will say "seas," and then will add, "without a
shore," and make it impossible for you to think of any sea that you
ever heard of.

Interviewer: What would you do with Emily Dickinson, then?
She's a woman who seems to work in the abstract.

Wilbur: Yes, she does. Toward the abstract, I would say, as David
Porter has recently shown so well. She writes a great many poems in
the riddle form, and some of them are the kind of riddle which has a
concrete answer. Many of them are. And she's brilliant in that kind of
extreme descriptive test. A poem like the one about the humming-
bird—how does it begin?: "A Route of Evanescence/With a revolving
Wheel." There's no problem about getting the answer to that riddle.
And she's a great describer in a lot of poems which aren't riddles; and
yet she keeps taking the qualities of sensible things and abstracting
them before your very eyes, and then sometimes combining qualities
taken from here and from there without giving you any objects to
look at. For instance, the way she uses purple. She draws purple
perhaps from the sunset more than any other place; also, from
associations with royalty. In "Success is counted sweetest" there's
purple, isn't there, associated with victory: "Not one of all the purple
Host/Who took the Flag today/ Can tell the definition/So clear of
Victory"—I think that's it. Purple, the purple throng. Surely they're

not colored purple; surely not dripping with blood, it wouldn't be purple in that sense. It must be the royal purple—

Interviewer: Or religious?

Wilbur: Yes, could be. Though she was a Congregationalist, I think she uses a broader religious vocabulary than that church would have entitled her to. I don't think they care much about vestments in the Congregational Church.

Interviewer: I've been wondering which female poets you think share your concern for precision and form—Carolyn Kizer and Ruth Stone, perhaps?

Wilbur: Yes, I like both of those poets. And I think that they are both very careful constructors of poems, careful choosers of words. I like Carolyn Kizer's "Blue Heron" poem, for example, very much, and with Ruth Stone's poems I have many favorites. I like her new book, *Cheap,* that recently came out.

Interviewer: Getting back to your new book, the title poem is a rather long one for you—

Wilbur: Yes, I don't know how many lines it is, but when printed in the small type of *The New York Review of Books* it filled a page in double column. When I looked at that page solid with my poem, it made me feel very productive, but of course it had taken me about a year to do it.

Interviewer: That's the poem that stems from the mind reader you saw in Rome years ago?

Wilbur: Yes. I'd been thinking about him for twenty-odd years.

Interviewer: Is an extended poem a greater effort? Is it somehow "more" of a poem?

Wilbur: I've never written a poem long enough to have to deal with the problem of density of language. I remember Robert Frost's giving a lecture at Bread Loaf on the exciting title, "The Dullness of Wordsworth," and everyone flocked in to hear whether he was going to insult Wordsworth in public, and, no, of course, he was going to praise him for being willing to produce prosaic bridge passages between his great moments. But my so-called long poems are at the worst eight-minute poems; so rightly or wrongly I don't feel that I have to come down off it into a more open style. So I continue, even in such longish poems as I've written, to have, I hope, more than one interesting word per line. I'm quoting Auden kind of obliquely. He said that in writing songs for music, or in translating *libretti,* as he and Chester Kallman often did together, you must restrict yourself to at most one interesting word per line. A singer cannot sing anything complex—or, at any rate, the music, and the presence of the singer, the costume of the singer and the situation of the plot, are going to provide sufficient complexity, so that if the line says, "I love you," that'll be quite an adequate statement.

Interviewer: How did the poem "The Writer" in your new book come about?

Wilbur: I expect it was done at some distance from the situation described in it. I've very, very seldom had the experience of encountering a raw event of some kind and immediately sitting down to write about it. The only time that ever happened to me that I can now recall was when I ran over a toad with a power mower, and for some reason was instantly ready to write about the toad and the associations of the toad. I must, indeed, have had a whole body of associations ready to which the dead toad became the center.

But in this case, heaven knows how many years before, the starling had in fact been trapped in that very room, and indeed that was the room in which my daughter wrote. . . . The poem tells the truth in general, but the chronology is probably not exact. People sometimes imagine that a rush of love for one's daughter might produce a poem. It's not that at all—it's that two ideas, two images come together, and then you've got something to work with.

Interviewer: Did you think about how your daughter would react to the poem? Do you ever think about your audience?

Wilbur: I did think a little bit about how she would react, but that wasn't at all what guided me in my choice of words and of tone. Even when one's writing a poem about someone that close, and my daughter and I are as close as it's possible to be, I don't think a poem is a message. It's a kind of performance; it's a kind of machine of feeling which other people can use. If I had thought too very much about my daughter there would have been things which wouldn't have been necessary to say. But in the poem, in so far as I'm talking to my daughter, I'm talking to her in public and therefore in a fuller, more explanatory way, and producing something which I hope other people can appropriate to their own lives. I don't think I've admitted anything to the poem which is so peculiar as to leave the average reader feeling that he's excluded from that kind of experience.

Indeed, one thing about that little poem that I've noticed is that there are people, when I read it to an audience, who come trotting up and say: "I had a robin in my house last week and had all hell getting rid of it!" If the poem is successful (I hope it is), this is the case of a poem which is fortunate in fitting Robert Frost's formula concerning the material of poetry. I'm going to misquote it, but he said something like this: that the material of poetry ideally should be common in experience, uncommon in literature. Everybody's had birds in the house and wanted to get them out without their bashing their heads against the glass. And yet, I think this is the only poem about it I have read.

Interviewer: Do you revise much?

Wilbur: No, I don't really have drafts. I do sometimes have false starts. Mostly I don't change my ground much, because usually a first line presents itself to me confidently and I go on from there. My revision consists mostly in refusing to put anything down until I think it will do; and then sometimes I will put a line down and I will scribble alternatives in the margin Emily Dickinson-fashion. And I don't keep notebooks, or a schedule, formally. Mostly I jot ideas on old envelopes and bits of paper.

Interviewer: You were telling us over lunch about the way Yeats approached a poem. . . .

Wilbur: Oh, well, I was just saying that I thought he was an extraordinarily willed poet. He claimed that a poem often began, for him, as a musical phrase, but I doubt that much of his work was wafted toward him on wings of song. I don't know in what sense he was tone deaf (he said he was); I know he had a marvelous kinetic sense; I don't sense any privation of music in his poetry. But clearly he was a man of no facility at all, and it took a lot of cold forethought and ambition to make his books. I do believe that he wrote a lot of poems to fill out his individual volumes, because there's almost always a unity to the individual volume. I think there are a lot of little poems which are outriders, as it were, destroyer-escorts of the big poems.

Interviewer: Do you do anything like that when you put a book together? Look for a unifying theme?

Wilbur: No. This is ridiculous to say, because I have no want of respect for Yeats, but I would abhor doing that. It wouldn't seem spontaneous enough; it would seem too calculating, too much like merchandising. It would be for me; it wasn't for Yeats. Yeats could make himself do things, the way some poets can make themselves write occasional poems. If it's the anniversary of the founding of Jamestown, there are some poets who can write those. . . .

Interviewer: The Bicentennial poet.

Wilbur: That's just exactly the last thing I could be. A publisher once had me down to New York and gave me lunch at the Plaza, and then over dessert said: "Well now, getting down to my idea. It seems to me it's many years since there's been a popular success like Stephen Vincent Benét's *John Brown's Body,* and we have an anniversary of Lincoln's death coming up, and if you could write a book-length poem about Lincoln, I could give you a $5,000 advance." I said: "Gee, it's been a nice lunch, but it's wasted on me. I can't do that kind of thing. The best I can do is to name to you the people whose long poem about Lincoln I might be interested to read," and I named some other people.

The other day I read, to my great amusement, that the same publisher offered the same deal to Auden, probably before he'd offered it to me. Can you imagine asking Auden to write a book like that on Lincoln?

Interviewer: You once said that no *one* poet influenced you most. Do other poets influence you? Do you ever read other poets before sitting down to write?

Wilbur: I don't want to do that. I know that all my life I've been reading Robert Frost, and sometimes that is visible. I don't want it to be. I try to get rid of the signs that show. But there have been, good heavens, outcroppings of Poe, involuntary ones. In that poem I wrote about the toad, about the time I was one-third into it, I had an odd feeling of having written a really resounding, splendid line; and I said to myself, "Good God, one shouldn't feel that way about one's poem. One shouldn't be so confident at this point." And I realized where I had gotten my confidence: I had borrowed two out of three adjectives from one of Poe's lines in "Dream-Land"! I think Yeats is catastrophic in this respect. If you become influenced by Yeats you do not sound like yourself. There's one poem of mine which I would

only one?
which one!?

have to throw out of a *Selected Poems*—perhaps there are two of
them, that are too touched by Yeats, too affected by the fact that I've
three times taught a seminar in Yeats. Yeats' poetry is gloriously
abnormal, but if you teach it for a semester it commences to seem
normal.

Still, it can be useful and safe to read someone like Robert Graves
who, as John Holmes said, is a great starter. You read Graves and he
reminds you how delightful poetry can be at its best, and what a fine
game it is—and it makes you want to write a poem. Not, however, a
poem by Robert Graves, but one of your own. I don't think I've ever
sounded like Graves, but I get the nicest nudges out of him.

Interviewer: Are you involved in any group of poets like the one
you used to have with John Ciardi and others?

Wilbur: No, no group. Every now and then there are certain
people to whom I show poems, and who show poems to me: Bill
Meredith, Bill Smith, John Brinnin, and Cal Lowell, when he's
around—we aren't in the same place at present. But that's just one-
on-one. The last time I found myself involved in anything groupy was
about seven years ago when Stephen Spender was staying at
Wesleyan and certain people on the Wesleyan faculty were interested
in reading poems to each other. Stephen, with his usual generosity—
of course this wasn't part of any deal he'd signed on to do—joined
the group. I suppose there were five or six meetings. We'd go around
in a circle and everybody would read at least one poem.

One evening Stephen invited I.A. Richards to come, and Richards
had not understood the character of the invitation. He hadn't realized
he was going to have to listen to a lot of people read poems, one
after the other, and then discuss them. And as soon as that became
clear, he did the most glorious thing. He simply stood up and said,
"Oh no, no, no, I'm sorry, no, I'm sorry, I can't. Good night! Good
night!" and out he went. He didn't have any evidence that any
particular, horrible poem was going to be read, but he thought the
chances were pretty good and he didn't see why, at his age, he had
to sit and listen to it.

Interviewer: What do you have planned for the future?

Wilbur: Well, I don't think I can resist it too much longer—my
wife's bullying me about writing some sustained prose books for
children. I have to write *one*, anyway. All the time my children were

growing up I told them great sagas about sets of characters who went through successive adventures, and I did take one of them and write a little book about him, *Loudmouse*. It's full of capitalized speeches which entitle the children or the reader to shout—they like that. Children love a moment of anarchy; they don't like sustained anarchy. They love violence in that sense, too, and too many children's books don't give them any of it, I think. Nothing scary, nothing disorderly, not enough that's crazy. So many children's books which come out are really just big picture-books, with a little bit of text, and bright-colored pictures of generous-bosomed, middle-European women in peasant costume cooking things. That's not the sort of thing that delights the heart of a child. I don't know who thinks all those Hungarian cooks are a delight to children.

Interviewer: Are there what one could call advantages to being a poet? *(goals, like being a child?)*

Wilbur: Well, one is allowed enormous license in behavior, one is forgiven everything, one can look as one likes, and one can travel around the country reading the same poems over and over; whereas if a scholar or critic wanted to travel around the country he'd have to write a number of fresh lectures, you see. You get to see a lot of the country on the same old material this way, and I like that. I'm being frivolous, I suppose. I don't know what disadvantages there are. I can't think of anything I'd rather do, hard as it is, isolating as it is, and unpleasant as it is to go stale and dead as you do periodically.

Interviewer: How do you feel then? And how do you overcome the dry spells, and your feelings about them?

Wilbur: Dead and guilty and ashamed; however, I say to myself, for what I suppose would now be the fiftieth time, this too will pass, you will write something again; and that helps a tiny bit. It doesn't help enough.

what one could now ask him? Getting ... silly?

Poetry as Performance: A Conversation between W.D. Snodgrass and Richard Wilbur

Walton Beacham/1979

From *New Virginia Review*, I (1979), 34-57. Reprinted by permission of Walton Beacham, Richard Wilbur and W.D. Snodgrass.

On April 12, 1978 the *New Virginia Review,* with the cooperation of Old Dominion University and in coordination with their Annual Poetry Jam, arranged the following conversation between W.D. Snodgrass and Richard Wilbur, two Pulitzer Prize winning poets. Walton Beacham, Poetry Editor of the *New Virginia Review,* moderated the conversation which was taped by WTGM Radio for National Public Broadcasting [on April 12, 1978] and aired in Tidewater, Virginia, on May 1, 1978.

Beacham: With me today are two of America's most distinguished poets, Richard Wilbur and W.D. Snodgrass. Richard Wilbur is the author of *The Beautiful Changes, Ceremony, Things of This World,* as well as a number of plays which have appeared on Broadway. With Leonard Bernstein he did the translation for *Candide;* he has translated *The Misanthrope, Tartuffe, The School for Wives, The Learned Ladies,* all by Molière, all of which have been performed in New York. He is an editor, a teacher, and one of the poets who influences other poets, as does W.D. Snodgrass, whose translations include *Gallows Songs* by Morgenstern, Medieval, Romantic and Renaissance songs, the ballad, various Medieval tales which tell stories of pain in life. Both of these men have a great deal in common and their careers have run parallel to each other. Both have won prestigious awards including the Pulitzer Prize, the Guggenheim Foundation Award; both are teachers in universities, both are products of classical educations, both are members of the National Institute of Arts and Letters, the Academy of American Poets, both practice other art forms to reach diversified audiences. Their work illustrates a number of common interests; they are both translators,

they both deal with dramatic poetry, especially as it includes voice
and personnae; they both insist on and include the other arts in their
own work; they are both formalists and they are craftsmen. One of
the things that Richard Wilbur and W.D. Snodgrass are bringing to
life in this part of the 20th century is the return of poetry as
performance. They are both interested in the voice with which poetry
is presented to an audience, and the ways in which the audience will
respond to it.

Mr. Snodgrass, certainly you are one of the best performers of your
own work among contemporary poets. How do you feel about
poetry as performance?

Snodgrass: For me it is terribly important. You know I teach oral
interpretation, and I really love doing that. For me the poem isn't
complete until it is performed, any more than a piece of music is
complete when I've got the score in my hand, or for most people a
play isn't complete until it's on the stage. Most people simply cannot
bring the thing to life really as a play when they read it, especially
when they read it silently to themselves.

Wilbur: That's true.

Snodgrass: You get a little further when you read the play out
loud. But again, the poem, it seems to me, isn't alive. . . . I really got
a shock last night. Some of my students were reading at a bar near
here and I suddenly realized that some of their pieces were better
than I'd thought. In spite of everything I've said I hadn't read those
pieces out loud; I'd thought, "I'm good enough to do this silently; I'll
get the sound." No; huh-uh. I'd missed the poem. For me, the silent
poem isn't the poem.

Beacham: How did your poems change when you began to take
voice lessons?

Snodgrass: That gets me off into autobiographical stuff, but I'll try.
It seems to me that now my poems are much less formal then they
used to be, and I think that comes from getting deeper into musical
study. You know I was a musician before I was a poet, and since; and
I think it has probably sunk to a much deeper level now than it ever
was before. So that . . . I feel more capable of finding a satisfactory
music for the poem without using a formal verse form. So I write a lot
more free verse than I used to, or at least things that look like free
verse.

Wilbur: I can see how that would happen. The more you think of your voice as an instrument which can carry a sufficient melody, and has a sufficiently emphatic beat . . . the less you will think of the voice as talking along and counterpointing itself against a metrical paradigm.

Snodgrass: Right. One of the funny things that happened with classes in oral interpretation is that when we stopped using a big square podium to read from and brought a music stand in, everybody suddenly got a whole lot better. (*Laughter*) Because they thought of it as an artistic performance then, and not . . . like telling people how to repair a tractor wheel, or get out there and sell, sell, sell, or something. Dick, what about yourself, how do you feel about performance?

Wilbur: Well, I think I'm a little different, perhaps because I'm a little more diffident about my voice as an instrument. When I was first writing, I know that I thought of the poem as something existing on the page, and I really didn't think at all of the poem as read aloud. I think I was somewhat tone deaf, through a failure to exercise my inner ear, and I wrote some lines which I find it now very difficult to articulate. And then, like everybody else, I began to give poetry readings, and got bolder and hammier. And now it's rather a different thing. It has had consequences for the way I write. I do think that, though I haven't heard you read recently, from the way you describe your reading I probably am a little more monotonous in my delivery than you.

Snodgrass: That's to say it in an ugly way. You are much more restrained and classical, I think, whereas I tend to be more florid and dramatic, which probably means I read better and worse. (*Laughter*) When I'm on I may be more on, but when I'm off I'm awful.

Wilbur: Yes, well that's bound to be the case if you in any degree act your poem.

Snodgrass: Sure.

Wilbur: Now I don't act them. I sort of intone them, and my voice makes, I suppose, little gestures in the direction of what I would do if I were to act the poems.

Snodgrass: Sure, sure.

Wilbur: But that's the method with which I am most at home. It can be irritating to some people. I recall once I was reading at NYU, and after I had read, Bob Bly, who was presiding, got up and said, "Are there any questions?" And an elderly woman stood up and said, "Young man, why do you sound like an Episcopal minister?" *(Laughter)*

Snodgrass: Let me tell you she is tone deaf. I heard you read yesterday. You do not sound like an Episcopal minister.

Beacham: That doesn't come from any philosophy about the poem . . . the poem ought to speak for itself, though, does it?

Wilbur: It does, to a certain extent. I feel that if you act a poem very fully, you are going to emphasize some of the words at the expense of others. I think that with a somewhat monotone delivery you deliver more of the words. And it's a little more like encountering the words on a page.

Snodgrass: Yeah.

Beacham: Well, with both of your poems, it seems to be that the visual experience is important, and when you begin to turn those poems into performance, how do you deal with that?

Snodgrass: When I was with a voice coach, that's one of the things we worked on most, ways to suggest the end of a line, for instance, without pausing. I approach the poem somewhat differently from Dick—I'm not saying this is better; it's just how I do it. When I read, I want to give a definite interpretation of the poem. It seems to me that I'm there specifically to sell that interpretation. You can wake up tomorrow and decide, "Well, he was all wrong—he just didn't understand the poem." I don't guarantee my interpretation is right—I only guarantee that I have one. I feel you've already got the words on the page. I'm here to give an interpretation of the emotion that underlies those words. The same thing that I go to a concert for. You know I've got the notes on the page. I want the performer to give me an interpretation of the emotion underlying them. But there are many people who don't feel that way.

Wilbur: I think we might differ slightly in degree, but I don't think we differ very much on this.

Snodgrass: I don't think so, either.

Wilbur: If a poem is read aloud well, I think it is bound to be a simplification and an enforcement of the interpretation. What you do often when reading a poem aloud . . . what one often does, is to make apparent the simple emotional spine of it. How intensely you do this is a matter of your own personal style, but I think it always happens when a poem is adequately read aloud.

Beacham: Do you trust yourself to interpret your own work?

Snodgrass: Oh, ahhh . . . *(Laughter)*

Beacham: Since the reading is an interpretation, of course.

Snodgrass: Sure, sure. As long as I think the audience realizes that they musn't take my interpretation as having any special authority. I am the person who has most reason to misunderstand my poems, because they probably show me in a bad light. If they are any good as poems they probably do. I am not the authority on this. Any more than I think that a musician ought to be the authority on the performance of his own piece. I don't want to hear Stravinsky conduct Stravinsky, I want to hear Van Karajan conduct Stravinsky. I want to hear another interpretation of it. The author gave it to me on the page.

Beacham: Since we are talking about the differences in your voices in the presentation of the poem, would each of you read a poem for us, and maybe that would help illustrate the difference in the voice that you are talking about.

Snodgrass: All right, sure. Richard, would you like to, like to read?

Wilbur: Yes. I haven't the foggiest idea of which one to read. Let's see. I'll read . . . because we're doing this in April, I'm going to read a poem called "Seed Leaves" about dicotyledonous plants, and how they first present us with leaves which take the shape of the seed case, then with true leaves. [Reads "Seed Leaves."]

Beacham: Wonderful reading, Mr. Wilbur. Mr. Snodgrass, will you give us a reading?

Snodgrass: After that I am afraid to read one of my own. I am going to read a translation, and get myself off the hook here. This is a little poem by Mihai Eminescu, the great Romanian poet, romantic poet. It's a little lullaby called "Somnoroase Păsărele," and I suspect that any Romanians in the audience are squirming with pain at my pronunciation. *(Laughter)* Try it. [Reads "Somnoroase Păsărele."]

Wilbur: Bravo!

Beacham: Bravo!

Snodgrass: I'm not sure that we proved our points with that, though. I have the suspicion that you read very dramatically and that I sounded very monotonous. (*Laughter*)

Wilbur: Not at all. No, we were very different.

Snodgrass: Were we?

Wilbur: And I was fascinated. You really performed that one.

Snodgrass: Yeah. I look on it much more as a performance, I think, than you do. Which isn't to say that one is better. It's like our different personalities, I think. Obviously when you set out to be a poet, you set out to do something that nobody else could do, and that ought to carry with it a way of performance, too.

Wilbur: Yes.

Beacham: How, Mr. Snodgrass, did you respond to the formality of Mr. Wilbur's poem as it was read and performed?

Snodgrass: Oh, I love it. You know.

Beacham: What does your ear hear when he reads? What do you begin to pick up?

Snodgrass: Well, one of the things I hear is a great admiration for the formality of the poem that brings a kind of sub-rational meaning, something that I can't gloss, but it says right away something about his concern for forms, for social forms, commitment toward something of that kind. Also, his concern for a kind of elegance of structure. It's very hard to talk about that, I think, because you're getting below the rational as soon as you get into form. Nobody knows exactly what form means. But right away that's suggesting something rich beyond the dictionary sense of the poem, something that enriches and orchestrates marvelously. And any reading that didn't convey that—I am sure that if I read his poem I would read it very differently, but I would have to get to the audience a sense of where the line endings are, where the rhymes come. As a matter of fact, I love to listen to poems in languages I don't understand, and in some ways I feel like, okay, if you get a good reading on this poem in another language, you almost get the poem more than if you got only the dictionary sense.

Wilbur: Yes. You know, I remember once in Paris, in 1948, I was talking with a young French poet named Henri Pichette. He didn't have any English, and he understood that Poe was a great poet, and wondered if I would read a poem of Poe's to him. So I read him

"Annabel Lee," and I pulled out all the stops (*laughter*), much more than I did in reading my own work just now. When I was finished he said, "*Formidable!*" Then he said, "Now, what does it say?" And I began translating some of the lines: and when I translated to him, "The moon never beams without bringing me dreams . . . " and so on, he said, "Oh, really! Is it as banal as that?" (*Laughter*) But I think his original response was right, that he was hearing the pure incantation which Poe had written—because, though the poem does say something, it doesn't say a great deal—*(laughter)* and that as soon as I began to translate I was somewhat falsifying the poem as ideally as we all ought to hear it.

Snodgrass: That interests me, Dick. Am I right in thinking that you feel freer to dramatize a poem that's somebody else's than your own?

Wilbur: Well, I feel freer to go crazy with a poem of Poe's, because of Poe's intentions. I think Poe is very little concerned with the precise dealing out of subject matter, or argument. I think he is an incantatory poet, and so within your limits you want to cast a spell when you read him.

Beacham: When you're trying to create such diverse voices other than the voice you may normally speak in your poems, such as the voice of a mouse in Mr. Wilbur's children's book entitled *Loudmouse*, or the voice of Magda Goebbels in a collection like Mr. Snodgrass' *The Führer Bunker,* how do you go about diversifying your normal voice and the voice of the persona that you are trying to pick up?

Snodgrass: Oh boy. (*Laughter*) Why don't you, Dick, you go ahead with that one.

Beacham: Let's hear it from the mouse. *(Laughter)*

Wilbur: What I would say is that, as someone who has read *The Führer Bunker* with admiration, but has not heard you read those poems, I should think it would be extremely hard to shift gears between Eva Braun and let's say the voice of Goebbels. Goebbels talks in rhyme, for example, whereas Eva Braun sings "Tea for Two" and then goes into quite another kind of verse from Goebbels. And of course she should have a different, lighter, more feminine voice. She has an altogether other sensibility. I would find that too great a challenge to my capacities. I think you could handle it a great deal better. When I read aloud my translations from Molière, I really don't try for total impersonations of the characters. I think it's partly because they're trading lines and half-lines of continuous verse, and it would be very hard for one reader to alter his tone and handle those line-breaks at the same time.

Snodgrass: Also, in Molière the form is really much more of the subject. When you do have something like those trading half-lines, that becomes very much a part of the subject, and if that's lost, you have nothing. It's destroyed.

Wilbur: Yes. Two good actors can do what's called for, or three good actors can do it, but I think that one reader can't very well retain the verse fabric and change his voice effectively.

Snodgrass: Well, as a matter of fact, the same thing happened to me the other night when I was up at Richmond with Walton giving a reading, and I did some of the "Bunker" poems, and for some of them I can do the switching back and forth. But I read a little poem of Magda Goebbels' where she's talking in two voices of her own and I had to have somebody read the second voice. But, no. I think you do impersonate the character probably more than you think. I had to leave before you read any of the Molière the other day, but I talked to people who heard you, and they knew . . . they knew the characters, they knew who you were reading, indeed.

Wilbur: I'm glad. (*Laughter*)

Snodgrass: It really was. Do you have a problem of getting the difference in character in there in composing, do you feel?

Wilbur: Well, I work so slowly, De, that I contemplate these people at leisure as they emerge in the play, and I think I have a pretty good sense of what they are like. I can't say whether I've in all cases fully endowed these people with what they had in the originals, but I have them in my mind's eye, and in my mind's ear.

Snodgrass: Sure.

Wilbur: And I think I hear a kind of ideal voice for each.

Beacham: How faithful do you feel you have to be to the actual characters you're creating, Goebbels or Hitler, or any of the characters which have appeared in Molière, which readers might have envisioned in their own mind as being certain kinds of people. Do you create your verse and try to recreate these characters faithfully?

Wilbur: Well, you do, don't you? In *The Führer Bunker.*

Snodgrass: In the "Bunker" poems I've done an awful lot of

research and generally speaking I tend to stick to it, although here
and there I have departed from facts and I've even put a couple of
things in that I know are wrong. That I'm fairly sure are factually
incorrect, anyway. Just because of the dramatic needs of the situation.
For instance, there is a creep named Fegelein who is being taken out *Ja!*
to be shot during the last days. And they take him out right through
the orgy that broke loose in the bunker, just before the Russians
came in. Well, I'm almost sure that that didn't really happen, they
probably would have led him out a back door, or stuffed him through
a window or something to take him out and shoot him. But it was
dramatically so enticing to take this guy who had been a creep, a
lecher, a super lecher, out through this orgy in which he very badly
wanted to be taking part. Instead, he's being taken out to be shot.
Who could resist imagining what would go through his mind? But
generally speaking I try to stick to the facts. I think in my translations
I'm somewhat freer than Dick is in his. We were talking about this
before we began, and it seems to me that both of us stay very close
to the dictionary sense of the poem. Neither of us make what we
would call imitations. But he is faithful to the poem, to the original, in
ways I don't try to be. This may be related to the fact that he really
reads the language he translates whereas I always work with friends
who read the language I'm working in. And it seems to me that he
tries to get the original all the way, you know, to the deepest
resonances of the language. I don't think I do. I stick to the dictionary
sense of the poem, but I figure that all the orchestration, all the
richness . . . ambiguities, puns, the way words rub against each other,
maybe even the verse form, will be different in mine from the
original. I figure I'm bringing the tune over, but I've got a different
orchestra, so I'm going to orchestrate it differently, and I'm going to
harmonize the thing differently, to fit the instruments I've got. Now I
think that Dick doesn't do that, but, maybe I'm wrong . . .

Wilbur: I wonder whether we differ as greatly in our practice
(*laughter*) as we may in our notion of what it is that we're doing, and
our feeling about what it is that we're doing. I pursue the illusion of
perfect fidelity and I perhaps kid myself very often that I've achieved
it. You seem to be more aware than I that it's impossible to translate
with perfect fidelity.

Snodgrass: Yeah, but now and then you do the impossible. By

God, if Molière didn't write the play that you translated, he should
have; shame on him.

Wilbur: The way in which I think we may differ a little, on the
basis of what you've just said, is that I do always try in English to find
the nearest measure, the nearest form to what there is in the original.
And when I translate a play of eighteen hundred lines, it comes out in
eighteen hundred lines. This is merely prudent to a certain extent,
and also it probably has to do with what languages I've worked from.
If you are translating French alexandrines the logical line, I think, in
which to catch and contain all the meanings of the original is the
English pentameter. If you try to do it as some people have done, in
tetrameter, you start leaving out words and ideas.

Beacham: To what extent are you trying to preserve the culture
out of which the original work comes?

Wilbur: You're speaking to me?

Beacham: Well, to both of you, but Mr. Wilbur . . .

Wilbur: That's right, the question could be asked of either of us.

Beacham: Mr. Snodgrass translating the Romanian and you
translating the French. Are you trying to give us some sense of what
these countries are and the culture . . .

Wilbur: I would be extremely annoyed if any translation of mine
from Molière sounded at any moment like a lecture on the culture of
the French seventeenth century. At the same time, I can't bear
anachronisms. I don't want the people in any of my Molière
translations to remind us for a moment that this is being done in the
twentieth century, so I aim (once again pursuing an illusion) at a
timeless language, at a transparent language which will make it
possible to some extent for the audience to move without struggle
into the pure temporal milieu of the play.

Snodgrass: Again I think that is a difference between us because
my first aim is to make a satisfactory English poem, or a satisfactory
English song, and one that people will listen to and feel as if it were
written in English. I mean that if you didn't tell them that it was a
translation, then they wouldn't know, and they would feel satisfied by
it. That's what I'm meaning to do, pursuing a different illusion.
(*Laughter*) And so I often take anachronisms; I'll put terms in that I
know the author wouldn't have known, and wouldn't have used.
Again I feel I'm probably losing so many things out of the original

that if my language and my culture come along and offer me an opportunity, I'd better grab it, because I lost so many things.

Wilbur: De, don't you think that's less dangerous with a lyric than with a play?

Snodgrass: That's probably true, especially when you're doing something like Molière, where the form is so much of the essence of the thing.

Wilbur: In a play like *The Learned Ladies,* which I just did, you have to think of the action in period, or the issue of how much women should be educated is going to be distorted.

Snodgrass: Absolutely. Certainly.

Wilbur: So that's why I avoid anything anachronistic; I don't want the play to be heard with a twentieth century feminist ear, and therefore misunderstood.

Snodgrass: Sure, sure.

Wilbur: But I think certainly in the case of a lyric . . .

Snodgrass: Certainly in the case of that play I would feel exactly the same way.

Wilbur: I'm sure you can take a lyric as far back as you like, you can take François Villon, for example, and use words which couldn't possibly have belonged to his vocabulary, and it's just fine. You're really transmitting him, you're updating him.

Snodgrass: Yeah, yeah.

Beacham: Is translating a different kind of creative activity than producing what we might call original poetry?

Wilbur: Yes.

Snodgrass: I guess so. It doesn't seem to me that involves the amount of strain. I do it for fun. I go to bed at night with a pad and a book of Romanian songs, or Hungarian songs, or troubadour songs or something and feel, "This is fun!" It's a game.

Wilbur: True, it's a game. It's a much more interesting game than doing crossword puzzles.

Snodgrass: Oh, boy.

Wilbur: In which they keep asking you the word for the sea eagle, you know . . . that damned erne that turns up in all those puzzles. (*Laughter*) You get tired of crossword puzzles and double-crostics, but you don't of the game of translating, which, of course, does involve a considerably greater imaginative investment, too. You have to impersonate the author to a certain extent, but thank God, he has figured out how it is going to end! (*Laughter*) That's the trouble with one's original work, or with mine at any rate, I so often find myself arrested four to five lines from the possible ending of the poem, unable to think my way to a close.

Snodgrass: Yeah, true. Your own poems take you into really dangerous and painful areas.

Wilbur: That's right.

Snodgrass: In a way that translations don't, although I find later on that I pick pieces to translate that were about exactly the things that were on my mind right then, even if I thought they weren't. Yet, that isn't painful or dangerous in the way that your own poems are. It doesn't involve so much regression, so much, oh, I don't know, dabbling in the dark areas of yourself.

Wilbur: And it doesn't involve so much danger of wasted effort.

Snodgrass: Yes! And how! Oh boy, are you right.

Wilbur: My guess is that we are both the sort of poets who throw a lot of their original work away.

Snodgrass: And how. Thank heavens! Going through all that garbage that's in your mind, all those lies you have to fight your way through. Yeah. So a lot of your work on your own stuff is exactly waste.

Wilbur: Yep.

Snodgrass: Necessary waste, but . . .

Wilbur: But it is very bitter. It is very bitter to have spent a week on something, or a month on something, and then to decide that it must go.

Snodgrass: And how. Yes indeed. (*Laughter*)

Beacham: Well, Mr. Snodgrass, your work has been publicly identified as being painful, or at least representing a painful process and perhaps a pained persona, and Mr. Wilbur, your work less so. I wonder why. Why do readers perceive that there may be less pain in your work than in Mr. Snodgrass'?

Wilbur: Oh, I don't know. Maybe it's those last five lines of poems that I was talking about. I confess frankly to being an optimist, and I hope not to be a shallow one. I come out always—not always, but most always—on the "Yes" side of things. I come out saying, "Nevertheless, it's all right." There are other poets like Randall Jarrell,

⚹ The Great Amelioration!

for example, who make it their life's business to point out the respects in which it's not all right. Everybody tells partial truths. My part of the truth is to stress what is hopeful.

Snodgrass: That seems right. As Alf Mapp said yesterday, you are a poet of delight. I guess I must not be. I mean I don't know how I seem. You know, I had a reading yesterday also, for some secondary school teachers. Afterwards one of them said, "Don't you ever write about anything you approve of?" (*Laughter*) All I could answer was that I don't think it matters whether I approve of things or not, the important thing is that I affirm them by putting them in the poem.

Wilbur: Yes. That's right. I was just listening to your voice, and there wasn't a touch of sadness in it. It's something often said, but nevertheless true, that all poetry is optative, since it has to do with exerting oneself, getting things said, getting them into forms.

Snodgrass: Yeah, and whether you think you approve of them or not really doesn't mean very much. Many of the people you think you hate you have some deep love tie to. And surely all of the people you think you love, and do indeed love, you have a good many hate ties to. And I think that the important thing is that you show that you affirm those things by getting as much of the world as you can in the poem.

Wilbur: Yes. What you are concerned with is much more important than what you vote for, or against.

Snodgrass: Oh, boy, do I think so!

Beacham: One critic, Mr. Wilbur, has said that perhaps you care too much for the things of the world. Would you . . .

Wilbur: For material objects?

Beacham: For the way material objects dominate your poems perhaps more than the personnae do.

Wilbur: Yes. I think that that is probably true. I've got more versified trees and animals than people, although the people are increasing in number as my poems go along. There are a lot more people, I think, in my last book than in my earlier ones. It's a little hard to talk in an either/or way about this, I think, because I know that I write poems about seed leaves, for example, in which there are human qualities and human problems discoverable in the description of the things or plants. I don't write a lot of nature poems in the sense that I'm writing about nature, though I do have a few of those. Much of the time when I'm talking about a tree, I'm also talking about people indirectly.

Beacham: How is your nature poetry distinct from, say, Robert Frost's nature poetry?

Wilbur: Well, I remember Frost saying once that he had only written one nature poem in his life. I thought hard about that, and I decided that he was right, and that the poem was a very early one called "In a Vale," a poem in which he claims that as a child he knew where the flower was before it grew, where the bird was before it flew. There he is saying that his spirit is continuous with that of nature, though he is saying it rather fancifully, in a way that almost negates what he is saying. Elsewhere, of course, in his poetry, Frost, though he gives us some of the most marvelous and loving evocations of natural things, is always saying that there is a dividing line between us and the world out there, and that our relations with it are unilateral. Now here I've talked entirely about him and not about me.

Snodgrass: (*Laughter*) Let me talk about you.

Wilbur: I think I'm a little more Emersonian than Mr. Frost in that I do think that we and the birds, we and the trees, are part of one scheme. Is that what you were going to say?

Snodgrass: No. What I was going to say is that this critic, I don't know who it is, thinking he was criticising you, seems to me to be giving you the highest kind of praise, and the most exactly right kind. Your poetry is full of the things of the world, and that's what love must call you to, if it is to be love. It better not be love of one's own voice, of one's self; it ought to be love of those things out there. But I also want to counteract a kind of criticism you were suggesting against your own poems. Your poems do see how difficult the world is. I'm thinking particularly about "Love Calls Us to the Things of This World." Even though there is that vision of angels, we all know we must get up and face the real world. The laundry is going onto the backs of thieves and of lovers who will indeed be undone. There is certainly a recognition of how really awful the world is, but nevertheless . . . Saying that those poems are full of things seems to me very high praise indeed.

Beacham: How, Mr. Snodgrass, do you think your poetry reflects the natural world?

Snodgrass: (*Laughter*) I sometimes refer to myself as the catheter poet, I am the first man to ever insert a catheter into a poem. I'm very proud of that. To get a detail into a poem that nobody ever put in before, you feel like, yeah, I've saved some of the world.

Beacham: Mr. Wilbur, could I ask a personal favor, which is will you read the poem "Year's End," and we can think about it in terms of the object reflecting the natural world in some way.

Wilbur: I'll see what I can do with it. That poem was written a long time ago, I think round about 1949, and we do alter and become estranged from our poems. We become, as De was saying earlier, perhaps less trustworthy interpreters of them than other people might be. Well, here's the poem. [Reads "Year's End."]

Beacham: Snodgrass: Bravo! Bravo!

Beacham: Do you hear yourself reading that poem more fervently and perhaps more passionately than you did "Seed Leaves"?

Wilbur: No. I don't think so. Except that of course there's an exclamation in this one. There's that "More time! More time!" I don't think that anything quite corresponds to that in "Seed Leaves." "Seed Leaves" is most certainly asserting something, but it's doing it more obliquely. Here, it's as if a whole lot of voices were crying out on New Year's Eve for another chance to get it right. Don't foreclose on us just yet.

Snodgrass: Yes. And this poem is more celebrant probably, whereas the other is more analytical.

Wilbur: Yes. And it involves a little sympathetic mockery.

Snodgrass: Yeah, yeah.

Beacham: In what ways are you a different poet now, Mr. Wilbur, than you were when you wrote that poem?

Wilbur: Well, in spite of the evidence you have just extorted, I think that I have become a more dramatic poet, perhaps as a result of translating plays, and that I do have more people talking out of disturbed conditions of mind, more straightforward expressions of emotion than I used to have. And also I think that I am very slowly developing a capacity to tell stories in poetry. My early poems, it seems to me, don't have much narrative character, and now, though

I'm never going to be everybody's favorite fireside yarn teller, I think I am developing an ability to build a poem in that way.

Beacham: And you, Mr. Snodgrass, are a real storyteller now, aren't you? You're telling the story of the end of World War II, and telling the stories of singers and Medieval cultures and the translations of . . .

Snodgrass: Well, I do translations, like the Romanian ballads which are four and five pages long; also there's a long, long Hungarian song about the battle at Eger against the Turks. So I tend to be translating stories a lot more. I don't think I'm writing any direct narratives myself, right now. But things have surely changed for me. I started out writing very personal, direct poems about my own most immediate problems, and certainly I'm not doing that anymore. And it looks as if I'm writing more free verse and less metered verse. I don't think that that's really true, it's just that originally I threw away lots of the free verse, and now I throw away a lot of metrical verse.

Beacham: So you don't think of yourself as telling the story of what happened the last week in Hitler's bunker?

Snodgrass: Well, in a way, but it certainly isn't a direct narrative, it's a series of monologues, and really what I'm trying to get at isn't the story of what happened, everybody knows that; I'm trying to get at what did those people think? What could they think that would lead them to do the things they did? At the time we all thought, oh, my God, how can this have happened, what could they have possibly been thinking? In the twenty years since, we find ourselves doing more and more things that suggest they weren't so different from us as we would like to believe. So I want to get at what was in the mind that made it possible or even necessary to do the horrifying things they did.

Beacham: You are creating character, then?

Snodgrass: Yeah, I think so. I'm not particularly interested in story as such. You know, the story of what went on in the bunker has already been filmed twice and I suppose it's been staged a number of times and it was a terrible flop. Simply because the things that happened in the outside world are just not interesting at all. Hitler yelling at his generals and carrying on—who cares about that? What was interesting, I think, I hope, I'm betting my life on this one, was what went on inside people's heads.

Wilbur: Yes, yes, I do have the feeling, reading your book, that what you're trying to do is to answer the question, "Were they human at all?" And one feels, yes, unfortunately, they were human, they were in some ways like me.

Snodgrass: Yeah; oh, thank you.

Wilbur: Like the reader at his worst. (*Laughter*)

Snodgrass: Yes, indeed. (*Laughter*)

Beacham: Mr. Snodgrass, could we hear a little of Eva Braun's voice in "Tea for Two?" Perhaps not the whole poem, which is rather long, but . . .

Snodgrass: Yeah, sure. I guess all I ought to say is that this takes place on April 22, after the Russians have started their attack on the city. She's in the bunker, she expects to die, they all know that they will die shortly. She had been very much neglected by Hitler and treated rather badly, and had a number of ways of getting revenge against him, as all lovers do of course. One of those was that she continually sang American songs; her favorite song was, indeed, "Tea for Two." She even translated it into German so that she could sing it in both languages. We should let Johnny Carson try it in German some night, perhaps. Anyway, the great thing that happened this day was that when she refused to leave the bunker, and insisted on staying there to die with him, he kissed her in public. That was the first public recognition she had ever had from him. [Reads "Eva Braun."]

Snodgrass: Now, I'll stop, break off there.

Beacham: Marvelous!

Wilbur: Yes.

Beacham: Any response to that, Mr. Wilbur?

Wilbur: Well, I think I'm going to take it back about the difficulties of changing voice in reading one's way through that book. I think De can do it. (*Laughter*)

Snodgrass: I never thought of this before, but I think I see a further difference in our aims. You can say there are two basic types of poetry: one kind tries to establish a tone and maintain it—like the poetry of Milton or Dryden. You seem very much in that tradition of maintaining a tone and voice and attitude. I tend to move much more in a tradition of, say, Sir Walter Raleigh and John Berryman—a poetry where you're continually opposing voices against each other.

Wilbur: That's right. That's right. I always play everything on my ocarina and you keep shifting from one instrument to another. *(Laughter)*

Snodgrass: Except for the ocarina part, I'll buy that.

Beacham: Mr. Wilbur, you once said that the power of the genie comes because he's been contained in the bottle.

Wilbur: Yes.

Beacham: What's the bottle?

Wilbur: That was written long ago, and I was justifying the use of formal means like meters, rhymes, stanzas. I think one could quarrel with that figure, with that spatial figure. Of course what I'm really saying is that if you make a lot of formal promises at the beginning of a poem, it slows you down, makes you put a good deal of choosy weight on every word that you write, and you arrive, therefore, if you write well, at a highly charged verbal structure. Good heavens! What a way to talk—verbal structure!

Beacham: Well, there will be a quiz tomorrow, Mr. Wilbur. *(Laughter)* Mr. Snodgrass, some of your "Bunker" poems are written in the shapes of bunkers.

Snodgrass: Oh, yeah.

Beacham: How did that happen and what effect does it have on the poem?

Snodgrass: Well, I was looking for a shape for Albert Speer's poems. They're made into stanzas where each line is longer than the one before; it's a kind of arbitrary growth, if you like. Which I saw as a part of his problem. You know, love of bigness, and then as his rationalizations about how much he was involved in the war and so forth. As his rationalizations start breaking down, those shapes break down. It was almost meant to imitate the shape of the stairs. He's almost always going either in or out. But also it's meant to imitate that kind of arbitrary growth. Such things get even worse in some poems that you haven't seen yet, in which the speaker is Heinrich Himmler. They have to be printed on graph paper, and in every line there are thirty letters and spaces, and then the whole poem is an alphabetical acrostic down the left hand margin. So, in other words, I'm looking for forms that will help convey what this person's character is like.

Wilbur: I'd like to hear you perform that alphabetical acrostic!

Snodgrass: *(Laughter)* Yeah, I'd like to hear that too! I don't think I can. I've been worrying about that quite a lot.

Wilbur: Quite often, though, there are little disciplines which are useful to the poet himself, in slowing down . . .

Snodgrass: Oh, sure, and making you take things out of your side vision, your night vision instead of your head-on vision. Wait, though, I've just belied my own statement, haven't I? Because I don't know how to read those poems of Heinrich Himmler's out loud. *(Laughter)* Which makes a lie out of my own theories.

Wilbur: Just an exception to your theories.

Snodgrass Oh! Okay. I just realized, though, what instrument it is for you. Since it isn't an ocarina, it is one of those fine modern John Challis harpsichords.

Wilbur: Oh. I like that.

Snodgrass: Ah, yeah, I think so. Not one of the old harpsichords; it's a good twentieth century harpsichord that you can also play jazz on and blue grass and rock and all kinds of stuff like that.

Wilbur: I'll settle.

Beacham: In concluding could I ask each of you to read a poem for us please? Mr. Wilbur?

Wilbur: Yes, I think I'll read what may be my chestnut, my anthology piece. It's called "Love Calls Us to the Things of This World." [Reads poem.]

Beacham: Thank you, Mr. Wilbur. Mr. Snodgrass?

Snodgrass: Yeah, this is a little poem called "Owls." I used to live outside of Syracuse, New York, way out in the woods, and there was a nest of great horned owls there that we watched all the time. We got very fond of them, even raised a couple of babies one year after the nest came down. This is a poem about the owls and their mating habits and so forth. The metric of the poem is the owl call, and variations of that call. It's just called "Owls." [Reads poem.]

Beacham: Thank you Mr. Snodgrass, Mr. Wilbur for being here and for your poetry.

Um > best thing he ever wrote!

Richard Wilbur
Nancy L. Bunge/1985

From *Finding the Words: Conversations with Writers Who Teach* (Athens: Ohio University Press, 1985), 171-81. Reprinted by permission of The Ohio University Press.

NB: You said that "Birches" "is happy in all the ways in which a poem can be happy" because it "does justice to world, to self, to literary tradition, and to a culture." What do your poetry students have the most trouble doing justice to?

RW: Like all young people, they are better at doing justice to self than to the world. I don't know whether you *can* do justice to yourself without doing justice to the world, but in any case there's a lot of self-absorption among young people and, most of the time, what one is doing in writing courses is pointing out moments of self-absorption. I have all my students get involved in the act of criticism. We present the poem of some student anonymously—twelve or thirteen copies, so that everyone can be staring at it—and everybody talks and *always,* unless it's the utterly successful poem which disarms criticism, *always* somebody says, "What were you trying to say in line six?" And the writer answers, in effect, "I did say it." And then the original critic, backed by perhaps two or three others now, says, "No, you didn't say it. No, it didn't come through to us. You were nudging your closest friend, maybe, but you weren't conveying it to the general reader." I suppose that's the most valuable thing that gets done in a half year of writing-teaching: people come to learn that they have to go to extraordinary lengths to compel a trained and willing reader to see something of what they want to show, think something of what they want thought. I remember Allen Tate saying in *The House of Fiction* that the commonest failing in the writing of amateur fiction could be called the "unwritten story." People think they have told the story; they haven't, they simply haven't told it.

The love of small vocabulary and incoherence that accompanied the sixties has made it harder for young writers now, even though everyone is trying to recover from that. You remember that expression, "You know, you know, you know"? It seems to me that

that expression was not just a tic, but a demand for reassurance that one belonged. "We understand each other without speaking, don't we?" I think that's what "you know" meant a lot of the time: "Aren't we all trustworthy and don't we all share the same likes and dislikes?" There was something conspiratorial or something of the shibboleth about "you know."

I think the students of the "Cambodian incursion" days were making a gesture of solidarity through that expression: affirming their mistrust of words and their respect for mute communion. Nowadays you can almost see bright people struggling to reinvent the complex sentence before your eyes. A friend of mine who is a college administrator every now and then has to say a complex sentence, and he will get into one of those morasses that begins, "I would hope that we would be able . . . " He never talked that way when I first met him, but even at his age, at his distance from the crisis in the lives of younger people, he's been to some extent alienated from easy speech.

All of this is reflected in writing courses and in a feeling among the students that it would be embarrassing to be too eloquent, too literary, too clear. It wouldn't be honest, in a certain debased sense of that word, because it would be showy. I suppose all of that is distilled in the familiar expression, "You talk like a book." (*Laughter.*) You'd think that it would or could be a compliment, but it never is. (*Laughter.*)

NB: One person I talked to said that he'd been accused of being literary. He thought that was a strange thing to accuse a poet of, but he had to agree he was.

RW: Yes. (*Laughter.*) I suppose poetry has become in good part sub-literary nowadays, and so one can understand very sharply what was meant by that man's critic. A number of years ago, the poem began to be confused with the rock lyric (*laughter*) by a great many people. And that meant shapelessness and want of grammar and any old kind of rhyming if one rhymed at all.

NB: Do you attempt to correct that attitude when you teach?

RW: I'm not very coersive; I guess I'm going to get more coersive this fall. It is, after all, 1981. I do want to encourage my students, not necessarily to understand scansion theoretically, but to try their hands, a least once, at some simple formal structure. There are always several people, sometimes more than that, who want to work in meters. I'm not complaining bitterly, but I think that I shouldn't let anybody get through the semester without brushing with that kind of discipline. I have in the past allowed people simply to try to do well in the manner that came easiest to them. And I can't explain why I'm now going to be a little more authoritarian, but I am. (*Laughter.*) I guess I'm just fed up. (*Laughter.*) I'm damned if I'm going to let any of my writing students be utterly ignorant of the literature of the past, or their work be utterly irrelevant to it.

NB: Do you give your writing students reading assignments?

RW: I pick different books in different years, sometimes an anthology containing a good deal of work from the past; but, in any case, I keep presenting them with mimeographed poems of the past and asking them to read in all ages and in as many languages as they can manage. To further that a little, I'll give them an exercise in translation: a French poem, accompanied by a literal translation and by a critical commentary borrowed from somebody, all of this to be worked up into a translation. I've even asked people to translate from less familiar languages because, with a sufficient amount of apparatus, I think it can be done. If the right sounds are made aloud, somehow that's a penetration of the poem's spirit. If they hear what kind of meter it is, that helps too.

I do think that there's a swing back now toward some sort of core curriculum, and so students are more and more picking up a sense of literary tradition. The period of disruption caused by the Vietnam War was disastrous in that respect. At many places I knew of, and at Wesleyan where I was teaching, many students got the idea that the past was indeed dead and that all they needed to learn was themselves. Oh, of course, they needed to learn also the things which they had appropriated to themselves, or decorated themselves with, such as William Blake and Hermann Hesse; there were certain things you were expected to have in your pocket, as you had a guitar in your hand during that period. (*Laughter.*) But I was most annoyed by the teachers who went along with it all and, indeed, fostered a great deal of it, told students that the past was irrelevant, accepted that nonsense word "relevance" as a way of acquitting students of making the acquaintance of humanity throughout its whole temporal range. Such a primitive notion: that you can ignore the past as a mob of strangers. Those people represent what one might again be, or what one still is. At Smith, a lot of my present students are pretty decently trained in the literary tradition. There are outstanding girls who really know it. Everybody has some sense of it, and you don't need to bully people into reading Chaucer; they will have read some Chaucer.

NB: You have said that it's hard to be a poet in a culture with no strong sense of community. Do you still believe that?

RW: For Americans, it's a problem. A country like France, for a contrast, feels itself to be monolithic, is violently conscious of its own culture and its own past and has one big cultural and governmental center. We're spread all over the place. That's good in a way; I'm not kicking about that, but we are. Los Angeles and Boston are remote from each other in more ways than one, and surely it's good for every place to have it's own character; but when one begins to think about the country, one has to think of something fragmented or incoherent; as Brooks Adams said, "The incoherence of American democracy." He thought America would have been more coherent in every sense if George Washington's notion of extending a canal from Washington to the Ohio had been put into action. That, he thought, would have made Washington not only the governmental, but also the commercial and the cultural center of the country.

NB: Your poems are very rich, but you sometimes wait a long time for them. Could you wait that long when you were twenty?

RW: Oh, yes. Yes, I did. I suppose I wrote a little faster than I write now, but I've always written very, very slowly and that's one reason there tends to be, for better or for worse, quite a lot in the individual line, why paraphrase would be hard. If you picked up the latest issue of the average poetry periodical nowadays, you'd find for the most part a density of language which is approximately that of prose. It is sometimes good in an affectingly sincere way, but because I'm a product of my time, it lacks for me the excitement that I look for in poetry. I look for the unparaphrasable; too many poems are now being written which are their own paraphrases.

NB: Can you persuade your students to wait the way you do?

RW: It's hard and unfair, isn't it, to do a thing like that, because part of my job is to bully them into writing eight poems and seven exercises in a semester. So I must keep the pressure on them. At the same time, I have to be understanding of blocks, because I would surely have a block if I were placed under my own demands. I do talk about how bad it is to spoil a good idea by executing it too rapidly. And I do as my students do in our group critiques; point out that such and such a line is pretty flat compared to the rest; but I think that's as far as I go with that kind of thing.

NB: Some people say that their writing students come into class believing that the most important aspect of a poem or story is its theme and that they have to think up something significant to say before they begin to write.

RW: I can recall student poems which seemed not to have arisen from the genuine concerns of the poet but simply from an effort to sound weighty. One student, way back there when I was first teaching at Harvard, said to me, "Mr. Wilbur, you're not an easy person to write for." And I said, "Great God, have you been writing for me all this semester?" I guess that many people do come into your class with the feeling that they are to some extent writing for you, and if they think that the English teacher wants them to adopt a theme of proven weight, there it comes: a poem which has been misconceived from the start. I often quote to my students that well-known bit of Auden's where he says that the most promising thing in a young writer is a hankering to play around with words, and that the most unpromising thing to hear from a young writer is, "I have a lot of ideas I want to express." (*Laughter.*)

NB: But you don't have any system for handling that.

RW: No. I think that if I ever say anything about the matter in class, I do so in the particular case. I might say, "We know by now that this writer is capable of something better than this. This appears to be a high-minded propaganda poem, or a poem on a supposedly obligatory weighty theme, and that's why it isn't any good." Not that one shouldn't start with some sense of a subject, but one shouldn't start with somebody else's subject.

NB: Do you regularly teach literature?

RW: I've always taught literature. In fact, I started out to be a teacher of literature; at any rate, that's what chiefly interested me when I was at Harvard. I really wouldn't enjoy teaching, if I were teaching only creative writing. I *like* teaching writing as a relaxation from the other kind of teaching, as another kind of relationship with the students—inevitably, a more personal one—and another way of connecting the literature of the past which interests me with the present.

NB: Most of the literature classes I had emphasized what you call "paraphrasable meaning," but I imagine that you focus on something else. What do you do in your literature classes?

RW: When I teach Milton, for example, I deal with him in all respects, spending a lot of time on matters of technique. You have to with a great technician, with the greatest verse architect in history; you cannot understand that "L'Allegro" and "Il Penseroso" are serious poems unless you worry the structure to death and discover the ideas implicit in the structure. And so I and the students wrestle for several days until we've found the structure of the two poems. You have to talk about theology too and to some extent, history. I've always been inclined to slack on that latter side of things because when I was in college, the New Criticism had just come along vivifying the reading process, but making some things impermissible. Biographical and historical information were considered dispensable at that time, and so if there's something I badly neglect, it's those two things. When I teach Poe, I'm always resistant to biographical interpretations of his stories, although Poe gives his own birthdate to William Wilson and the tales contain all kinds of sly references to his life. I probably have a certain culpable blindness to the pertinence of biography.

NB: Do you read aloud in class?

RW: I do that a great deal, both when I'm teaching literature and when I'm teaching writing. I think there's no substitute for it. You read something aloud as well as you can, and I think you thereby give a new sense of its measure as well as of its meaning. If you're reading a student poem aloud to your students, they all know that you're going to do as well by it as you can. And if it doesn't quite work, they have a fresh sense of where and why it doesn't work. I read things as long as "Lycidas" aloud to my classes when I'm teaching literature; the musical and emotional dimensions can't be got in any better way, and also a feeling of the poem as a whole. If one is talking at it and explicating little corners of it, one can lose what they call "the big picture"; one can simplify wonderfully by reading. I try to get students to read aloud too, a thing they're often scared to do because they haven't been asked to do it in any primary or secondary school. I wish that that were done more in the earlier stages of schooling; everyone should have a competence in that.

NB: How did you happen to write on Poe, or to write criticism at all?

RW: The thing that excited me most as an undergraduate at Amherst was the impact on my teachers of the New Criticism. So I became excited, not only about the sort of literature to which the New Critics pointed, but also by the New Critics themselves and the idea of criticism. To think of looking at a poem and conveying what you see in it to a third person was very exciting. So I had an itch to be a scholar and critic when I was an undergraduate at Amherst, and when I was in graduate school at Harvard, and I would have been very sorry not to write some criticism, even after poetry and translation had more or less taken me over. Poe was someone I read as an adolescent—I suppose even younger than that—for the first time. During World War II I had among other things a beat-up little paperback of Poe in my knapsack; when I was in a foxhole at Monte Cassino, I started reading Poe and all of a sudden got a sense of submerged meaning in some of his stories: a very sure sense that it was there. Not that I knew what it was, but that it was there. So I began reading him with that conviction in mind. After the war, when I was at Harvard, had done my M.A. and decided not to go for the doctorate but be a junior fellow, I started teaching Poe again—hard. And I wrote most of a book on Poe which I had to throw away because I was not able to find the right terms for describing what was going on underneath the surface. But I did teach a course in him at the time, and since then, once or twice, I've taught courses in him—always seminar-sized courses, so that everybody could mull freely and collectively and make discoveries. And now and then I've done an introduction, a job of editing, an essay.

NB: I read your introduction to the Laurel edition of Poe's poetry almost twenty years ago. Your discussion of Poe's fascination with Supernal Beauty has made a lot of sense to me and to my students. Without it, the tales become simply horror stories which illustrate the use of techniques like the unreliable narrator.

RW: Well, it always *is* interesting to talk about the narrators in Poe; but since Poe himself argued that all imaginative literature has undercurrents of meaning, I think it's too bad not to go for those undercurrents, even though it involves a lot of wild conjecture and subjectivity.

NB: What is the difference between writing poetry and writing prose? Is it easier for you to write prose?

RW: I suppose prose is an easier thing for me to write than verse, but both are hard for me. If your main business is writing poetry, you find it hard not to write a somewhat incrusted prose or, at any rate, a prose you've worried pretty hard. I write prose very slowly, just as I do verse. I think slowly, and write slowly, and I wish I were able to do what my wife does, which is write a damned good letter very fast and get it into the mail. I've never been able to kid myself into doing that, even by sticking the paper directly into the typewriter and hammering it out. Mostly I find myself, if it's a serious letter, writing a few notes in pencil before I ever get to the typewriter. That slows matters down. As I've confessed here and there, it's sometimes taken me five years to finish a poem. Fortunately, it's never taken me five days to finish a letter. (*Laughter.*)

NB: When you write prose, do you make notes or outline before you write?

RW: I don't outline. Well, I suppose I'd better not lie. Sometimes I have tried to outline, but I've never outlined before starting. I've always started, then discovered that I was in a mess, and then made a little list of what points I ought to make and in what order. That, I suppose, is an outline. I've never used the "I" and "A" and "B" and "C" kind of outline, but I have gone so far as to sketch a structure in the margin of the page to clarify the confusion I've gotten into.

NB: It sounds like you write prose the way you write poetry, just following . . .

RW: I just try to see which idea logically comes next. I don't know what the rule for the paragraph is, but I think I know what a paragraph is. (*Laughter.*)

NB: The student you mentioned who knew all the grammatical rules but couldn't use them is a wonderful example of why there's no point in learning those rules.

RW: The advantage to the rule is that if you're telling someone where he is wrong . . .

NB: You can identify it.

RW: That's why, when I teach a poetry writing course, I give the

first day of talking about meters, rhymes and stanzas. I discuss all of
the technical terms, and the point is not that the students will then
know how to put five feet together and get a pentameter, but that
when they're criticizing the poems I hand out at the next meeting,
they'll be able to say: "There seems to be a foot lacking here."
(*Laughter.*)

NB: What part of your education was most helpful to your writing?

RW: Certain of my literature courses presented me excitingly with
writing which made me want to "do something like that." The same
is true of the courses I've taught. The courses most useful to me have
been the ones which excited me by putting me into the presence of
things which I wanted not so much to copy as to equal in art and
vitality.

NB: If there had been a lot of writing programs around when you
were a student, do you think it would have been a good idea for you
to go to one?

RW: Probably not a good idea at all. I went to Amherst. Amherst is
a place I'm terribly fond of, and so I shall probably exaggerate its
virtues, but the air of Amherst is full of approval for poetry and for
writing, and always has been. You can't solve the matter by saying,
"Oh, Emily Dickinson lived in that town," or "Oh, Robert Frost was
on the faculty for a while." It's no one thing, it's no number of things
that you can add up, it's just there. There was a great deal of extra-
curricular excitement about writing when I was a student there, and
all of one's teachers were glad to look at anything in the way of a
poem or a story and criticize it. They were always very encouraging,
and with all that encouragement, it wasn't necessary to burrow into a
writing course. A number of my friends did take the one writing
course then offered at Amherst, but I didn't see the necessity. I visited
it once; it seemed OK, but I felt I would learn more somewhere else.

NB: Some people have said that it hurts literature to have so many
people become writers by going through writing programs.

RW: I think it's hurting a lot of people, and that it's hurting the
whole scene. I'm not alone in having this cranky feeling. Too many
people are failing to study what they *should* study by concentrating
too much on creative writing courses. There are so many schools in
which people are allowed to major in creative writing, right through
to a B.A. They go through impoverished, knowing, as Yeats said,

"nothing but their blind, stupified hearts." And so often, having become defective and specialized in this way, they go on to graduate school in creative writing, and then drift on out into the M.F.A. market looking for jobs, not too many of which are there. Until recently, the government has been providing them with poetry in the schools programs, occasional fellowships and subsidized little magazines in which they can publish. It's a lamentably "supportive" world in which far too many people are encouraged to imagine themselves poets beyond the point at which they should wake up and decide to do something useful. One consequence of all this over-encouragement and subsidizing is that we have quantities of little magazines full of bad poetry, depressing poetry, around us. Standards are lowered as soon as you have a whole lot of creative writing courses, because you can't ask for the highest performance of young people who have had much experience as writers and have no strong calling. Insensibly, you lower your standard. And standards are lowered on the graduate level, because there are so many people going to these competing schools of writing. I think that the cessation or lessening of government support for poetry is not going to be a bad thing. I have no desire to make anybody stop writing poetry, but I think it would be a favor to many people and to poetry if some people stopped thinking of themselves primarily as young poets and kept on writing on the side.

It affects everybody if a whole lot of bad work in any art is being published and supported. If there are magazines all around us full of poems which start, "I turn off the television," and so on—that sort of loose-jointed, prosaic, supposedly sincere poem that says what you have done in the last five minutes—it's going to affect the general sense of what poetry ought to be doing.

NB: I'd like to ask about "The Writer," the poem you wrote to your daughter. What did you mean by "It is always a matter of life . . . and death"?

RW: Getting oneself off one's chest, writing. I'm wishing her a lucky passage, and it's a passage both in the sense of making connections with the world, getting out of oneself, and of writing a good paragraph. When one is dealing with young writers, one almost always has both those feelings going: you're hoping that the young writer will do well, will write a good story or a good poem; you're also hoping that the doing of that will be a successful coming to terms with the world by way of the common means of language.

NB: Is there anything you'd like to add?

RW: Yes. Since many of my remarks have been a bit negative or tart, I'd like to right the balance by saying that there is, in fact, much good poetry being written these days, that year after year I encounter students who are truly gifted, and that a course in writing can be stimulating and salutary. As for anyone's taking *two* such courses, or three, at the cost of neglecting Geology or Latin, I have my doubts.

Poet-to-Poet: A Conversation between Richard Wilbur and Linda Pastan

Howard County Poetry and Literature Society/1986

Sponsored by the Howard County Poetry and Literature Society, videotaped by Cable 8 TV Studio of Howard Community College in Columbia, Maryland in the Fall of 1986. Reprinted by permission of the Howard County Poetry and Literature Society.

Wilbur: Linda, I suppose we have certain things in common. I know that we were around Radcliffe and Harvard at the same time. And then we have both taken to writing poems since then—maybe before then—but at any rate noticeably since then. And then we're both married poets with spouses and children. Does that exhaust our similarities?

Pastan: No, we do each have a daughter who has taken to writing, which at least for me has made me start thinking about the life of a writer and the choices of such a life. I fell into it but my daughter is thinking about actually choosing it.

Wilbur: Yes, that's a big difference, isn't it? To resolve to be a writer and to figure out how life should practically be organized in order for one to be a writer. I just fell into it too myself, and so I can't say that I've made practical arrangements to write. I've just lived a life and been stubborn about going on writing, I suppose.

Pastan: I love your poem about your daughter writing. I don't think I've ever tried that as a subject, but maybe you could read that for us?

Wilbur: I haven't written an awful lot of daughter poems, but I'm glad to have written one poem about someone I'm as fond of as I am of my daughter. She was always writing short stories, poems too, but the short stories were what were distinguished from the start. And this poem you refer to, the one called "The Writer," is about my daughter Ellen as she was back in an old Victorian ark of a house. And she had the best lighted room in the house, a second floor bedroom that looked out on American linden and European linden. It was a nice place to write. Still, there was a lot of struggle and doubt about it for her at that stage and that's in this poem.

In her room at the prow of the house
Where light breaks, and the windows are tossed with linden,
My daughter is writing a story.

I pause in the stairwell, hearing
From her shut door a commotion of typewriter-keys
Like a chain hauled over a gunwale

Young as she is, the stuff
Of her life is a great cargo, and some of it heavy:
I wish her a lucky passage

But now it is she who pauses,
As if to reject my thought and its easy figure.
A stillness greatens, in which

The whole house seems to be thinking,
And then she is at it again with a bunched clamor
Of strokes, and again is silent.

I remember the dazed starling
Which was trapped in that very room, two years ago;
How we stole in, lifted a sash

And retreated, not to affright it;
And how for a helpless hour, through the crack of the door,
We watched the sleek, wild, dark

And iridescent creature
Batter against the brilliance, drop like a glove
To the hard floor, or the desk-top,

And wait then, humped and bloody,
For the wits to try it again; and how our spirits
Rose when, suddenly sure,

It lifted off from a chair-back,
Beating a smooth course for the right window
And clearing the sill of the world.

It is always a matter, my darling,
Of life or death, as I had forgotten. I wish
What I wished you before, but harder.

I remember that a critic in *The New York Times* lit into my last lines
in that poem. He said that to say it is always a matter of life or death
is a little bit flat, a little bit banal. And it was very odd that he should
be saucy about those particular lines, because I'd felt so pleased with

getting that close to the colloquial norm. It seemed to me like straight talk rather than banality. But there's a fine line, isn't there, between the two?

Pastan: I'm not sure critics always see these fine lines. . . .

Wilbur: Have you got a daughter poem or a child poem?

Pastan: Well, I have many daughter poems. I don't have one about my daughter as a writer, but I have one about the naming of my daughter, and I think that the preoccupation of writers with naming might actually influence the children who are so named. Her name is Rachel, which literally means a ewe, a female sheep, and this poem is about the naming of Rachel. "Rachel":

> We named you
> for the sake
> of the syllables
> and for the small boat
> that followed the Pequod,
> gathering lost children
> of the sea.
>
> We named you
> for the dark-eyed girl
> who waited at the well
> while her lover
> worked seven years
> and again
> seven.
>
> We named you
> for the small daughters
> of the Holocaust
> who followed their six-pointed stars
> to death
> and were all of them
> known as
> Rachel.

Wilbur: Your poems are very good, as they say, "reading poems," very good reading aloud poems. They get straight across. I don't think I'd heard that poem read, and I think I just swallowed it whole. The name Rachel is always associated with grieving, isn't it? Amongst other things.

Pastan: Well, Rachel grieving for her lost children, but I think I was very influenced by Thomas Mann's Rachel in *Joseph and His Brothers,* who was the most fetching heroine.

Wilbur: Yes.

Pastan: I had read that book quite, quite soon before my daughter was born.

Wilbur: I think you were saying before you started reading that, out of our preoccupation with naming we writers imagine, perhaps correctly, that if we name a child Daisy, she's going to be something like a daisy. Robert Frost has a poem called "Maple," not one of his best or best-known poems, but it has that theme. A girl is named Maple and she grows up to be all the nice things that a maple tree is. It's bound to be coercive, what you're named. Now I was named Richard by my parents, and it wasn't a family name; it was a name they liked so they just picked it out of the air and gave it to me. But of course I had to think about it. I've had to think whether I was really lion-hearted or not.

Pastan: I actually have a poem which I hadn't thought about reading, but will, about the subject of naming. It's a poem that I wrote for a cousin named Susan who changed her name to Shoshana and the poem is called "A Name."

> David means beloved.
> Peter is a rock. They named me
> Linda which means beautiful
> in Spanish—a language
> I never learned.
> Even naked
> we wear our names.
> In the end we leave them behind
> carved into desktops
> and gravestones, inscribed
> on the flyleaf of Bibles
> where on another page
> God names the generations
> of Shem, Ham, and Japheth.
>
> Homer cast a spell with names
> giving us the list
> of warriors and their ships
> I read my children to sleep by.
> There are as many names underfoot
> as leaves in October;

they burn as briefly on the tongue,
and their smoke could darken
the morning sky to dusk.
Remember the boy of seven
who wandered the Holocaust alone
and lost not his life
but his name? Or the prince whose name
was stolen with his kingdom?

When I took my husband's name
and fastened it to mine
I was as changed
as a child
when the priest sprinkles it
with water and a name
that saves it a place in heaven.
My grandfather gave me a name
in Hebrew I never heard,
but it died with him.
If I had taken that name
who would I be,
and if he calls me now
how will I know to answer?

Wilbur: It's bottomless the question of names, what we feel about names. Some of the things we feel are pretty superstitious. I feel that if I don't know that that's philodendron, I have less control over it. I assume it's philodendron. Somehow, if I have a thing by the name I almost have it by the scruff of the neck.

Pastan: I suppose that's why we write poems, in a sense, to get those things named and by the scruff of their necks.

Wilbur: Yes, makes things quiet down a little and organize themselves. Well I certainly like that poem. A friend of yours changed her name from Susan to?

Pastan: To Shoshana.

Wilbur: Sh-su. I can't say it.

Pastan: Right. I couldn't say it either—

Wilbur: Is it a Hebrew name?

Pastan: It's a Hebrew name. And I would giggle when introducing her and the poem was written sort of as an apology to her.

Wilbur: Some names take a little practice before you can say them. Shoshana is a little bit of a tongue twister or something like

that. I stayed once for a couple of days, for about three days, with a
poet in Finland whose name was Aarvo Turtiainen and it took me
three days to be able to speak his name. During the first two days he
was a little irritated at me for not measuring up. I have at last come to
say it, as you can see I like to show off by saying it. Well now, do I get
to read a poem?

Pastan: Absolutely.

Wilbur: I think I'll read another family poem since we started that
way. One of my sons was just married two days ago and I think I'd
like to read "A Wedding Toast," which I wrote for the wedding of my
eldest son fifteen years ago.

> St. John tells how, at Cana's wedding-feast,
> The water-pots poured wine in such amount
> That by his sober count
> There were a hundred gallons at the least.
>
> It made no earthly sense, unless to show
> How whatsoever love elects to bless
> Brims to a sweet excess
> That can without depletion overflow.
>
> Which is to say that what love sees is true;
> That the world's fullness is not made but found.
> Life hungers to abound
> And pour its plenty out for such as you.
>
> Now, if your loves will lend an ear to mine,
> I toast you both, good son and dear new daughter.
> May you not lack for water,
> And may that water smack of Cana's wine.

I sent that poem somewhere—perhaps to *The New Yorker?*—
somewhere that didn't print it. It seems to me that the editor of
whatever magazine initially rejected it said that the word "depletion"
had been spoiled for a time because readers couldn't look at it
without thinking of Texas and the oil depletion allowance.

Pastan: My goodness.

Wilbur: I wrote back and said we musn't let words be spoiled, that
we must always figure that we can redeem anything that has been
used and misused, however badly. Don't you feel that way about it?
That we ought to write out of all the words that are in and out of the
dictionary?

Pastan: Absolutely, and I get very angry when people tell me what I can and can't write about, and what words to use. They are doing it all the time.

Wilbur: Not everything that you write has to be "Linda." Not everything has to be beautiful and written in words like lagoon or cellar door or whatever people think are euphonious or pretty.

Pastan: Your poems are wonderfully musical and yet you're one of the poets—and there aren't many—who can use all the music of the traditional forms without ever making us feel that we're listening to something old fashioned.

Wilbur: Well, bless you for saying that. If it's true that's exactly what I would like because the last thing I would want to seem is a sort of timid home-sticker who's using old forms in the sort of antiquarian spirit. I don't want my poems to be a kind of aesthetic Williamsburg.

Pastan: I do have something I meant to ask you, which is, do you think which form you're going to use before you begin, or does each poem come to you more in terms of language and subject and then find the form. . . .

Wilbur: Now, I know that you sometimes worked in so-called forms and sometimes not, but I'll bet that we write in exactly the same way, even though perhaps a greater percentage of my poems come out metrical and rhymed. I certainly never say to myself, "Now let's write a sonnet," or "Wouldn't it be grand to try the ballade form." Nothing like that. I start talking in poems. I find some words that are interesting and that have a kind of rhythm, and they constitute a first line. We know where to break, when to start another line. And after a while a stanza appears, if it's going to appear; if it's a freer sort of poem that won't happen. Sometimes I have found myself writing things like ballades and rondeaus, but only because those forms have gotten into my memory and my blood so that I could as naturally blunder into writing a ballade as I could suddenly start whistling a waltz without knowing that that was what I was doing. I don't think any of this is good unless it's second nature.

Pastan: Well, it is quite different for me, really, since in the majority of cases I construct the form, which is what free verse really is; it's inventing a new form for each poem. But then occasionally I'll get taken over by a form, so that it's the form that's in my mind and I'll have to find the poem to fit it rather than the other way around,

which is quite strange. Last year I couldn't stop writing sonnets. I
wrote six or seven sonnets about the Garden of Eden and nothing
else would come except sonnets.

Wilbur: But surely you weren't enamoured of making some kind
of repeated technical experiment? It must've been more like having a
tune in your mind.

Pastan: It was like having a tune, right. Right.

Wilbur: You know what I wish you'd read? I wish you'd read a
poem I heard you read at Pittsburgh recently, the pantun, if you've
got it around.

Pastan: Yes. That actually is an example of what I was saying. I
heard somebody read a pantun and the form, the repetitive form
without any words, was in my head for such a long time that I had to
sit down and try it myself. This is a form without rhyme or meter, but
where the lines keep repeating in a very specified pattern. It's called
"Something About the Trees":

> I remember what my father told me:
> There is an age when you are most yourself.
> He was just past fifty then,
> Was it something about the trees that made him speak?
>
> There is an age when you are most yourself.
> I know more now than I did once.
> Was it something about the trees that made him speak?
> Only a single leaf had turned so far.
>
> I know more now than I did once.
> I used to think he'd always be the surgeon.
> Only a single leaf had turned so far,
> Even his body kept its secrets.
>
> I used to think he'd always be the surgeon,
> My mother was the perfect surgeon's wife.
> Even his body kept its secrets.
> I thought they both would live forever.
>
> My mother was the perfect surgeon's wife,
> I still can see her face at thirty.
> I thought they both would live forever,
> I thought I'd always be their child.
>
> I still can see her face at thirty.
> When will I be most myself?

I thought I'd always be their child.
In my sleep it's never winter.

When will I be most myself?
I remember what my father told me.
In my sleep it's never winter.
He was just past fifty then.

Wilbur: That's a dandy. I remember the effect it had on our audience at Pittsburgh. They all took it and, complex though the form is, it's fed to the hearer at an assimilable rate I think because, well, you're talking about something most universal. You're talking about it very simply and yet in wonderful phrases. I love the line, "When will I be most myself?" Yes; I think I could start saying that to myself and haunt myself for weeks with it. It's an insoluble question for everybody.

Pastan: Recently, it seems to me, just by looking in the literary magazines and in the commercial magazines like *The New Yorker* and *The Atlantic*, that many more poets are coming back to form. And I wondered what you thought about that?

Wilbur: It seems to be everybody's opinion that there's a revival of interest in form, so called, and the use of traditional means. I think it's so. I must say I don't scour all the magazines to find out, but I keep noticing that so-and-so, who used to be exclusively a sort of Iowa free verse poet, has now discovered that there's something for him in rhyming a bit, using a truly metrical stanzaic pattern. One such poet wrote me a couple of years ago and said, "How have I been so blind to the gaiety of form?" He had apparently always associated it with stuffiness. He didn't know what every kindergarten child knows, he'd forgotten what every kindergarten child knows, that there's a lot of primitive fun in making the same sound over again, repeating and yet varying a rhythm. I don't really think there's a profound reason for this change that's occurring. I suspect that things go tidally in the world of the arts. That people get tired of doing one thing and think, well maybe I'll do another. Also, any impulse wears itself out. I think Ezra Pound himself said that he thought that the possibilities of free verse were going to be exhausted before the end of the twentieth century. And many people, many writers, must feel that, for them at any rate, the possibilities of free verse have been exhausted. And now they'd like to perk up their poems in some other way. More and

more, it seems to me, people are becoming aware that the use of
rhyme and of meter can be as perfectly natural and organic as the
use of any of its techniques by free verse. I don't think there's a kind
of prejudice against artifice which there was for a time, in the 1960s,
for example. It's funny to be annoyed by artifice in art, but a lot of
people were for a while there.

Pastan: I know that people say that you're not allowed to write
poems about writing, for example. I seem to have a number of them
scattered here and there. Do you have any on that subject? Have you
avoided that?

Wilbur: I think I have very few poems about writing. I have one
poem about the Etruscan poets because I visited some Etruscan
tombs in Italy and I began to be burdened by the thought of how it
would be to have committed all of your best ideas, all of your best
sounds and movements, to a language now utterly dead. That's a
little poem, let me read that. "To the Etruscan Poets":

> Dream fluently, still brothers, who when young
> Took with your mothers' milk the mother tongue.
>
> In which pure matrix, joining world and mind,
> You strove to leave some line of verse behind.
>
> Like a fresh track across a field of snow,
> Not reckoning that all could melt and go.

I don't know. Do you think that's true about why poets write? Do
they write something in order to leave something behind?

Pastan: I don't think it's certainly a conscious thing that makes
one write.

Wilbur: No, it seems to me as something that might cross your
mind after you'd written fifty poems or so. You might say, how nice if
one of these should be read twelve weeks from now, or twelve years
from now. But it surely isn't the primary urge of the poet. What I say
about the motive of the Etruscans in that poem is really not their
motive but the way I'm thinking about them.

Pastan: I think one of the motives has to be the way one can
make use of everything in the world around you. Nothing has to be
wasted. I sometimes think of it as being thrifty. Everything can be
finally used in a poem.

Wilbur: You want to use it up. Use up the world and use up the
language too. I know that there are certain words I've always wanted

to use and haven't gotten around to it yet. And it annoys me to find that I'm repeating some of the same words I've used before. I suppose it depends on how showily you use certain words. If you use words rather showily sometimes you don't want to repeat a showy use of them. I remember Dick Eberhart saying to me one time, "You can't say monument again, you've said that in such and such a poem." Well, now, we're running out of time. Have you got a poem that you'd like to sort of close this out with?

Pastan: Let me see. Maybe I'll read my "Ethics" poem as a final poem. It grew out of many years of ethics class.

Wilbur: Oh, I think I've heard this one, yes.

Pastan:

> In ethics class so many years ago
> our teacher asked this question every fall:
> if there were a fire in a museum
> which would you save, a Rembrandt painting
> or an old woman who hadn't many
> years left anyhow? Restless on hard chairs
> caring little for pictures or old age
> we'd opt one year for life, the next for art
> and always half-heartedly. Sometimes
> the woman borrowed my grandmother's face
> leaving her usual kitchen to wander
> some drafty, half-imagined museum.
> One year, feeling clever, I replied
> why not let the woman decide herself?
> Linda, the teacher would report, eschews
> the burdens of responsibility.
> This fall in a real museum I stand
> before a real Rembrandt, old woman,
> or nearly so, myself. The colors
> within this frame are darker than autumn,
> darker even than winter—the browns of earth,
> though earth's most radiant elements burn
> through the canvas. I know now that woman
> and painting and season are almost one
> and all beyond saving by children.

Wilbur: Yes. That's still a nice poem. One thing I thought hearing you read is how a large part of the fun of writing poetry is seeing if without exclamation points, without quotation marks, without any hoking of it in any way, you can shift your voice from one tone to the other, and out into another. There's some amusement in that poem and you didn't change your voice while you were reading it—it just transpired from the words.

Pastan: Do you have one you'd like to finish us with?

Wilbur: I don't think there's time for us to finish. I think we'd better end by my just thanking you for that one. Thank you.

Pastan: Thank you.

Afternoon Delight: Brian Bedford and Friends Reading Great Scenes from Molière

Howard County Poetry and Literature Society/1988

Sponsored by the Howard County Poetry and Literature Society, videotaped by Cable 8 TV Studio of Howard Community College at the Smith Theatre in Columbia, Maryland on May 3, 1988. Reprinted by permission of the Howard County Poetry and Literature Society.

Molière is to the French what Shakespeare is to the English: their great man of the theatre. At his peak, the seventeenth century actor and playwright was under the patronage of Louis XIV. Molière's company performed at Versailles and in Paris was the forerunner of today's French National Theatre, the Comédie-Française. To confer with his patron, Molière was sometimes asked to breakfast with the Sun King and his courtiers in the royal bed chamber. Molière's great comedies of character spring to life in modern conversational rhymed English thanks to Richard Wilbur. *Tartuffe, The Misanthrope,* and *School for Wives,* translated with fidelity and charm, are a continuous delight from beginning to end.

During his year as Poet Laureate, Mr. Wilbur hosted a program of staged readings from his Molière at Smith Theatre, Columbia, Maryland. Leading the cast was Brian Bedford, who created the role of Arnolphe in *School for Wives* on Broadway, winning a Tony Award. After the readings, Mr. Wilbur will join Mr. Bedford downstage for a discussion with the audience. And now, Richard Wilbur.

[Wilbur presents actor Brian Bedford and actresses Helen Carey and Michele Farr. He introduces *Tartuffe* and the plot elements leading up to the scene performed.]

[*The Misanthrope* introduced and performed.]

[*The School for Wives* introduced and performed.]

Bedford: Anybody curious about anything?

Question: My question would be for either one of you. It seems to me that Molière has had a real resurgence in the last three or four

years. It seems that everyone, the campus theatre, professional
theatres, they're doing so much more Molière than previously. What
do you think the reason is for that?

Bedford: Well, I think Richard Wilbur should answer that, but I'll
tell you the reason is because of Richard Wilbur. Because he has
made these plays accessible to and relevant to audiences in 1988.
Molière, of course, was a great genius, but he was very, very lucky—
wherever he is floating around up there—very lucky for this man to
have crossed his path because, unfortunately, equally great writers,
dramatists, great in different ways, for instance Chekhov and Ibsen,
they have not found their Richard Wilbur, and so unfortunately we
don't have access to these plays. But this man has made them
accessible to us and I think Richard should continue that. Do you
have any feeling why Molière . . . [Laughter]

Wilbur: I love your reasons and I'm certainly not going to hasten
to deny them. I think we also should give Molière credit for being
timeless and generally human in ways in which many dramatists are
not. The other person I've translated is Racine and he's a very great
dramatist. But it is harder, I think, to be faithful to him and at the
same time bring him close to a contemporary audience. Why?
Because there are qualities of belief and feeling in Racine that put
him back in the seventeenth century, amongst the stern Jansenists
and those who believe that we have no free will. There's no such
impediment in the attitude of Molière toward the world. I think we
can understand instantly in each of his plays that there's some central
character, like Arnolphe or Tartuffe, who is behaving in a distorted
and unbalanced way, in a way that Molière didn't consider natural,
nor would we consider natural. It's very easy to understand what he
thinks is wrong with his chief characters and to understand the impact
they have on a world which really isn't very strange to us. I think the
world of seventeenth century France is quite intelligible to our
twentieth century American world.

Bedford: The extraordinary thing also is, as Richard said, that he
captured a way of behavior which he didn't consider natural. But in
point of fact, it was the way he himself behaved, wasn't it? [Laughter]

Wilbur: You mean Molière himself?

Bedford: Yes.

Wilbur: Oh, yes, yes!

Bedford: That's one of the extraordinary things, you know. That, like Arnolphe, Molière in middle age fell desperately in love with a very, very young girl . . . For instance, in *The Misanthrope,* which is patently him, and again he's mad about Celimene, the delicious young creature who drives him absolutely mad and he's going insane with jealousy. He experienced all these things, and what amazes me is that he can remove himself sufficiently to see the absurdity of his own behavior.

Wilbur: And play the part!

Bedford: And then play the part! But not only him playing the part, the girl he was mad about in real life was the girl playing the part that he was mad about in the play!

Question: I would just like to ask Mr. Wilbur, just for a minute, if he would speak briefly about the difference of the French language and the English language as he's experienced it?

Wilbur: I think for the translator of French classic plays there are lots of built-in difficulties. You cannot imitate the rhythm of a French line because the French language simply unrolls in a syllabic manner different from English, which is highly accentual. The basic French meter is a twelve-syllable line, the Alexandrine; our basic meter is the pentameter. And they really don't make the same kind of waves, but fidelity consists I think in unpacking the French Alexandrine and accomodating its materials thought by thought in the pentameter. There's a built-in infidelity here. You're taking a language which moves in gentle waves and putting it into a language which comes down hard on its stressed syllables. One thing that makes you worry about this while you're translating is that if you're rhyming, as the original does, and as you should out of fidelity to Molière and the spirit of comedy, you're going to be coming down hard on your rhyme sounds at the ends of the lines in a way in which the French does not do. You're going to seem to be asking for laughs in a way in which the original, which is less emphatic, doesn't do. So you have to be aware of that and to try to keep every couplet from going bang and begging applause. There are other things, no doubt, that I could think of that are just basic differences between one language and another. And one simply alertly seeks out something parallel and avoids the folly of seeking to translate it directly—to produce something that is the same. You could never produce a translation that is identical to the original.

Bedford: Is this why, conversely, the French have problems with translating Shakespeare?

Wilbur: I suppose that they do.

Bedford: I'm told that the German translations of Shakespeare are absolutely superb because of the similarity between the two languages, but the difficulty of French people, of capturing the iambic pentameter, makes it—

Wilbur: I think they probably don't try to capture our pentameter, but try to adapt it to their basic meters.

Bedford: But the French versions of Shakespeare are not very successful, are they?

Wilbur: Well, I'm sure that it is very much easier for the Germans or the Russians to capture the movement, the very sinewy movement, of Shakespeare's lines.

Bedford: But one of Richard's achievements is that in rehearsal at times we have had a copy of the French text, and of course had Richard's version, because that's the one that we were performing, but when you go through it you find that precisely the same thing he said in his version . . . within that line it's exactly what's said. I think that's one of his achievements.

Wilbur: I think that the big thing you aim for in any translation is tone. To get the tone of it right. And secondly, I think, one sets aside the idea of word-for-word fidelity, because that makes you write in a language which does not exist anywhere. But one insists upon a thought-for-thought fidelity and it is possible, it simply is possible, given an open colloquial writer like Molière, to take him thought for thought out of his Alexandrines and put them into our five-footers.

Bedford: I once directed *Tartuffe* at the Kennedy Center and CBS—or NBC or one of these people—were putting some money into the production because they wanted an option to tape it for TV. And so they were calling the shots and they would not allow Wilbur's version to be used because they thought that the TV viewers would be put off by the rhyming couplets. And so, as a result of this, I commissioned Simon Grey, who is a very, very, very talented playwright. And he did a prose version—he said, you know I can't possibly do a verse version. He did a prose version, and as good as it was, it was stale, flat and unprofitable because it didn't have the ebullience . . . somehow, it *needs* these rhyming couplets and it's like the couplets keep it like a ping pong ball on a spout of water . . . it keeps it up there in a light and delicious way and the prose does not do it justice . . . even good prose.

Wilbur: I think if you translate Molière's verse plays faithfully in prose many of the speeches suddenly seem long-winded.

Bedford: They do. It's strange.

Wilbur: Whereas if you're doing it in five-footers, even if you vary the treatment of the basic meter, what happens is that the phrases of the argument get measured out to you at an assimilable rate.

Bedford: And also it becomes heavy going, the play. Because it is rather a heavy play in a way. You know, a middle-aged man's obsession with who he considers is a guru, but is obviously a great phony, and the phony is bringing down the institution of the family and everything. It's a heavy play, and so it needs that balancing to retain its comedic quality. It needs the balance of this lovely language, and the verse—not only the verse but the rhyming-ness of the verse.

Wilbur: I do think that's right. I think it's the dancing of the verse that makes absolutely certain that a play like *Tartuffe* won't collapse, as it might in the wrong hands, into bourgeois melodrama. We're worried about whether Mariane's arm is going to be twisted or poor Orgon is going to lose his money and his house. Who cares about all that? Let's get to the point.

Question: Are there more modern plays written in verse that have achieved any kind of credibility and, if not, can you speculate why?

Wilbur: I recall that just a very few years before I first got the notion of translating Molière, there was a lot of somewhat localized excitement about poetry on the stage. Eliot's *Cocktail Party* appeared on the stage in New York with a very fine cast.

Bedford: Thank you. You don't mean that one, though, do you? You mean the other one.

Wilbur: What did I say? I said *The Cocktail Party.*

Bedford: Yes. I was wondering if you meant the production that was done at the APA or the original one . . .

Wilbur: Well, I'm speaking of the original, damn it. [Laughter] You did the Guiness Row.

Bedford: Well I take back the thank you then. [Laughter]

Wilbur: Well, I was dating this around the late 40s, I guess. Isn't that when *The Cocktail Party* broke? And then there was *The Lady's Not for Burning,* which was a species of poetic play—at any rate it had a lot of metaphors in it.

Bedford: I'll say.

Wilbur: Around Cambridge where I was at the time, there were an awful lot of people, most of them associated with something called The Poet's Theatre, who were writing in poetry for the stage and were staging things like Yeat's poetic plays, his sort of "no plays," MacLeish's poetic plays. There was a good deal of vitality and hope going into it. I think those high hopes have somewhat faded now, but I know there are some stubborn folk around who would like to revive them. Can you say something further about verse on the stage, Brian?

Bedford: Well, of course I spend I suppose most of my time doing verse on the stage, but Shakespeare, you know. The most modern I've come are the plays that he's mentioned, *The Cocktail Party* and the Eliot plays . . . Are you a writer of verse plays?

Questioner: Not yet!

Bedford: But you intend to be. Well, I think you should pursue it . . . Actually, speaking of verse plays, did you see the Carol Churchill play that was in rhyming couplets, if you please, about the stock market in England? Yes. It was very clever. It sort of ran out of steam. Do you know the one I mean?

Wilbur: No, did it come over here to New York?

Bedford: Yes, it came over here to New York and was hugely successful off Broadway, then they took it to Broadway and it failed miserably. But in England it was a huge success. And it was in rhyming couplets!

Wilbur: Well, it certainly can be done, and so people should not give up hope.

Question: We've seen a selection from one Molière play which I found, before Mr. Wilbur's translation, very inaccessible to me because of its ending and its dependence upon an external source to sort of solve things. But the scene that we saw was wonderful, and I wondered if that isn't the beauty for an actor, to have a hypocrite abandon his role. It's the only time when he really, voluntarily, gives this—it's the one time in the whole play when Tartuffe becomes human.

Bedford: Well, listen, like a lot of us, his downfall is sex. [Laughter] Like a lot of us in high places. Actually, this is one of the reasons, I said, when we were talking about this program, I said to Mrs. Kennedy—because we didn't do *Tartuffe* at the arena—I said, we've got to do *Tartuffe* at this moment in our lives. You know, that's his Achilles' heel. What Shakespeare in *The Merchant of Venice* calls "woolly breeding."

Wilbur: I love that. It's a very cheerful scene, I think, in which Tartuffe cannot resist nature. Long live nature; the coercion and exploitation of the world by such villains won't really work because they'll all turn out to be hungry, lusty, or something else.

Bedford: But what is so brilliant about that scene is if, like Damis, you were actually listening in a cupboard, it could be construed as an ecclesiastical conversation just because it's all bliss . . . and it's very, very clever.

Wilbur: Yes, the very first lines you say got the *Book of Common Prayer* in them.

Bedford: But regarding the *deux ex machina,* do you have any feelings about that? You know of course that *Tartuffe* was banned for 14 years and we don't know exactly, do we, what the original version actually consisted of?

Wilbur: No. I think it was a three act-er originally.

Bedford: I think it was three acts. But it's quite possible that, you know, the *deux ex machina* at the end, who is Louis XIV, that that could've just been put in to sweeten things up a bit.

Wilbur: I'm sure it had to do with the difficulties the play had undergone and with the fact that the king really was Molière's protector in this case as in several other cases. But I like what the critic Jacques Guicharnaud said about this, that however silly the ending may seem, however forced or opportunistic it may seem, we nevertheless at the end of the play are asked to contrast the domestic tyrant Orgon with the wise monarch, Louis, with the idea of wise monarchy. And I do think that makes a certain amount of sense. I think it's really in the words of the play at that point.

Moderator: May I thank you for the wonderful afternoon you've given us?

An Interview with Richard Wilbur
William Butts/1988

From *Esprit,* Vol. IV, No. 1 (Fall 1988), 1-8. Reprinted by permission of *Esprit.*

Richard Wilbur, winner of the Pulitzer Prize for Poetry and the National Book Award, stands as tall amid the melee of modern poetry as he does in the flesh. The poise and authority of his highly structured verse in an array of traditional forms have made him the despair of many a modernist, but few would deny that Wilbur's mellifluous voice of reason is charged with a wit and intelligence difficult to match. He recently completed his term as our nation's second poet laureate. The following interview was conducted by mail.

Your father was an artist. Did this provide any special climate at home that prompted you to start writing poetry?
   My father worked his way through the Art Students' League, studying with such masters as Bellows and Henri, and initially supported himself as a commercial artist: magazine covers and illustrations, Red Cross posters, advertisements, that sort of thing. In his New York studio he employed professional models, among them such worthies-to-be as Frederic March and Charles Atlas, but out in rural New Jersey, where we lived, he often drew on family talent. I can remember holding still, for a very long time, in the posture of a boy running ecstatically home from the store with a loaf of Ward Bread under his arm. Once financially secure, my father freed his pallette from the color limitations of lithography and became an excellent portrait artist who also did landscapes and seascapes in various media. Our household was not arty; the beret-beard-and-smock sort of thing was mistrusted; but anything my brother or I did in the way of drawing or writing was encouraged, and I relished my father's craftsmanship and invention as well as my mother's gift for words. It was also formative that I grew up amongst farms and woods, knowing the names of natural things, and that a measure of rural solitariness made me learn to amuse myself.

254

Are you happy you became a poet? Any regrets?

Yes to the first question, although I am not sure that I *became* a poet. I *was* one, and unexpected critical approval confirmed me in it. Of course, I have been a number of things: a teacher, critic, editor, poet, translator, Broadway lyricist, writer of children's books. I am sorry not also to have been a cartoonist, a finished linguist, and a better scholar of 17th century art and letters. My various undertakings have contributed to each other, and they have also interfered with each other. Regrets are inevitable; I am glad to have produced faithful and actable versions of Molière and Racine, but I am sorry that the translation of three plays in the past decade has left me struggling to recover the habit of making my own poems. Friends and readers are forever telling me that what I do is all very well, but that I ought to do more of this or that. They collectively echo my own divergent feelings, and I am deeply grateful that they give a damn. Reverting to your first question, and broadening it, I feel lucky to have done very little that I didn't want to do.

Didn't your years of teaching at Wesleyan and Smith College distract much from time you would have spent otherwise?

Of course. Everything, as I just said, has interfered with everything else. Teaching and writing have been hard, enjoyable tasks for me. It was always clear to me that writing was the more important, but I couldn't at all times compel myself to act accordingly. Why? Because the demands of teaching are obvious and definite. If you are a teacher, you must be ready, by Tuesday at ten o'clock, to help your students—let's say—distinguish between Mannerism and the Ba-roque. When you sit down to write a poem, your obligations are less certain: there is no deadline, nobody asked you to do it, the subject will not be fully known until you've finished, the beneficiaries of your work are conjectural. Furthermore, a poem may come to nothing; but what you are to say on Tuesday at ten had better be something. All of these considerations can confuse what administrators call your "priorities."

What is the biggest change in your writing from The Beautiful Changes *to your recent work?*

That's really for critics to say. I don't give myself talkings-to, and consciously resolve to change; time, experience, and the need to interest oneself take care of that. But even I can see that my language is plainer, that my formal high-jinks are fewer, and that the influence of theatre work has brought me closer to dramatic speech.

You attribute this then to your work on Molière and Racine? Any other benefits translating drama holds for a poet?

It can help you to broaden your expressive range, I think. Translating drama involves impersonation, the imitation of attitudes and emotions. There's undoubtedly some transference from such practice to one's own work; more of oneself becomes articulate.

Are you surprised how much your work has changed? How would you describe those changes?

It doesn't surprise me that I've changed, because one can't write poems over a period of decades without continually refreshing one's approach to inveterate concerns. What I mean is that new words must be found for new understandings. Modifications of style and technique follow naturally from that.

What is your relationship to your creative moments? Do you have to court your muse?

There is no recognizable state of mind in which poetry gets written, or at any rate I can't recognize such a state in myself. All I know is that vatic moods are not promising, and that it's of no use to be grimly businesslike. The best thing is to be frequently idle, and thus available to the impulse should it come.

What are the conditions you write under? Do you require quiet, chaos or what?

Youthful self-absorption once made me able to write in an air-raid, or a living room full of spirited children. Now I do better in a deep chair, in a quiet room with a limited view and no telephone.

Does your silo/study offer this ideal environment?

Yes. My only bothers there are tending the Franklin stove and the humidifier. I do have a phone, but it doesn't ring. A buzzer from the main house lets me know when some call *must* be answered—when some dreadful person is about to say, "I'm afraid I'm taking you from your work."

Do your first drafts come quickly?

Only rarely does anything come quickly, and I try to make the first draft—on which I may work for months or years—the last draft. Because I work slowly, revising as I go, I must take care not to lose the flow and speed and openness of speech.

Do you write one poem at a time, or do poems come to you in larger groups?

In general I work on one poem at a time, though some of the words and phrases which blacken the margin of the page may lead in time to other poems. If I thought in groups and suites I would doubtless be more prolific, but I can't shake the habit of trying to use up, within a single poem, my present sense of its subject.

What sort of poetry are you interested in at the moment?

I'm interested in seeing what my next poem, if any, will look like.

You seem resigned to the notion that a poet's ability may dry up and blow away at any moment. Shouldn't a poet who feels this has happened to him persist? Some think, for instance, that Auden continued publishing after his well had dried. Agree?

There's nothing good about boxing when your legs are gone and you've lost your hand-speed. However, writing poetry isn't *just* like boxing. Lucky poets can survive dry periods and write again, perhaps in a changed manner, right to the end; and the only way to find out if you're lucky is to keep trying. But by "trying" I don't mean joyless drudgery; good poems won't come of that. Auden's last books are not up to his best earlier work, but in *About the House* he found a voice for his aging self, and I wouldn't be without it.

Do you have any idea where your work is heading now?

Not the foggiest. At sixty-six years of age, any lyric poet must be prepared to find that his latest block is going to last. But I hope that won't happen just yet. If it does, I have other projects which will preserve me from puttering.

Do you feel you have written poetry that will endure?

Every poet says with Catullus, *quod, o patrona virgo,/ plus uno maneat perenne saeclo.** I don't think, however, that the hope that one's best work may last a while is based on any confident fore-glimpse of the future and its tastes in art. Who knows? The future may belong to rock videos, or whatever they're called. The hope that something may endure is based on a sense that it is well-made and useful. A good boot or hammer is *capable* of lasting; so is a good poem. Had I not written a few of those, I'd have quit long ago.

Do you feel a strong kinship with certain other poets of your generation? Or do you feel closer, perhaps, to some dead poets?

*Oh virgin protectress, let it persevere for more than a single age. *Editor.*

My feelings of kinship—with certain young poets and with many who are roughly of my generation—are too many to mention. I don't, actually, feel myself to be part of any school or phalanx, and I can be heartened by really good work of any kind. Seldom, however, do I now find myself moved to write, or moved to write in a certain way, by the work of the living. Those who spurred me on in the first place—my immediate American elders, and a host of poets, of all times and tongues—are still my main prompters. In this I am like most poets of sixty-odd.

Any unsung heroes of the generation preceding yours you would like to name?

All of them dead, all of them sufficiently sung.

Publisher's Weekly *recently featured an article about the "Key West literary environment." Yourself and several other poets are mentioned. Anything to this notion?*

It's nonsense to say that there is anything like a Key West school, though there are many good writers on the island, year-round or in the "season." All of the Key West writers I know learned their trades elsewhere, and persist in their own peculiarities while enjoying each other's company. Some were drawn to the place for particular reasons: to fish, to be with their friends, to enjoy its human diversity or bohemian license. What pleases them all, I think, is the island's charming blend of beauty and crumminess, and the fact (as Jane O'Reilly once said) that it is a small town with city advantages. And for all it is a place where one can be warm, comfortable, and unavailable.

What do you tell students they should try to avoid in their writing of poetry?

I tell them to read the poetry of all ages, so as not to be copycats of the contemporary. I tell them not to succumb to any one influence, but to take pleasure and prompting from a hundred sources. Since any poem is in part begotten by other poems, originality requires a flexible responsiveness to diverse models.

As a teacher, did you stress a thorough knowledge of meter and verse forms before encouraging your pupils to take off in their own direction?

I always gave the first two hours of a poetry-writing course to discussing the time-tested instruments of poetry, and illustrating—by quotation from the masters—what power and control those instruments can provide, if rightly used. It wasn't possible to insist on a "thorough knowledge" of poetic form, since even my best students tended, initially, to know little or nothing about it. What I accomplished by the two-hour discussion of meters, rhyme and verse forms was to introduce my students to technical terms without which they would be unable to praise or fault each other's work in a precise way. I also asked my students to buy some handbook of poetic terms—Babette Deutsch's very often—and to attempt at least one poem in meter and rhyme. Not a villanelle; something more manageable, such as a few quatrains.

In judging a poem, do you take into consideration the poet's attempt, along with his finished product, or is it simply a matter of the best achieved poetry? Does ambition, potential, or degree of difficulty enter the picture at all?

A teacher judging a student's poem will be pleased if it shows ambition and promise. A reader encountering a bad poem may sometimes be touched by some human quality which he glimpses in it: decency, sympathy, grief, youthful charm. But, severe as it sounds to say it, what really matters, for reader or critic, is whether or not the poem is "achieved," as you say, in itself. At a poorish opera, one may compensate oneself by looking at the sets, the costumes, the audience. A poor poem offers no such compensations.

Has having taught for so many years actually contributed anything to your work?

Yes, by forcing me to read many books for my literature courses, and to learn to enjoy some things not initially attractive.

Do you have any thoughts on why there seems to be so little political commitment in American poetry, when in parts of Europe the opposite is true?

In the Soviet Union, to take the most salient example, two things incline poetry toward political commitment. Three things, rather. The state, which controls publication, expects all art to support, in some measure, the socialist experiment. It is also an historic expectation of the Russian people that poets will serve as the national conscience. And finally, political awareness is not excludable from the consciousness of any Russian; you can't get away from it. There was a certain daring in those early poems of Yevtushenko and Voznesensky which concerned themselves with the merely personal life.

Americans, and American poets, enjoy the luxury of focussing, to a great extent, upon private experience: love, sex, family, nature, religion. This can have splendid consequences, as in Emily Dickinson. It can also result in a poetry of shrunken scope and value. We have lately had a good deal of protest poetry: the Vietnam war provoked much right-minded verse which was also simple-minded and dull; minority poets, and feminist poets, have swelled the literature of protest. But protest and "political commitment" are not precisely the same thing. Political commitment would entail something like Archibald MacLeish's loyal-and-critical concern for the health of our institutions; I wish that were not so rare.

How do politics fit into a poem?

As one important aspect of life. Propaganda poetry can be good, but only so good. Poetry does best by politics when it acknowledges complexity, tells the whole truth, and authenticates the political by treating it not in isolation but in conjunction with all else that the poet knows of life.

Have you felt any compulsion to be socially responsive to any group or movement?

I've picketed, I've marched, I've handed out literature at factory gates, I've read poems at anti-war rallies. There are times when that sort of thing is called for, as during the long agitation for civil rights. But more important than any kind of single-issue behavior is the supporting of good candidates within our party system.

Yet you're not generally thought of as an activist poet in the way that Yevtushenko is.

That's true.

How closely do you pay attention to your critics?

I don't pretend not to read my critics, and it matters to me what they say. If a criticism is intelligent, I am pleased to have had the attention of an intelligent person, even if he gives me a hard time. If all my critics denounced me, I think that I would be somewhat disheartened and would write somewhat less. When I am praised by someone I respect, it makes me want to write more. No criticism, however, has had the effect of making me strive to please by writing this way or that; I am stuck with my own tastes, themes, and capacities.

Do you ever feel that your poetry's aesthetic perfection is at odds with our own nuclear age?

Beauty in art is a by-product of adequacy to the subject, is it not? But perhaps I misunderstand you: perhaps you are saying that technical finish may be out-of-place in certain ages, like a tailcoat on a battlefield? I don't think so. If the technique properly serves the words, the argument then the words are the clearer and the stronger for it. Thomas Nashe, writing in a time of pestilence, did not feel that his verse should be accordingly spotty. Would my poem "Advice to a Prophet" deal better with the threat of nuclear war if it were "sincerely" incoherent and dispensed with all supporting artifice? Nope. There is a goofy argument going around, to the effect that metrical writing tempts one to make strong closures, and that strong closures are fraudulent in an age of doubt and confusion. To which I can only say that poets are not bound to conform to anyone else's notion of the age, and that a few iambs and trochees never led an able poet to say more than he meant.

When you look around in American poetry today, what do you see? What do you like, what do you not like?

I like the work of individual fine poets, of whom we have a fair number, thank heaven.

Do you think America's laureateship will broaden the readership of poetry in this country? It isn't often that you find a serious poet in the pages of People *magazine.*

The new title is a good thing because it does honor to American poetry. I can't guess whether the attendant publicity, which gives a minor and fleeting celebrity status to individual poets, will boost the circulation of *Poetry* magazine, or lengthen the poetry shelves of our chain bookstores.

Index

262